THE VIDEO GAME DEBATE

Do video games cause violent, aggressive behavior? Can online games help us learn? When it comes to video games, these are often the types of questions raised by popular media, policy makers, scholars, and the general public. In this collection, international experts review the latest research findings in the field of digital game studies and weigh in on the actual physical, social, and psychological effects of video games. Taking a broad view of the industry from the moral panic of its early days up to recent controversies surrounding games like *Grand Theft Auto*, contributors explore the effects of games through a range of topics including health hazards/benefits, education, violence and aggression, addiction, cognitive performance, and gaming communities. Interdisciplinary and accessibly written, *The Video Game Debate* reveals that the arguments surrounding the game industry are far from black and white, and opens the door to richer conversation and debate amongst students, policy makers, and scholars alike.

Rachel Kowert received her PhD in Psychology from the University of York (UK), where her research focused on the relationships between social competence and online video game involvement.

Thorsten Quandt holds the chair of Online Communication at the University of Münster (Germany) and is a distinguished scientist with extensive experience in digital games research.

THE VIDEO GAME DEBATE

Unravelling the Physical, Social, and Psychological Effects of Digital Games

Edited by Rachel Kowert and Thorsten Quandt

Routledge
Taylor & Francis Group

NEW YORK AND LONDON

First published 2016
by Routledge
711 Third Avenue, New York, NY 10017

and by Routledge
2 Park Square, Milton Park, Abingdon, Oxon OX14 4RN

Routledge is an imprint of the Taylor & Francis Group, an informa business

Library of Congress Cataloging in Publication Data
The video game debate : unravelling the physical, social, and psychological effects of digital games / edited by Rachel Kowert and Thorsten Quandt.
  pages cm
Includes bibliographical references and index.
1. Video games—History. 2. Video games—Social aspects. 3. Video games—Psychological aspects. I. Kowert, Rachel. II. Quandt, Thorsten.
GV1469.3.V5225 2015
794.809—dc23   2015013347

ISBN: 978-1-138-83160-5 (hbk)
ISBN: 978-1-138-83163-6 (pbk)
ISBN: 978-1-315-73649-5 (ebk)

Typeset in Bembo
by Keystroke, Station Road, Codsall, Wolverhampton

Printed and bound in the United States of America by Publishers Graphics, LLC on sustainably sourced paper.

CONTENTS

ACKNOWLEDGMENTS

The editors would like to give special thanks to all of the authors who contributed to this volume. For almost a decade, we have wanted to create a volume that collates the latest research in game studies. Our primary aim was to produce a book that could be used to inform parents, policy makers, clinicians, and other scholars about the state of research within the field. *The Video Game Debate* has achieved that goal. We thank you for your hard work in helping bring this dream to reality.

1

A BRIEF HISTORY OF VIDEO GAMES

James D. Ivory

Evolutionary biologists use a term called "convergent evolution" to explain the existence of similar traits in living organisms that are otherwise markedly different and only distantly related.[1] For example, similarities between the body types of fish, marine mammals such as dolphins and whales, and the extinct ichthyosaur may give the impression that these animals share a similar biological class even though other less superficial characteristics of these animals clearly identify them as members of separate animal classes. Similarly, bats may seem more closely related to birds than to other mammals because of their shared wings and ability to fly even though bats have little else in common with birds, including the anatomical location of their wings (bats' wings are essentially long webbed fingers, while the feathers of birds' wings are attached to the equivalent of the forearm and wrist). In these and other examples, it is all too easy to misperceive beasts that have little in common as part of one family.

So it is with video games. The social, cultural, and economic presence of video games is so overwhelming in the electronic media milieu, and the term "video game" is so often used as a talismanic catch-all for nearly any form of interactive digital entertainment, that it is easy to assume that the technological and social developments leading to what we now call "video games" are not composed of a single evolutionary pathway. Instead, the video games of today represent a convergence of substantially different trajectories of technological developments providing discrepant forms of entertainment to audiences with different needs. The result is a medium that is very diverse in its functions, content, and audiences – so diverse, in fact, that like birds and bats or dolphins and fish, many shared characteristics among some video games may be only superficial. Just as organisms described as examples of convergent evolution are very different creatures who seem more similar than they are because of a shared functional trait, many video games are actually very different entertainment products with different technological and social histories distinguished from other electronic media only by their shared primary function of providing interactive entertainment to their users. This kludge of technological and social bloodlines and audiences under the loosely defined blanket term "video games" is a challenge for those seeking to understand the impact of the medium. The impact of video games is great, but it is far from uniform because video games are far from uniform.

The Converging Ancestry of Video Games

Nuclear Roots: Action Simulations from Oscilloscopes to Arcades to Consoles

The First Video Games

The most resounding impact William "Willy" Higinbotham had on the world had nothing to do with video games. Higinbotham worked on the team that developed the first atomic bomb at Los Alamos Laboratory (now Los Alamos Research Laboratory), and after that experience he became a leading figure in the nuclear non-proliferation movement as a founder and chair of the Federation of American Scientists.[2] As a relative footnote to his role in such pivotal global events, Higinbotham is also known for having arguably developed the first electronic video game. While serving as a senior physicist at Brookhaven National Laboratory, Higinbotham was aware that even though the innovations his facility was producing could be world-changing, they were not necessarily impressive on display to visitors (his work in Los Alamos being a notable exception). To entertain attendees at an annual public visitors' day in 1958, he spent a few hours developing a rudimentary tennis simulation using analog computer technology designed to track missile trajectories and a pair of 5-inch oscilloscope screens.[2] The result, *Tennis for Two*, was a popular feature for visitors, but appeared only once more at the next annual visitors' day. Higinbotham couldn't even be bothered to pursue a patent for his patched-together diversion, which was based in technology that was already on its way to obsolescence; digital computers had already begun to appear, and much larger cathode ray tube displays were in use in household televisions. Only more than a decade later, when the eerily similar *Pong* burst onto the commercial scene, did the significance of Higinbotham's *Tennis for Two* as a milestone in video game history become apparent.[3]

As with most remembered milestones in the history of communication technology, the actual story of the first video game is not so clear-cut as Higinbotham and *Tennis for Two*. Just as tales of Alexander Graham Bell's telephone and Samuel Morse's telegraph are famous, but oversimplified by the absence of references to earlier prototypes and competing developments,[4] there were other prototypes that could be called electronic games that were developed before Higinbotham's 1958 demonstration. *OXO*, a simulation of the popular pencil-and-paper game called "Noughts and Crosses" or "Tic Tac Toe," was developed in 1952 as part of Alexander "Sandy" Douglas' doctoral work at the University of Cambridge.[5] While the program ran on a digital computer (the Electronic Delay Storage Automatic Calculator, or EDSAC) and used a cathode ray tube display, *OXO* often eludes credit as the first video game because it lacked a moving graphic display. A similar effort was a *draughts* (checkers) simulation made in 1951 by Christopher Strachey at England's National Physical Laboratory in London, which was a pioneering artificial intelligence program.[6] British engineering firm Ferranti exhibited a computer developed to play the game *Nim* using a series of lights as an interface at the Festival of Britain in 1951,[7] and famed British mathematician Alan Turing worked with Dietrich Prinz on a rudimentary chess simulation that had no visual interface and was programmed by Prinz in 1951.[8]

Another argument for the earliest origin of the video game can be based on a patent for a "Cathode Ray Tube Amusement Device" filed in 1947 and issued in 1948.[9] That device, developed by Thomas T. Goldsmith, Jr. and Estle Ray Mann at Dumont Laboratories in Upper Montclair, New Jersey, allowed users to control a dot on a screen to aim at paper overlay targets, with successful targeting tracked mechanically rather than by computer processing. While sharing some visual display traits with Higinbotham's *Tennis for Two* game, Goldsmith and Mann's device was completely mechanical and used no computer program or memory. There is therefore a good case for *Tennis for Two* as the first video game prototype because earlier putative "first" video games lacked either a graphical motion display (e.g., *Nim*, *OXO*) or computing technology (e.g., the Cathode Ray Tube Amusement Device). Bragging rights regarding which invention might truly be called the first video game notwithstanding, it is notable that all of these early precursors and prototypes simulated a game or sport, and of these the graphical motion display is frequently cited as a necessary criterion for an early prototype to be called a "video game." Thus, even retrospective glances at video game history place a heavy emphasis on action and simulation as defining characteristics of video games.

Tennis for Two and its various predecessors were never widely played or released commercially; they were either produced only as working prototypes or exhibited to the public at isolated events. The first video game to find a large audience and be available beyond a single exhibition was *Spacewar!* Initially developed by three students at the Massachusetts Institute of Technology, Stephen R. "Slug" Russell, J. Martin Graetz, and Wayne Witanen (with help from others at later stages), in 1962, *Spacewar!* allowed two players to control dueling spaceships and attempt to shoot each other with torpedoes while orbiting a black hole.[10] *Spacewar!*, played using a cathode ray tube display and custom-built controllers on the Digital Equipment Corporation's PDP-1 computer, also featured a score display, a player-friendly feature not available on the oscilloscope display used by *Tennis for Two*. This and other competition-oriented features ensured that *Spacewar!* was a hit. Within a year of its 1962 demonstration at the Massachusetts Institute of Technology's annual Science Open House in May, 1962, copies and variations of the *Spacewar!* program began to emerge at research laboratories across the United States, and the game was being played not only on PDP-1 computers but on other computers that used a cathode ray tube display as well.

A much more polished video game than *Tennis for Two*, *Spacewar!* might also be considered the first video game, especially as *Spacewar!* used digital computing hardware rather than analog technology. More relevant to the video game industry boom to come, *Spacewar!* was certainly the first video game to be commercialized. While the actual *Spacewar!* game as originally programmed could not be commercialized because it was played on expensive research computers that were usually inaccessible to the public, the first coin-operated arcade games were both adaptations of *Spacewar!*: *Galaxy Game*, a one-of-a-kind arcade unit that debuted on the Stanford University campus in Palo Alto, California in 1971 and was the first coin-operated video game, and *Computer Space*, a mass-produced coin-operated arcade game released later the same year throughout the United States.[11] Therefore, whatever early device is credited as the first video game, there's no debating that *Spacewar!* accomplished two milestones important to the scalability of the video game as a mass medium: it was the first video game to be played on more than one machine, and the first video game to be adapted for commercialization.

While the technologies employed to create the first video game prototypes and their predecessors varied, some conceptual themes are apparent across all of these early games. Each had a basis in simulating competition, either competitive action simulations or simulations of competitive strategy games. While some of the early precursors imitated competitive board games and parlor games (*OXO*, chess, draughts/checkers, *Nim*), the prototypes most often referred to as actual video games and the first video game to evidence the medium's commercial potential featured competitive action simulations of sport or combat (Cathode Ray Tube Amusement Device, *Tennis for Two*, *Spacewar!*). Therefore, even in the earliest roots of video games an emphasis is established on conceptual inspiration from simulation of competitive games and other competitive activities, sometimes based only in strategic competitions like board games or parlor games but more often based in action simulations of sport or combat.

Commercial Success in Arcades and the Home

Just as the first video game prototypes were conceptually rooted in simulating the themes of competitive enterprises from board games to sport to war, the biggest early commercial successes in video game history drew from the same sources of inspiration. While *Spacewar!* adaptation *Computer Space* was not commercially successful as the first mass-produced commercial arcade game, the release of *Pong* by Atari, Inc. the following year in 1972 met commercial success immediately beginning with its well-received introduction at a local watering hole called Andy Capp's Tavern.[12] *Pong* held to the same tennis theme as *Tennis for Two*, continuing the tradition of video games' reliance on simulations of competitive activities. The year 1972 also saw the release of the first commercial home video game console, the Magnavox Odyssey, which featured sport and shooting games among its game titles.[13] The Odyssey console used light signals combined with overlays placed on the users' television screens to simulate graphics and featured predominantly sports and action games, though some games featured other simulations such as roulette. Other successful arcade and home consoles would follow, once again with action sport and combat simulations predominant in their themes. In fact, the popular Atari Video Computer system (VCS, later renamed the Atari 2600 as later console versions were developed) was released with a game titled *Combat* that featured 27 combat games such as tank and biplane duels.[14] Oddly enough, the first video game industry crash in 1977 was precipitated in part by a glut of *Pong* copycats on the arcade market.[15]

Action games also defined the video game industry's recovery from its 1977 crash, most notably the iconic *Pac-Man* coin-operated arcade game released by Namco in 1980. *Pac-Man*'s simple action hunt-and-chase play made the game a commercial success and a cultural phenomenon.[16] In fact, *Pac-Man* was so popular that after the arcade game sparked a resurgence from the 1977 industry crash, the let-down from a much-anticipated but poorly produced console version of *Pac-Man* contributed to a second video game industry crash in 1983.[17] The early 1980s also saw a rise in personal computer ownership and a corresponding rise in video game play on those computers, including the popular game-friendly Commodore 64 home computer released in 1982.[18] (Sales of personal computer hardware and software used to play video games may have been something of an exception to the game industry recession of 1983, though considering the multiple household functions of most home computers it is difficult to assess how much personal computer hardware at the time was bought partially or wholly for the purpose of playing video games.) In any case, the recovery of the industry was led by Nintendo and its Nintendo Entertainment Center home console, which rose to fame on the whimsical action play of its flagship *Super Mario Brothers* game, first released in Japan in 1985.[19] While advances in graphics from the first video games allowed direct sport and combat simulations to give way to fantasy themes in *Pac-Man*, *Super Mario Brothers*, and a host of other titles by the 1980s, the presence of action-based themes related to sport and combat continued to dominate these arcade and console hits as well.

Since the Nintendo-led recovery from the infamous 1983 crash of the video game industry, home consoles and computers have continued to erode the arcade video game market. While access to licensed adaptations of arcade hits was an integral part of video game console makers' success in the early 1980s, the growing success of consoles and the development by Nintendo and other companies of popular console game characters and franchises not based in arcade games limited console makers' reliance on arcade hits by the latter half of that decade.[20] In the years since, the trend has continued, with home console and personal computer games burgeoning at the expense of a flagging arcade market.[21] The 1990s saw home video games begin to feature expanded production budgets and innovations such as three-dimensional graphics, faster processors, a shift from game software using ROM cartridges to optical CDs that could hold much more program data, and the ability to hold multi-player sessions using Local Area Network (LAN) connections and the Internet. The pace of innovation has continued since, with multiple "generations" of home game consoles piggybacking incremental advances in game consoles' graphical realism, data storage and processing capacity, control interfaces, and online accessibility.[22] The parallel development of a variation on the home console, the handheld mobile game device, has followed a similar technological trajectory over the decades, starting with early handheld devices in the late 1970s that featured simple LED arrays for displays and beeps for sound feedback to approximate competitions such as auto races and American football games and eventually evolving into modern handheld consoles offering parallel versions of home console hits – as well as games released for play on mobile phones and tablets.

Through so much technological advancement over decades, though, the video game industry's most popular titles remain heavily fixed in the themes of simulating sport and combat that inspired the first video game prototypes. The top ten best-selling video games in the United States in 2013 included two games from the perennially popular military-themed *Call of Duty* franchise (*Call of Duty: Ghosts,* and *Call of Duty: Black Ops II*), as well as *Battlefield 4,* another entry from a popular military-themed series. Two more video games, chart-topping *Grand Theft Auto V* and *Assassin's Creed IV: Black Flag,* included combat simulation as a heavy component of their themes. Madden *NFL 25* and *NBA 2K14* represented annual releases from sporting franchises (the annual entry from the popular *FIFA* video game series a notable omission from the U.S. list given its popularity in much of the rest of the world), with *Just Dance 2014* arguably something of a sporting simulation as well. Of the top ten sellers in the United States, then, only the console edition of *Minecraft* and *Disney Infinity* were not primarily action simulations of war, combat, or sport.[23]

While video games' technological history provides a classic example of a "spin-off" media technology, with the medium emerging from computing technologies developed for much more serious purposes,[4] the themes of video games throughout their history demonstrate the medium's solid grounding in an ancestry of simulating combat and war, and to a lesser extent strategy games. Given that much of the cultural history of sport is arguably based in imitation of war,[24] and given that war was an inspiration for many historical strategy games such as chess and its predecessors,[25] video games' emphasis on action simulations of sport and war can be viewed as the product of received thematic ancestry based in many centuries of structured games and leisure activities devised to simulate the action of mortal combat. If sport and parlor games both have germs of inspiration in simulating war, then much of the history of video games bears the marks of a pedigree based in simulating all three – with as much action and photorealism as possible.

Alternate Ancestry: Narrative Role-Playing from Tolkien to Dungeons and Dragons to World of Warcraft

The First Online Role-playing Games

While the conceptual roots of video games in action simulations of sport and war are deep, they do not tell the entire story of modern video games' lineage. Midway through the decades-long process of video games' development from rudimentary simulations of tennis and spacecraft battles to blockbuster simulations of American football and war in the Middle East, another branch of video games' conceptual DNA emerged. As with the nascent moments of video games' history in action simulations, a second key ancestor of today's video games also rose from the primordial environment of academic computer research facilities. This second branch of video games' family tree focused not on fast-paced competitive simulation rendered on a visual display, but on something in many ways quite the opposite: an interactive adventure tale scrawled in text on a computer screen.

In 1978, just as the arcade game industry was reeling from an economic crash and the home video game console industry was beginning its first boom on the back of the success of the Atari VCS console, two British computer science students at the University of Essex called Roy Trubshaw and Richard Bartle finished the first functioning version of a very different kind of game that they would continue to refine and develop through two more versions through 1980.[26] While even the term "video game" indicates the importance of rich graphical representations to most examples of the medium, Trubshaw and Bartle's game had no graphics at all. Their game, *MUD* (Multi-User Dungeon), instead relied on interactive text commands and automatically generated text feedback for all of players' interactions with the game program, as well as between players using the game at the same time.

MUD's text-only input and output format might seem a rudimentary interface even compared to the commercial video games popular around the same time, such as the colorful and noisy spectacle of the *Pac-Man* arcade hit that was released in 1980, the same year that the finished third version of *MUD* became available online when Essex University became connected to Internet precursor ARPAnet. Even so, *MUD* became popular enough that it spawned an entire genre of text-based online games (so much so that *MUD* came to be referred to as *MUD1* to differentiate it from its many adaptations, as well as from a later successor dubbed *MUD2*) and influenced some of today's most popular graphical video games.[27]

To play *MUD*, users connected to the game online by creating and logging into character accounts with names and statistics describing attributes such as stamina. Using these characters, which existed in the game solely as text descriptions like all of the games' other elements, players then navigated a vast game environment by typing commands to travel from location to location, interact with objects and features of the environment, talk to other players, and fight with both other players and computer-controlled characters.[28] The game's program responded to the commands with text feedback such as descriptions of places, characters, and objects, as well as feedback describing the results of attempts to carry out actions such as picking up an object or attacking a foe. Aside from indulging in these game dynamics, players could also have conversations with each other via text, either privately or in view of other players. Such conversations might be focused on the game's dynamics, such as threats or offers to cooperate, or they might be discussions about topics unrelated to games altogether.[29] In some cases, this feedback was based on randomly generated outcomes using probability weighting, such as the result of an attempt to strike a weak or strong enemy with a given weapon. Thus, beneath the seemingly crude text interface of *MUD* was a richly described virtual space, a complex array of game mechanics mixing chance with strategy, and a bandwidth-lean modality that allowed online game play all over the world long before the Internet was even well-known outside of university research labs.

While in many ways unprecedented, *MUD* was based on existing text-based games that could be played by single users on computers not connected to any online network. One inspiration for *MUD* was *Zork*,[30] a text-based computer game published in 1977 and developed by a group of researchers at the Massachusetts Institute of Technology.[31] Another was *Colossal Cave Adventure*, a text game that was originally programmed in 1975 and 1976 by Will Crowther, a programmer at technology company Bolt, Beranek and Newman, and then developed into an expanded version that would become better known in 1977 by Don Woods, a graduate student at Stanford.[32] Both of these games shared the same text interface as *MUD*, but a key difference between MUD and previous text-based computer games was that *Colossal Cave Adventure* and *Zork* were programmed to be played by a single user on one computer. While Trubshaw and Bartle borrowed some elements from these games in developing *MUD*, they intended for their game's plot to be an open-ended one determined by users playing with each other rather than a predetermined adventure arc programmed into the game in advance for a single user.[30]

The popularity of *MUD* spawned an eponymous genre throughout the 1980s as *MUD* fans developed their own "MUD" games and, eventually, open-source code platforms to be used for creating even more games. As the number of MUDs grew, their themes and game mechanics also became increasingly diverse, so much so that different acronyms became used to describe some MUD variants. For example, some games focused on long sessions of extensive typewritten "role-play," with players taking turns typing rich descriptions of their characters' actions and dialogue to tell a collaborative story in conjunction with their use of game commands to govern actions such as travel and combat.[33] MUDs with such a role-playing focus came to be described by some with the term "MUSH" (Multi-User Shared Hallucination) to distinguish their role-play focus from other MUDs whose users relied more on game commands alone and less on typed role-playing "poses."[34] Similarly, games prioritizing users' extensive access to creating new objects and spaces to expand and redefine the game environment were called MOOs (Mud, Object-Oriented).[35] A range of MUD variant categories emerged based on other distinguishing features, described by acronyms such as MUCK, MUSE, and DUM, and sometimes collectively referred to as MU★s, but all retained elements of structure and style from the original *MUD* game's creation of a text-based world related to the user by descriptions of places and objects, and navigable by simple commands.[36]

While this genre of online text-based games evolved largely from the original *MUD* game and the earlier text games that inspired *MUD* itself, an even earlier conceptual lineage can be identified for these games. An acknowledged inspiration for both *Zork* and *Colossal Cave Adventure*, the pioneering "offline" text-based games that influenced Trubshaw and Bartle's seminal online *MUD* game (so much so that the "Dungeons" part of the *MUD* acronym was in part an homage to a *Zork* adaptation called *Dungeon*),[30] was the paper-and-pencil and dice-based "tabletop" role-playing game *Dungeons and Dragons*, which was first published by Gary Gygax and Dave Arneson in 1974.[37] Created as a partial adaptation of existing strategy war games, but with players controlling individual characters instead of military units, *Dungeons and Dragons* was the first commercial role-playing game, and has remained a dominant fixture in the genre since.[38] *Dungeons and Dragons*' devoted player audience included creators of both the *Zork*[39] and *Colossal Cave Adventure*[40] games. While the original *MUD* game's roots in *Dungeons and Dragons* were therefore somewhat indirect via the tabletop game's influence on earlier text games (Trubshaw and Bartle were not directly inspired by *Dungeons and Dragons* when creating their game), some influential subsequent MUD games developed in the 1980s relied on *Dungeons and Dragons* more directly as a source of both themes and game mechanics. The popularity of *Dungeons and Dragons* themes and mechanics in MUD games was perhaps predictable considering that *Dungeons and Dragons* players were using online networks as a rudimentary communication tool to facilitate playing their tabletop games across distance even before *MUD* was created.[41]

There is, however, a much deeper ancestral vein for both MUDs and *Dungeons and Dragons*, in the form of one of the most well-known authors of the last century. A key source of thematic inspiration for *Dungeons and Dragons* was the famed work of J. R. R. Tolkien, a British professor at Oxford University who produced influential scholarship on topics such as the Old English epic poem *Beowulf*[42] and who achieved much popular fame by penning best-selling fantasy novels such as *The Hobbit*[43] and *The Lord of the Rings*.[44] Tolkien's work, a popular culture staple by the 1970s, had a heavy imprint on the themes of *Dungeons and Dragons*, as is best evidenced by the inclusion of several fantastic creature species (including Tolkien's iconic hobbits) from Tolkien's stories in the original version of the game before legal threats by representatives of the Tolkien estate forced their removal.[45] Popular themes for many of the MUDs and MU★s that sprang up on the years following the release of the original *MUD* game include fantasy themes reminiscent of Tolkien's stories, including some MU★ games set overtly in the Tolkien literary universe.[46]

Just as an evolutionary path can be traced from arcade and console video games to simulations of sport and combat, then, a separate pedigree can be identified tying the text-based online role-playing games not to early video game prototypes like *Tennis for Two* or *Spacewar!*, but to the narratives and fantasy settings of beloved literary classics. While the trajectories of both display-based video games and text-based online role-playing games have a background in board and tabletop games ranging from chess to *Dungeons and Dragons*, and while both types of games are based in prototypes from universities and research centers ranging from Brookhaven National Laboratory to the University of Essex, their conceptual heritage is otherwise mostly distinct. On one hand, there is a tradition of video games based in efforts to simulate the action of sport and combat, and on the other, there is a tradition of text-based online games based in creating a shared experience of a narrative fantasy story.

Commercial Success of MUDs, MMOs, and Virtual Worlds

Despite the popularity and rapid proliferation of MUDs in the years following the first availability of online access to Trubshaw and Bartle's *MUD* game, the genre was not initially a commercial presence. Tolkien's novels sold millions of copies, *Dungeons and Dragons* was a best-selling game spawning edition after edition and adaptation after adaptation, and *Zork* and *Colossal Cave Adventure* were eventually commercialized in 1979[47] and 1981,[48] respectively, but the *MUD* game and its first successors did not charge players a fee to access and play. In fact, Bartle chose to explicitly release the *MUD* name and concept into the public domain in 1985.[49] Many subsequent MUDs have held to the same non-commercial principles, likely in part because creators and administrators have supported the idea of keeping their communities free to the public but also because many MUD games borrow from themes, characters, settings, and plot lines of existing intellectual properties.[50] Many of the most popular MUD games are based to varying degrees on popular novels, films, television programs, comic books, and other popular culture staples; while most have been tolerated, implicitly or explicitly, by the owners of those intellectual properties as non-commercial fan communities, commercializing MUDs based on valuable intellectual commodities such as *Lord of the Rings*, *Harry Potter*, *Star Wars*, or *A Song of Ice and Fire* would be legally problematic to say the least.

Trubshaw and Bartle's MUD game did eventually receive a commercial release in 1985 when it was licensed for use on early commercial online service provider networks, which provided much broader access than the research- and business-oriented networks used to access *MUD* during its earlier years.[30] Around the mid-1980s, even while non-commercial MUDs were proliferating, various other commercial MUDs also began to appear. As with the eventually commercialized version of *MUD* these commercial MUDs relied on a business model based on licensing the games to online service providers, who in turn charged users hourly rates for access and could therefore make substantial revenue from users who habitually played MUD games online. Among the first prominent commercial MUDs was *Scepter of Goth*, a game that was released for commercial play in 1983 while its creator, Alan Klietz, was an undergraduate student at the University of Minnesota.[26] Klietz, who was inspired by the same offline text-based games that influenced *MUD*, as well as by *Dungeons and Dragons*, had begun developing early versions of the game as early as 1978 while still in secondary school. A noteworthy development in the evolution of commercial MUDs was the release of *Islands of Kesmai*, another MUD inspired by *Dungeons and Dragons* that was released in 1985 and which departed slightly from MUDs' text-based format by approximating graphics with text characters arranged to resemble crude maps of the game setting, characters, and objects.[51]

The procession of online role-playing games from text-based MUDs to more graphics-based descendants continued from there. *Habitat*, a Lucasfilm product created by Chip Morningstar and Randall Farmer in 1985 and released online in 1986, allowed players to interact with each other and the environment via text commands and also represented characters, objects, and settings with simple graphics.[52] Rather than a fantastic setting, the *Habitat* game environment included more mundane elements such as apartments and bank machines. The graphics of *Habitat* were mostly static, and the game play and interaction between users was mostly driven by text commands and text chat. In 1991, Stormfront Studios and Strategic Simulations released *Neverwinter Nights,* which brought more dynamic graphics that portrayed movement each time a player moved the character avatar with a keyboard arrow key and provided feedback about the results of characters' actions in battles. The game was successful with a peak subscriber total of more than 100,000 by 1997, and its graphical advancements have earned it retrospective recognition as the first graphical version of the "Massively Multi-player Online Role-Playing Game" genre.[53] *Neverwinter Nights* was not simply inspired by *Dungeons and Dragons* like many MUDs, but actually based in a setting of the *Dungeons and Dragons* intellectual property. *Meridian 59*, developed by brothers Andrew and Chris Kirmse while they were students at the Massachusetts Institute of Technology and Virginia Tech, respectively, and released as an unpolished version in 1995 by Archetype Interactive before a more complete commercial launch in 1996 by The 3DO company, upgraded the emerging "graphical MUD" genre with 3D graphics.[54] While an online game boasting 3D graphics might seem to have little in common with early text-based online games, the relationship between *Meridian 59* and its MUD ancestors is indisputable as the Kirmse brothers acknowledge *Scepter of Goth* as their game's original inspiration.[55]

While *Meridian 59* was groundbreaking, its commercial scale was not vast. The game never claimed more than some 12,000 subscribers at any time.[56] *Ultima Online*, released in 1997 by Origin Systems and Electronic Arts, adapted the medieval theme of Richard Garriott's already-popular *Ultima* computer game series[57] to find unprecedented commercial success for an online role-playing game as the first such game to amass 200,000 subscribers.[58] *Ultima Online* popularized the MMORPG genre and encouraged commercial imitators, but nonetheless had deep roots in the MUD tradition; Raph Koster, its lead designer, was an experienced MUD creator and administrator.[59] *Ultima Online* was closely followed by other successful MMORPG games. *Lineage*, a South Korean MMORPG designed by Jake Song and released in 1998, had a peak membership of as many as 4 million subscribers and remains active in South Korea.[58] In the West, the release of *EverQuest* in 1999 by Sony's Verant Interactive brand eclipsed *Ultima Online*'s marks for success by attracting more than 400,000 subscribers.[58] Another 1999 MMORPG release, *Asheron's Call* from Turbine and Microsoft, accumulated more than 200,000 subscribers.[58] *Ultima Online*, *EverQuest*, and *Asheron's Call* have been described as the "big three" MMORPGs because of their impact on the commercial popularization of the genre in the United States and the West.[60] Despite their innovations and success, though, all three games and other MMORPGs were still routinely referred to as "improved MUDs" at the height of their success,[60] a clear testament to the cultural influence of the MUD genre on the MMORPG genre.[61] In fact, while *EverQuest* was an MMORPG with 3D graphics, it shared so many similarities in its mechanics with the text-based *DikuMUD* that *EverQuest* has been described by *MUD* co-creator Richard Bartle as "basically a DikuMUD with a graphical front end bolted on."[30(p33)] In response to a minor controversy over the games' apparent similarities, *EverQuest*'s designers provided *DikuMUD*'s administrators with a signed statement testifying that *EverQuest* was not based in code poached from *DikuMUD*.[62]

By the first years of the twenty-first century, the popularity of early MMORPGs had opened the floodgates for waves of emulators, some successful and some short-lived in a crowded market. Many were based on popular films, television programs, and literature such as *Star Wars*, *The Matrix*, *Star Trek*, and *Conan the Barbarian*, or successful video game franchises such as *Final Fantasy* and *The Sims*, though some MMORPGs were original intellectual properties. In 2004, though, the MMORPG market was well and truly dominated by the arrival of Blizzard's *World of Warcraft*, which was a spin-off of the longstanding *Warcraft* video game series that blended conventional MMORPG features (including many inherited similarities with the MUD genre) with new innovations and elements designed to make the game more accessible to players not familiar with MMORPGs.[27] Within 24 hours of its release, *World of Warcraft* had drawn more than 200,000 subscribers, and more than a million were playing within a few months.[63] *World of Warcraft*'s player population peaked at more than 12 million, and the game holds a majority share of the world's MMORPG player market.[56] Despite *World of Warcraft*'s brobdingnagian presence on the MMORPG landscape, though, several dozen other commercial MMORPG games have continued to emerge and ebb and flow in popularity in its shadow in recent years.[64]

While online role-playing games have undergone a dramatic makeover in terms of both their appearance and audience in the decades since *Zork* and *Colossal Cave Adventure* first began to be passed from computer to computer and *MUD* first became available online, modern MMORPGs' themes and functions remain firmly grounded in the same base of fantasy adventure stories that drove those first text-based games. Many of the aforementioned milestone-reaching online role-playing games described above were inspired or based in part on MUDs and the *Dungeons and Dragons* tabletop role-playing game that preceded them, which in turn was influenced directly by the fantasy literature of J. R. R. Tolkien. In fact, one currently popular MMORPG game from Turbine is based on the *Dungeons and Dragons* franchise, and another from the same company is based on Tolkien's *The Lord of the Rings* novel series. Just as elements of *Colossal Cave Adventure* have been described as "Tolkienesque,"[65] and the *Dungeons and Dragons* tabletop game that inspired so many MUDs and MMORPGs in a direct or indirect manner originally included Tolkien-created species, *World of Warcraft* has also been described as "Tolkienesque" for its high fantasy setting[66] and the inclusion of species such as orcs and elves in its bestiary.[67] "Tolkienesque" themes have also been the norm across the majority of popular MUDs and MMORPGs throughout the genres' histories.[68]

Just as a line of popular arcade, computer, console, and mobile video games have a firm pedigree in action simulations of sport and combat, online role-playing games such as modern MMORPGs have a parallel ancestry in historical attempts to create a fantastic adventure narrative ranging from text-based computer games to tabletop role-playing games to fantasy literature. In fact, considering that one of Tolkien's aims was to create a legendary universe to accommodate for England's lack of a comprehensive mythology,[69] online role-playing games even have a distant (albeit tenuous) tie to the epic works such as *Beowulf* that inspired Tolkien's fiction.

The Current Economic Position and Audience of the Games Industry

This chapter's description of a dual ancestry for video games (see Figure 1.1) only partially describes the medium's myriad roots and developments. While more than two evolutionary pathways have likely served as tributaries feeding the modern video game medium, the two routes described above explain the background of many of the most popular and culturally significant video games today. Most importantly, identifying these dual pedigrees for the modern video game exemplifies that whether or not there are more key pathways of ancestry for the medium, there is certainly more than one received genetic blueprint for the conceptual themes that video games seek to emulate. Therefore, we must conclude that what we call the medium of "video games" is actually a kludge of at least two distinct streams of communication technology conceptualization, innovation, and commercialization. Far from a monolithic economic and social

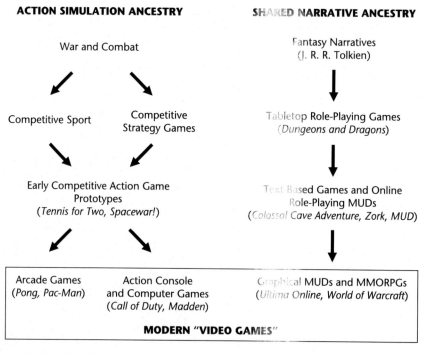

ACTION SIMULATION ANCESTRY   **SHARED NARRATIVE ANCESTRY**

War and Combat

Fantasy Narratives
(J. R. R. Tolkien)

Competitive Sport   Competitive Strategy Games

Tabletop Role-Playing Games
(*Dungeons and Dragons*)

Early Competitive Action Game Prototypes
(*Tennis for Two, Spacewar!*)

Text Based Games and Online Role-Playing MUDs
(*Colossal Cave Adventure, Zork, MUD*)

Arcade Games
(*Pong, Pac-Man*)   Action Console and Computer Games
(*Call of Duty, Madden*)

Graphical MUDs and MMORPGs
(*Ultima Online, World of Warcraft*)

MODERN "VIDEO GAMES"

FIGURE 1.1   Dual Evolutionary Pathways Leading to Modern Video Games

force, video games are actually in many ways more than one medium, and the meaning of the word "video game" varies widely depending on which video games are referenced. For some, a video game aims to provide the thrill and competition of sport or combat as richly as can be enjoyed; for others a video game is there to engender the creation of a shared narrative adventure story.

Given the catch-all nature of the term "video game," then, clear articulations of the medium's economic impact and audience are elusive given that the diversity in the range of technologies, forms, and themes described as video games is mirrored by diversity in their range of business models and users. Some current estimates of the total revenue of the worldwide video game market are in the neighborhood of $81.5 billion[70] to $93 billion USD,[71] with continued growth predicted in the coming years. As much as a quarter of this revenue is generated by the industry in the United States.

Estimates of the global market are difficult to make with precision, though, as video game industry revenue sources vary widely across game types. Traditionally, the video game industry is heavily reliant on "hits,"[17] even compared to some other hits-dominated media industries. While independent games developed by an individual or a small studio can be profitable, the bulk of the industry's profits are generated by a very small number of smash hits based on years of development by a huge staff. For example, the best-selling video game of 2013, *Grand Theft Auto V*, grossed more than $1 billion USD in three days; more than two weeks quicker than the 19 days it took for the three biggest film releases of all time to reach the same milestone.[72] While many MMORPG games and other developing game formats such as mobile phone and tablet games are also dominated by popular titles, their income is more skewed toward ongoing revenue such as subscriptions and purchases of "virtual items."[73] In fact, many successful MMORPG games have switched to free-to-play and "freemium" models where access is free and all revenue comes from either option premium fees or "microtransactions" from virtual item sales – a stark contrast to the reliance on blockbuster opening-week sales of action games such as *Grand Theft Auto V*.

Identifying the global video game audience is as nebulous as estimating the industry's economic scope, but one estimate places the audience at more than 1.2 billion souls.[74] Again, though, the habits of this audience are diverse. While only a slight majority of worldwide game users are male, trends in players' game preferences differ by gender; action and sport titles are most popular among males and puzzle and quiz games more popular among females. Within the MMORPG genre, meanwhile, there is evidence that the audience is much more male-dominated, with males comprising as much as 80–85 percent of that genre's audience.[56] Game users' habits also differ markedly depending on what devices they use to play games. In the United States, action games are the most popular genre of games played on video game consoles, while strategy games are most popular on computers and casual and social games are most popular on mobile devices.[75] As with the split ancestry of video games, the varied patterns in the industry's economics and audience are also evidence that video games can be best understood as a combination of different media with different conceptual traditions, cultural contributions, and social impact.

The Evolution of Research on Video Games and Societal Concerns

The remaining chapters of this volume provide a detailed account of the state of research dealing with a number of potential societal concerns related to video games, so this chapter will not address that research in depth. To preface those thorough explanations of social research topics that follow, though, this chapter will follow up on the above historical overview of video games' evolution with a very brief glance at the evolution of trends in research on the social impact of video games over the medium's lifespan.

Historically, it has been typical for the arrival of a new media technology to be followed by a spike in research on that medium's potential effects on children.[76] There has also been a predictable pattern in the trajectory of the focus of that research, with the specific focus of research on social harms tending to move over time from initial concerns about children's time spent with the medium to concerns about effects of specific content.[77] The research on video games over the past few decades has tended to follow that pattern as well.

While video games were commercially popular by the late 1970s, early research on social issues with games is relatively absent until the early part of the following decade. That early research includes a focus on how children's overall time spent with video games affected their personality[78] and socialization[79] and whether video game play was an "addictive" habit[80] interfering with other healthy activities.[81] Aggression was an outcome also explored in early research on video games' social effects, either as a form of delinquency potentially associated with heavy use[82] or as an outcome in controlled laboratory research.[83]

Much of the early research on societal issues with video games also investigated effects of video game exposure generally without regard to content. Through the 1980s and into the 1990s, even research dealing with the question of whether the violence in video games influenced players was often conducted by measuring video game exposure in general,[84] though there were also a number of studies that isolated violent or "aggressive" content to examine its possible effects.[85] Through much of the 1990s and 2000s, though, research increasingly focused on effects of violent content specifically, particularly in terms of its effects on measures related to aggression in users.[86] Similarly, while early research on video game "addiction" and problematic use tended to explore effects of overall video game exposure,[87] in the last decade more research on "addiction" and problematic behavior has begun to focus on specific types of video games such as online games[88] and specific genres such as MMORPGs.[89]

Therefore, while early research on societal concerns about video games has tended to lump together the different types of games that all fall under the "video game" banner, the research has tended to evolve toward studies isolating specific types of games and content to explore possible content-specific and genre-specific effects. There is, however, much room for improvement in tailoring research to fit the broad range of video game types and player experiences that exist. For example, while the video game play experience has increasingly become a social experience shared between players online,[90] research conceptualizations and designs have tended to focus somewhat myopically on effects of game content without regard to other dynamics of video game play settings and experiences. Also, violence has been a primary focus; content associated with other social concerns, such as the potential effects of portrayals of women, has received less attention, with exceptions.[91] Scholarly approaches that better accommodate the differences between types of video games and the different ways people play them, as well as an increased focus on the way players use video games to interact with each other as well as with game content,[92] are likely to provide more comprehensive answers to societal worries about video games.

Conclusion

While video games are a powerful social and economic force in the media landscape, they are not a monolithic one. The medium we call "video games" today can actually be seen as a diverse array of entertainment forms with roots in a history of more than one evolutionary stream of conceptualization and innovation. The better we remember that there is variety in the inspirations and innovations leading to the modern video game landscape, the better we will be equipped to try to understand the current societal role of video games.

References

1. Shubin N, Tabin C, Carroll S. Fossils, genes and the evolution of animal limbs. *Nature*. 1997; 388: 639–648. doi:10.1038/41710
2. Sullivan R. William A. Higinbotham, 84; Helped build first atomic bomb. *New York Times*. November 15, 1994. Available at: www.nytimes.com/1994/11/15/obituaries/william-a-higinbotham-84-helped-build-first-atomic-bomb.html
3. Anderson J. Who really invented the video game? *Creative Computing: Video and Arcade Games*. Spring 1983; 1(1): 8. Available at: www.atarimagazines.com/cva/v1n1/inventedgames.php
4. Winston B. *Media Technology and Society: A History: From the Telegraph to the Internet*. New York: Routledge; 1998.
5. Kirriemuir J. A history of digital games. In: Rutter J, Bryce J, eds. *Understanding Digital Games*. London: Sage; 2006: 21–35.
6. Campbell-Kelly M. The history of the history of software. *Ann Hist Comput, IEEE*. 2007; 29(4): 40–51. doi:10.1109/MAHC.2007.67

7. Baker C. Nimrod, the world's first gaming computer. *Wired*. June 2, 2010. Available at: www.wired.com/2010/06/replay/

8. Copeland BJ, Proudfoot D. What Turing did after he invented the Universal Turing Machine. *J Logic Lang Inf.* 2000; 9(4): 491–509. doi:10.1023/A:1008371426608

9. Goldsmith TT Jr, Mann ER. *U.S. Patent No. 2455992 A.* Washington, D.C.: U.S. Patent and Trademark Office; December 14, 1948.

10. Graetz JM. The origin of Spacewar. *Creative Computing.* August 1981; 7(8): 56–67.

11. Lowood H. A brief biography of computer games. In: Vorderer P, Bryant J, eds. *Playing Video Games: Motives, Responses, and Consequences.* Mahwah, New Jersey: Erlbaum; 2006: 25–41.

12. Lowood H. Videogames in Computer Space: The complex history of Pong. *IEEE Ann Hist Comput.* 2009; 31(3): 5–19. doi:10.1353/ahc.0.0076

13. Pelovitz R. The 2014 IEEE Edison Medal recipient: Meet the father of video games. *Consumer Electronics Magazine.* April 2014; 3(2): 18–24. doi:10.1109/MCE.2013.2296997

14. Montfort N. Combat in context. *Game Stud.* December 2006; 6(1). Available at: http://gamestudies.org/0601/articles/montfort

15. Ernkvist M. Down many times but still playing the game: Creative destruction and industry crashes in the early video game industry 1971–1986. In: Gratzer K, Stiefel D, eds. *History of Insolvency and Bankruptcy from an International Perspective.* Stockholm, Sweden: Södertörns Högskola; 2008: 161–192.

16. Pac-Man fever. *Time.* April 5, 1982. Available at: http://content.time.com/time/magazine/article/0,9171,921174,00.html

17. Williams D. Structure and competition in the U.S. home video game industry. *J Media Manag.* 2002; 4: 41–54. doi:10.1080/14241270209389979

18. Collins K. In the loop: Creativity and constraint in 8-bit video game audio. *Twentieth-Century Music.* 2007; 4: 209–227. doi:10.1017/S1478572208000510

19. Cifaldi F. Sad but true: We can't prove when Super Mario Bros. came out. *Gamasutra.* March 28, 2012. Available at: www.gamasutra.com/view/feature/167392/sad_but_true_we_cant_prove_when_.php

20. Gallagher S. Innovation and competition in standard-based industries: A historical analysis of the US home video game market. *IEEE Trans Eng Manag.* February 2002; 49(1): 67–82. doi:10.1109/17.985749

21. Jörnmark J, Axelsson A-S, Ernkvist M. Wherever hardware, there'll be games: The evolution of hardware and shifting industrial leadership in the gaming industry. *Proc Digit Games Res Assoc Int Conf (DiGRA) 2005,* Vancouver, Canada; 2005. Available at: http://summit.sfu.ca/item/255

22. Wolf MJP, ed. *The Video Game Explosion: A History from Pong to Playstation and Beyond.* Westport, Connecticut: Greenwood; 2008.

23. Crossley R. NDP: Best-selling US games of 2013 revealed. *Computer and Video Games.* January 17, 2014. Available at: www.computerandvideogames.com/445780/npd-best-selling-us-games-of-2013-revealed/

24. Fischer N. Competitive sport's imitation of war: Imaging the completeness of virtue. *J Philos Sport,* 2002; 29: 16–37. doi:10.1080/00948705.2002.9714620

25. Smith R. The long history of gaming in military training. *Simulation Gaming.* 2010; 41: 6–19. doi:10.1177/1046878109334330

26. Bartle RA. *Designing Virtual Worlds.* Indianapolis, IN: New Riders; 2003.

27. Mortensen TE. WoW is the new MUD: Social gaming from text to video. *Games Cult.* 2006; 1: 397–413. doi:10.1177/1555412006292622

28. Thomas S. Real, live MUD! *Personal Computer World.* August 1984; 134–135. Available at: http://mud.co.uk/richard/pcwaug84.htm

29. Machin D. MUD, MUD GLORIOUS MUD. *Big K.* October 1984; 46. Available at: http://mud.co.uk/richard/bkoct84.htm

30. Bartle RA. From MUDs to MMORPGs: The history of virtual worlds. In: Hunsinger J, Klastrup L, Allen M, eds. *International Handbook of Internet Research*. Dordrecht: Springer; 2010: 23–39. doi:10.1007/978-1-4020-9789-8_2

31. Lebling PD, Blank MS, Anderson TA. Zork: A computerized fantasy simulation game. *IEEE Comput Mag.* April 1979; 12(4): 51–59.

32. Seegert A. "Doing there" vs. "being there": Performing presence in interactive fiction. *J Gaming Virtual Worlds*. 2009; 1: 23–37. doi:10.1386/jgvw.1.1.23/1

33. Turkle, S. Constructions and reconstructions of self in virtual reality: Playing in the MUDs. *Mind Cult Act*. 1994; 1: 158–167. doi: 10.1080/10749039409524667

34. McKenna KYA, Bargh, JA. Plan 9 from cyberspace: The implications of the Internet for personality and social psychology. *Pers Soc Psychol Rev*. 2000; 4: 57–75. doi:10.1207/S15327957PSPR0401_6

35. Lindlof TR, Shatzer MJ. Media ethnography in virtual space: Strategies, limits, and possibilities. *J Broadcasting Electron Media*. 1998; 42: 170–189. doi:10.1080/08838159809364442

36. Mann C, Stewart F. *Internet Communication and Qualitative Research: A Handbook for Researching Online*. London: Sage; 2000.

37. Gygax G, Arneson D. *Dungeons and Dragons*. Lake Geneva, WI: Tactical Studies Rules; 1974.

38. Rignall J. Dave Lebling on the genesis of the adventure game – and the creation of Zork. *USGamer*. August 22, 2014. Available at: www.usgamer.net/articles/dave-lebling-interview

39. Copier M. Connecting worlds: Fantasy role-playing games, ritual acts and the magic circle. *Proc Digit Games Res Assoc Int Conf (DiGRA) 2005*, Vancouver, Canada; 2005. Available at: http://summit.sfu.ca/item/215

40. Rockwell G. Gore galore: Literary theory and computer games. *Comput Humanit*. 2002; 36: 345–358. doi:10.1023/A:1016174116399

41. Cox A, Campbell M. Multi-user dungeons. *Interactive Fantasy*. 1994; 2: 15–20. Available at: http://mud.co.uk/richard/ifan294.htm

42. Tolkien JRR. *Beowulf*: The monsters and the critics. *Proc Br Acad*. 1936; 22: 245–295.

43. Tolkien JRR. *The Hobbit: Or, There and Back Again*. London: George Allen and Unwin; 1937.

44. Tolkien JRR. *The Fellowship of the Ring: Being the First Part of the Lord of the Rings*. London: George Allen and Unwin; 1954. Tolkien JRR. *The Two Towers: Being the Second Part of the Lord of the Rings*. London: George Allen and Unwin; 1954. Tolkien JRR. *The Return of the King: Being the Third Part of the Lord of the Rings*. London: George Allen and Unwin; 1955.

45. Booker CM. Byte-sized Middle Ages: Tolkien, film, and the digital imagination. *Comitatus: J Medieval Renaissance Stud*. 2004; 35: 145–174.

46. Ekman F. Tolkien MUDs and other online games. *The Tolkien Computer Games Pages*. n.d. Available at: www.lysator.liu.se/tolkien-games/mud.html

47. Loguidice B, Barton M. *Vintage Games: An Insider Look at the History of Grand Theft Auto, Super Mario, and the Most Influential Games of All Time*. Burlington, MA: Focal; 2009.

48. Lemmons P. The IBM Personal Computer: First impressions. *BYTE*. October 1981; 6(10): 26–34.

49. Bartle RA. *Artificial Intelligence and Computer Games*. London: Century Communications; 1985.

50. Ivory JD. Technological developments and transitions in virtual worlds. In: Heider D, ed. *Living Virtually: Researching New Worlds*. New York: Peter Lang; 2009: 11–22.

51. Mulligan J, Patrovsky B. *Developing Online Games: An Insider's Guide*. Indianapolis, IN: New Riders; 2003.

52. Morningstar C., Farmer FR. The lessons of Lucasfilm's Habitat. In: Benedikt ML, ed. *Cyberspace: First Steps.* Cambridge, MA: MIT Press; 1991: 273–302.

53. Langshaw M. Retro corner: "Neverwinter Nights." *Digital Spy.* September 8, 2010. Available at: www.digitalspy.com/gaming/levelup/a404663/retro-corner-neverwinter-nights.html

54. Ludlow P, Wallace M. *The Second Life Herald: The Virtual Tabloid that Witnessed the Dawn of the Metaverse.* Cambridge, MA: MIT Press; 2007.

55. Kirmse A. *History of Meridian 59, 1994–2000.* May 2000. Available at: www.meridian59.com/about-early-history.php

56. Ivory JD. *Virtual Lives: A Reference Handbook.* Santa Barbara: CA: ABC CLIO; 2012.

57. Inside Ultima IV. *Computer Gaming World.* March 1986; 18–21. Available at: www.cgwmuseum.org/galleries/issues/cgw_26.pdf

58. Castronova E. *On Virtual Economies.* CESifo Working Paper No. 752. July 2002. Available at: http://ssrn.com/abstract=338500.

59. Tingle A. Raph Koster on the past, present, and future. *MMORPG.com.* August 28, 2013. Available at: www.mmorpg.com/showFeature.cfm/feature/7716/General-Raph-Koster-on-the-Past-Present-and-Future.html

60. King B. Games started off without a bang. *Wired.* July 15, 2002. Available at: http://archive.wired.com/gaming/gamingreviews/news/2002/07/53765

61. Axelsson A-S, Regan T. *How Belonging in an Online Group Affects Social Behavior – A Case Study of Asheron's Call.* (Technical Report) Redmond, WA: Microsoft Research; January 29. 2002. Available at: http://research.microsoft.com/pubs/69910/tr-2002-07.pdf

62. DikuMUD *Sworn Statement.* April 25, 2003. Available at: www.dikumud.com/Everquest/Sworn.aspx

63. Ducheneaut N, Yee N, Nickell E, Moore RJ. Alone together? Exploring the social dynamics of massively multiplayer online games. *Proc SIGCHI Conf Hum Factors Comput Syst.* New York: ACM Press; 2006: 407–416. doi:10.1145/1124772.1124834

64. Van Geel I. *MMOData.net: Keeping Track of the MMORPG Scene.* 2013. Available at: http://mmodata.blogspot.com/

65. Sihvonen T. *Players Unleashed! Modding The Sims and the Culture of Gaming.* Amsterdam: Amsterdam University Press; 2011.

66. Nardi B, Harris J. Strangers and friends: Collaborative play in World of Warcraft. In: Hunsinger J, Klastrup L, Allen M, eds. *International Handbook of Internet Research.* Dordrecht: Springer; 2010: 395–410. doi:10.1007/978-1-4020-9789-8_24

67. Schmieder C. World of Maskcraft vs. World of Queercraft? Communication, sex and gender in the online role-playing game *World of Warcraft. J Gaming Virtual Worlds.* 2009; 1: 5–21. doi:10.1386/jgvw.1.1.5_1

68. Lastowka FG, Hunter D. The laws of virtual worlds. *California Law Review.* 2004; 92: 1–73.

69. Chance J. *Tolkien's Art: A Mythology for England.* New York: St. Martin's Press; 1979.

70. Ohannessian K. U.S. leads the world in video game revenue. *Tech Times.* June 27, 2014. Available at: www.techtimes.com/articles/9270/20140627/america-china-japan-video-games-revenue.htm

71. Molina B. Gartner: Global video game market to hit $93B this year. *USA Today.* October 29, 2013. Available at: www.usatoday.com/story/tech/gaming/2013/10/29/gartner-worldwide-video-game-market/3294591/

72. Kain E. "Grand Theft Auto V" crosses $1B in sales, biggest entertainment launch in history. *Forbes.* September 20, 2013. Available at: www.forbes.com/sites/erikkain/2013/09/20/grand-theft-auto-v-crosses-1b-in-sales-biggest-entertainment-launch-in-history/

73. White G, Searle N. Commercial business models for a fast changing industry. In: Hotho S, McGregor N, eds. *Changing the Rules of the Game: Economic, Management,*

and Emerging Issues in the Computer Games Industry. New York: Palgrave Macmillan; 2013: 28–47.

74. Takahashi D. More than 1.2 billion people are playing games. *VentureBeat.* November 25, 2013. Available at: http://venturebeat.com/2013/11/25/more-than-1-2-billion-people-are-playing-games/

75. Entertainment Software Association. *2014 Sales, Demographics, and Usage Data: Essential Facts about the Computer and Video Game Industry.* 2014. Available at: www.theesa.com/facts/pdfs/esa_ef_2014.pdf

76. Wartella E, Reeves B. Historical trends in research on children and the media: 1900–1960. *J Commun.* 1985; 35: 118–133. doi:10.1111/j.1460-2466.1985.tb02238.x

77. Wartella EA, Jennings NA. Children and computers: New technology – old concerns. *Future Child.* 2000; 10(2): 31–43.

78. Gibb GD, Bailey JR, Lambirth TT, Wilson WP. Personality differences between high and low electronic video game users. *J Psychol.* 1983; 114: 159–165. doi:10.1080/0 0223980.1983.9915409

79. Selnow G. Playing videogames: The electronic friend. *J Commun.* 1984; 34: 148–156. doi:10.1111/j.1460-2466.1984.tb02166.x

80. Braun CM, Giroux J. Arcade video games: Proxemix, cognitive, and content analyses. *J Leisure Res.* 1989; 21: 92–105.

81. Egli EA, Myers LS. The role of video game playing in adolescent life: Is there reason to be concerned? *Bull Psychon Soc.* 1984; 22: 309–312. doi:10.3758/BF03333828

82. Dominick JR. Videogames, television violence, and aggression in teenagers. *J Commun.* 1984; 34, 136–147. doi:10.1111/j.1460-2466.1984.tb02165.x

83. Cooper J, Mackie D. Video games and aggression in children. *J Appl Soc Psychol.* 1986; 16: 726–744. doi:10.1111/j.1559-1816.1986.tb01755.x

84. Griffiths MD. Violent video games and aggression: A review of the literature. *Aggression Violent Behav.* 1999; 4: 203–212. doi:10.1016/S1359-1789(97)00055-4

85. Dill KE, Dill JC. Video game violence: A review of the empirical literature. *Aggression Violent Behav.* 1998; 3: 407–428. doi:10.1016/S1359-1789(97)00001-3

86. Anderson CA, Shibuya A, Ihori N, et al. Violent video game effects on aggression, empathy, and prosocial behavior in Eastern and Western countries: A meta-analytic review. *Psychol Bull.* 2010; 136: 151–173. doi:10.1037/a0018251

87. Griffiths MD, Hunt NH. Dependence on computer games by adolescents. *Psychol Rep.* 1998; 82: 475–480. doi:10.2466/PR0.82.2.475-480

88. Kuss DJ, Griffiths MD. Internet gaming addiction: A systematic review of empirical research. *Int J Ment Health Addict.* 2012; 10: 278-296. doi:10.1007/s11469-011-9318-5

89. Hussain Z, Griffiths MD. Excessive use of massively multi-player online role-playing games: A pilot study. *Int J Ment Health Addict.* 2009; 7: 563–571. doi:10.1007/s11469-009-9202-8

90. Williams D. Why game studies now? Gamers don't bowl alone. *Games Cult.* 2006; 1: 13–16. doi:10.1177/1555412005281774

91. Behm-Morawitz E, Mastro, D. The effects of the sexualization of female video game characters on gender stereotyping and female self-concept. *Sex Roles.* 2009; 61: 808–823. doi:10.1007/s11199-009-9683-8

92. Elson M, Breuer J, Ivory JD, Quandt T. More than stories with buttons: Narrative, mechanics, and context as determinants of player experience in digital games. *J Commun.* 2014; 64: 521–542. doi:10.1111/jcom.12096

2

THE RISE (AND REFINEMENT) OF MORAL PANIC*

Nicholas D. Bowman

The following chapter provides an overview of the dominant approaches to understanding the impact of mediation on media consumers. Before approaching the topic regarding video games however, it is important to plot the trajectory of how we have historically understood moral panics from the media. To this end, the chapter will cover five main areas of thought: a definition of moral panic, early accounts of media fears, the rise of moral panics as a result of mass communication, the refinement of media effects as individual processing, interactivity as a key igniter of the moral panic debate, and a contemporary view of media effects as the interaction of messages and the idiosyncratic ways they are processed.

Moral Panic, Defined

As a social science, the study of media psychology aims to untangle the "complex relationship between humans and the evolving digital environment."[1] If we were to remove the term "digital" from this definition, we can broadly explain that the goal of media psychology is to better understand how individuals use and are affected by mediated messages. By effects, we are referring to how media might impact people at the cognitive (thoughts), affective (feelings), and behavioral (actions) levels.

While not by definition, most scholarly and public interest tends to focus on the potential for negative media effects – that is, as a whole we are driven to

* The author would like to recognize James Abdallah (West Virginia University) for his editorial and formatting assistance with this manuscript.

understand how media usage (often considered as a voluntary pursuit) might have a corrosive impact on how we think, feel and behave towards each.[2] Some of this focus might be the result of an evolutionary tendency – at both the individual and societal level – to identify and minimize risk.[3]

Focusing on risk mitigation is not an inherently faulty practice, but in practice such an approach brings with it a need for researchers to adopt a more normative approach to science. Researchers are required to assume that the effects they are looking for are (a) present and (b) dangerous, which often results in the adoption of a moral stance. Writing for *The British Journal of Psychiatry*, Elson and Ferguson explain potential pitfalls with this approach:

> In a moral panic, a part of society considers certain behaviors or lifestyle choices of another part to be a significant threat to society as a whole. *In this environment, moral beliefs can substantially influence scientific research, and its results are readily used as confirmation for what has been suspected.* (emphasis added)[4] (p 32)

Early Moral Panics

> Appraisal: All have said the stated proposition to be foolish and absurd in Philosophy; and formally heretical since it expressly contradicts the sense of sacred scripture in many places . . .[5]

In 1616, the Roman Inquisition of Pope Paul V issued the above ruling in a heresy case against famed Italian scientist Galileo Galilei for his public writings about the heliocentric structure of the solar system – a view that directly contrasts several passages in the Catholic Bible suggesting the Earth, as created by God, to be the "height of the stars" (Job 22:12). Galileo was later committed to a lifetime of house arrest after mocking Pope Urban VIII as the Simplicio (simpleton) in further writing on the topic in 1633.[6] While certainly not the only scientist to be persecuted by Church authorities – indeed a portion of the *Pontificale Romanum* (the oath taken by Roman Catholic bishops at their consecration) requires any ordained bishop "to the utmost of [their] power, persecute and attack heretics, schismatics, and rebels against the same our Lord or his aforesaid successors" – Galileo's case is compelling in that his scientific views were accurate. Later work by scientists empirically confirmed his theories by demonstrating the Earth's orbital patterns around the Sun, and Vatican leaders later apologized for their treatment of Galileo, with Pope John Paul II issuing an official apology on behalf of the Catholic Church nearly 360 years after the original ruling.[7]

Importantly for our discussion, scientists were not the only ones persecuted by the Church. Thomsett writes that nearly 75 years prior to Galileo's trials, the 1564 Council of Trent formalized their guidelines for adding published books to the *Librorum Prohibitorum* – a list that eventually grew to include over 4,300 works on science, philosophy, and popular culture (the list was not abolished until 1966, by decree of Pope Paul VI).[8] While not all of the authors were punished, their works were severely restricted for containing views against Church doctrine. Works such as Victor Hugo's *Les Miserables* and Alexander Dumas' *The Count of Monte Cristo* and *The Three Musketeers* are only a small sampling of volumes on the Index that, while shunned in their time, are celebrated today. Indeed in the late 1700s, German theologian and historian Johann Gottfried Hoche wrote extensively on the societal dangers of reading adventure novels, claiming that they led to compulsions that were a foolish and harmful waste of time – particularly for children, but also for housewives who might be distracted from their other domestic duties.[9]

Our focus on the Catholic Church above is done to illustrate an important point raised by Elson and Ferguson: when part of a society (the Church) considers another part (the scientist) to be a threat or risk to the greater social good, perspectives are severely limited.[4] As written by Thomsett: "It would not have been possible for science to progress as long as the Church held the power to silence anyone it chose."[8] From a moral panic standpoint, and certainly from the standpoint of Hugo and Dumas, the same could be said about literature: when one aspect of society deems another to be heretical, expression becomes impossible.

The persecution of Galileo, Hugo, and Dumas for their "immoral" teachings (or at least, teachings incompatible with Church doctrine) share a unique common factor that makes each a key for the study of media psychology: each published books, for the general public, written in a common language (Italian in the case of Galileo, French in the case of Hugo and Dumas). That is, the Church was not so much concerned about the individual authors as they were about the impact of their works on the thoughts, feelings, and actions of the larger social structure. The printing of a book allowed for the authors' thoughts to be spread in an unadulterated form, and writing these thoughts in a common language allowed them to be understood and discussed by a mass audience.

As far back as the ancient Greeks, fears of written language – one of the first forms of mass media – were expressed. In his *Phaedrus*, the famed philosopher Plato emulates the thoughts of his mentor Socrates, who denounced written words as antithetical to learning, suggesting that as writing spreads, people will begin "sowing words which can neither speak for themselves nor teach the truth adequately to others."[10] Those early philosophers feared that written words would ruin education because they would present singular answers to complex problems, and such a perspective again fits Elson and Ferguson: the dominant perspective on education during the time of Socrates and Plato (argumentation and rhetoric) was challenged by an emerging perspective that privileged the written word.[4] Indeed in the modern education system, both speech and writing are equally treasured.

Fast-forwarding nearly 1800 years from these debates (and skipping over the previously discussed controversies with the *Librorum Prohibitorum*), we can find a number of examples of media products that faced early moral scrutiny. Connor gives an account of the "enslaving" (para. 4) allure of the newspaper crossword puzzles in 1920s North America (the USA and Canada, namely),[11] citing a variety of accounts in which editorials written in English newspapers espoused the corrosive impact of crosswords on laborers and housewives (distracting them from their economic or domestic duties, similar to Hoche's fears about reading in 1794) and encouraging a marked decline in reading and intelligent conversation. One editorial, entitled 'Cross-Word Puzzles. An Enslaved America,' claims that crosswords "have dealt the final blow to the art of conversation, and have been known to break up homes" (*Tamworth Herald*, 1924, as cited by Connor). To some extent, the roots of this moral panic can be traced back to a Puritan approach to media entertainment (cf. Zillmann) in which "idle hands are the Devil's playthings."[12]

Mass Audiences Give Rise to Mass Panic

As media technology progressed into the twentieth century, so did public fears about its impact. Parker explains that the early adoption of the electronic telephone systems in the late 1800s was met with fears that the technology was invasive (allowing for others to spy on private conversations by intercepting telephone signals) and potentially dangerous (its electronic signals might permanently deafen the user).[13] Eber suggests that others were concerned that telephones would prove to be incessant distractions – so much so that Alexander Graham Bell himself (the inventor of the device) refused to have a phone in his own workshop.[14] Many would claim later that the source of some of these fears may have been telegraph companies, who were encouraged to incite moral panics about a (not-so) dangerous technology in order to slow its growth.[13]

Perhaps the first scientific study into moral panics can be traced to the Payne Fund studies of the 1930s. Funded by noted Ohio philanthropist Frances Payne Bolton, these studies looked to establish a learned opinion to address societal concerns about the influence of motion pictures on their largely adolescent audiences – concerns fueled by newspaper editorials and magazine articles similar to those denouncing the evils of the crossword puzzle.[15] As written by Charters (1933):

> No one in this country up to the present time has known in any general and impersonal manner just what effect motion pictures have upon children. Meanwhile children clamor to attend the movies as often as they are allowed to go.[16]

For Charters and his colleagues, the best way to address the moral panics associated with motion pictures was not through argumentation and rhetoric, but instead through an impartial scientific lens in which effects could be observed and understood without the biased perspective of any one investigator.[15] Broadly, the Payne Fund studies were broken into (1) an analysis of film content and (2) investigations into the impact of that content. In analyzing over 1,500 films in the time period of 1925 to 1935, Payne Fund scholars reported that nearly three-fourths of films featured crime, sex, and love as central plotlines, with the use of tobacco and alcohol being openly portrayed (as Lowery and DeFleur note, during a time of Prohibition). Moreover, a variety of experimental and interview techniques showed that not only did children react physiologically to films (such as increased arousal when watching action and horror sequences) but they also expressed attitudes and opinions that aligned with on-screen content (such as more liberal views on crime, sex, and love). Such findings led Charters to later conclude that "the commercial movies are an unsavory mess."[17] The fact that his conclusions were seemingly based on (at the time) state-of-the art science seemed to justify the larger public's concern that motion pictures were a root cause of juvenile corruption.

So, if the Payne Fund studies were done using the objective lens of science, then do their conclusions support 1920s moral panic over motion pictures? Hardly. For example, Sproule (1997) discussed that many of the studies themselves – such as the content analysis study – were designed from a moralist perspective; at one point, the authors of that study concluded that (then) contemporary film contained themes "at variance with the views that we are trying to develop in the schools, homes and churches" (Dale, as cited by Sproule).[17] Noted social scientist Samuel Stouffer similarly critiqued the methods of using anecdotes as proof of causal and generalizable phenomenon.[17] Finally, Lowery and DeFleur suggest that while the Payne Fund studies did provide evidence of motion pictures' corrosive impact on children, they also provided evidence about prosocial impacts – for example, studies on children's perspectives towards minorities (such as ethnic Chinese) were found to improve in the short and long term following exposure to a film that showed those minorities in a positive (vs. a negative) light.[15] That is, the best conclusion of the Payne Fund studies – although not a popular conclusion among media critics and others caught in the moral panic – was simply that: "films were an influence on attitudes; they provided models for behavior; they shaped interpretations of life. They probably had as many prosocial influences (or at least harmless influences) as those that disturbed adults of the time."[15]

Almost directly mirroring the motion picture debate, the 1950s saw a similar debate involving the negative impact of popular entertainment media on young minds – this time, pulling comic books into the bulls-eye of a moral panic. An article in *Collier's Magazine* entitled "Horror in the Nursery" offered a six-page feature on the work of US psychiatrist Fredric Wertham, who claimed to have clinical evidence of the impact of comic book illustrations and narratives on juvenile delinquency rates across the nation.[18] To Wertham, comics "are demoralizing the morals of youth" and he saw his role in this research "not as a psychiatrist, but as a voice for the thousands of troubled parents who, like myself, are concerned primarily with their children's welfare."[19] Wertham and his team content analyzed selected comic books of the time and found them to contain themes of crime, sex, horror, misogyny, and violence (many of the same themes found by Payne Fund scholars in the 1920s), and his follow-up interviews with children in juvenile detention found many of them to be avid comic book readers. From this, Wertham confirmed comic books to be a form of dangerous entertainment media in need of regulation – eventually leading to an industry self-regulation (the Comics Code Authority) that held from 1954 (the publication of Wertham's *Seduction of the Innocent* volume) until January 2011.[20] Later, much of Wertham's research was discredited for not adhering to basic standards of the scientific method – for example, neither his sampling of comic books for analysis nor his interviews with children were random – but for industry, the damage was done. In offering a comprehensive and critical analysis of Wertham, Tilley best summarizes his research as:

> filled with examples like the preceding ones in which Wertham shifted responsibility for young people's behavioral disorders and other patholo-gies from the broader social, cultural, and organic physical contexts of these children's lives to the recreational pastime of reading comics.[21]

Looking back, contemporary media psychologists refer to studies such as the Payne Fund and the Seduction of the Innocent as examples of a magic bullet effect: a model of media effects that assumes media content to have a direct, powerful, and universal impact on the individual audience member. In truth, it is unlikely that any of these researchers honestly claimed that effects were so simple; at the same time, their studies placed a heavy focus on media as the causal agent in corroding individual thoughts, actions, and behaviors. However, as best stated by Joseph Klapper: "mass communication ordinarily does not serve as a necessary and sufficient cause of audience effects, but rather functions among and through a nexus of mediating factors and influences."[22]

Klapper's perspective, often called the limited effects paradigm, perhaps aligns most closely with the modern definition of media psychology offered earlier in this chapter: in both definitions, the impact of a media message cannot be understood unless we better understand the person consuming it, requiring a deep understanding of both individuals and their evolving media environment. Conversely, this deep understanding does not require (and is not assisted by) a moral panic perspective that diminishes the role of the individual as an active creator of meaning. Unfortunately for Plato (and Socrates), research and common practice has long disproven the notion that mediated messages are closed for interpretation, such as Taylor's cloze tests for readability and Barthes' discussions of the dual agency of author and reader.[23,24]

Yet, while we might suggest that such strict adherence to a magic bullet effect was never really present in the social sciences, many suggest that these early studies – even after they were reinterpreted as being less damning than initially drafted – established a legacy of fear for mass media effects that continues to dominate the scientific examination of media effects into the digital age.

Interactivity and the "Murder Simulator"

By most accounts, the first video game subjected to moral panic was the 1976 driving simulator *Death Race*, an arcade machine in which players, sitting at the controls of a physical steering wheel and gas pedal, earn points for using their on-screen car as a weapon to run over "gremlins."[25] The game sparked controversy for essentially encouraging players to use their cars in an aggressive manner, awarding them points for committing vehicular homicide reminiscent of the 1975 film *Death Race 2000* (which the game was loosely inspired by). In an interview with *The New York Times*, a psychiatrist from the US National Security Council by the name of Gerald Driessen offered a simple-yet-powerful statement on the matter in stating his group's concern over the interactive nature of video games, suggesting that while television violence is passive, "in [Death Race], a player takes the first step to creating violence. The player is no longer just a spectator. He's an actor in the process."[26]

As a video game, *Death Race* was not particularly innovative – it presented simple black-and-white pixel graphics, rudimentary even for their time. However, Kocurek suggests the controversy surrounding the game set a course for video game fears that persisted far beyond the 500 *Death Race* arcade cabinets that were eventually manufactured (far beyond developer Exidy's original sales projections).[27] For Kocurek, the *Death Race* controversy inextricably linked video games and violence in the public mind, as well as drawing specific attention to the potentially dangerous role of interactivity in video games. Walker discussed similar concerns over the 1982 pornographic game *Custer's Revenge*, in which players navigated an arrow field in order to force themself upon a Native American woman tied to a cactus – the pornographic elements (given technological limitations of the time) were incredibly rudimentary, but the game required players to digitally enact an on-screen rape in order to win.[25] In replicating Driessen's panics, Dworkin claimed that the game had "generated many gang rapes of Native American women" although this claim was supported with a lone anecdote.[28]

Perhaps the most prominent illustration of the limits of what the public would be willing to accept in a violent video game can be found in the 1992 release of the arcade fighter *Mortal Kombat*. Perhaps best stated by Narcisse, *Mortal Kombat* "broke an implicit taboo about what was okay to put in video games" – such as the game's use of motion-capture technology to display realistic human body movement, the intense focus on blood and gore during in game fights, and the (not so) secret "Fatality" special moves where players could brutally kill each other through a series of beatings, beheadings, and disembowelments (based on the talents of the gamer as well as their in-game character).[29] Although the game's reputation in arcades had drawn some criticism from activist groups, it was the game's home release on September 20, 1993 (or "Mortal Monday" as labeled in a $10 million advertising campaign by producer Acclaim – at the time the largest advertising campaign ever for a video game) that was most concerning for a critical public.[30] As described by *Time Magazine*:

> Johnny Cage kills his victims with a bloody, decapitating uppercut. Rayden favors electrocution. Kano will punch through his opponent's chest and rip out a still-beating heart. Sub-Zero likes to tear his foe's head off and hold it up in victory, spinal cord twitching as it dangles from the neck . . . these are characters from Mortal Kombat, America's top-grossing arcade game last year and the focus of a growing debate about whether violence in video games has finally gone too far.[31]

To some extent, video game manufacturers had already anticipated criticism of the home versions of *Mortal Kombat*. Prior to release, Nintendo censored out the blood and violence and altered the Fatality moves to make them less graphic in their Super Nintendo version of the game. While not editing the original game code (except to make it compatible with their system), SEGA chose instead to label the game packaging with a "MA-13" as not appropriate for children under the age of 13.[32] However, in the face of intensifying Congressional scrutiny to answer questions about whether or not games were training killers and encouraging graphic violence, the two companies instead chose to debate each other's relative moral stance: SEGA claiming moral superiority because their games were labeled for concerned parents, and Nintendo claiming moral superiority because their products were never allowed to contain such violence as a matter of internal corporate policy.[33] Further complicating these debates was a complete lack of any scientific data on the potential impact of video games on aggression, leaving all sides of the argument with little more than empty rhetoric on which to base their claims. In the face of mounting public, governmental, and industry pressure to address the moral panic caused by *Mortal Kombat*, 1994 saw the creation of the Entertainment Software Rating Boards – an independent organization funded by the gaming industry and designed "to empower consumers, especially parents, with guidance that allows them to make informed decisions about the age-appropriateness and suitability of video games."[34] Looking back on the controversy caused by his creation, *Mortal Kombat* creator Ed Boon expressed in an interview that he somewhat sympathized with critics of his game, saying that "[Back in 1992] there was no ratings system when the first one came out, and to me it makes sense – I wouldn't want my ten-year-old kid playing a game like that."[35] Perhaps unsurprisingly, *Mortal Kombat* was the first game ever assigned ESRB's "M" rating (for "mature audiences only"). As stated by Korucek, games such as *Death Race* and *Mortal Kombat* served to stoke public fears about the presence of interactive video game violence, and the response *du jour* seemed to be a heightened awareness of the adult-nature of video game content; that is, the implementation of a ratings system so that consumers could be better informed as to the content of their desired media products.[27] Ratings were not new to entertainment media, as the Motion Picture Association of America (MPAA) had been rating US films since 1968. However, it was clear (as mentioned by Narcisse) that audience expectations and perceptions of violence in films and video games differed substantially, a claim empirically supported in later literature.[29,36]

However, an established ratings system did little to quell moral panics related to video game violence, and a series of high-profile school shootings in the US re-ignited concerns that video games served as interactive murder simulations. Investigations into the causes of tragic incidents in Paducah, Kentucky (December 1, 1997) and Columbine, Colorado (April 20, 1999) by politicians such as then-US Attorney General John Ashcroft implicated video games as a root cause.[37] On the surface, linking violent video games to school shootings was a simple matter of observational deduction, given the increased popularity of the first-person shooting game in the 1990s. Games such as *Wolfenstein* 3D (released by id Software in 1992) and *DOOM* (1993) ushered in a genre of video games in which the player was effectively placed in the shoes of the main protagonist (a Nazi prisoner in the former, and a space Marine in the latter), armed with high-powered weapons and challenged with navigating a series of mazes and puzzles while being attacked on all sides by enemy soldiers and demons. Ashcroft mirrored many other public opinions when he suggested that shooting games have the ability to train players not only to think about violence as an acceptable form of reprisal for pent-up aggression (a process empirically supported by Anderson and Bushman, albeit challenged by Ferguson), but that games also have the capacity to teach someone how to use a weapon effectively – such as how to load, aim, and fire a military-grade weapon.[38,39] While the debate still rages about the relative contribution of video game violence to human aggression (see Chapter 4 in this volume), the latter behavioral effects seem dubious given the non-familiarity between game controls and actual weapons. As written by the 6th US Court of Appeals (in reference to the Paducah shooting): "We find that it is simply too far a leap from shooting characters on a video screen (an activity undertaken by millions) to shooting people in a classroom (an activity undertaken by a handful, at most) ..."[40]

As games gained in popularity, the content of games became increasingly scandalous – likely in an effort for games to stand out among an increasingly crowded marketplace, UK-based Rockstar Studios released one of the most commercially and critically successful games in the medium's history with *Grand Theft Auto*. While early iterations of the game enjoyed moderate popularity, the 2001 release of *Grand Theft Auto III* popularized the sandbox genre of video games: games in which the player has the ability to navigate the environment as if it were real (in this case the sprawling city of "Liberty City" modeled loosely after New York City). In this game, and its subsequent iterations, players adopt the role of a criminal involved in any number of organized crime activities from (as the title implies) car theft to drug-running, prostitution, and murder. While these games were meant to satire popular gangster films – such as Francis Ford Coppola's acclaimed *Godfather* trilogy (cf. Bowman) – their content is decidedly dark, "from the theft of vehicles to get from one mission to the next to the murder of rival crime bosses, police officers and innocent bystanders who might interfere with the player's objectives."[41]

While games such as *Wolfenstein* and the *Doom* and *Grand Theft Auto* series have incurred little recourse beyond public ire and scrutiny, there have been video games that have been banned for their overtly violent content, such as the prison violence game *Manhunt* which was banned in New Zealand and Germany, and refused a rating by Australia's Classification Review Board (effectively banning the game) for containing elements "beyond those set out in the classification guidelines."[42] In an interview, former Rockstar programmer Jeff Williams explained his feelings about the game, suggesting that unlike the satirical nature of the *Grand Theft Auto* games:

> *Manhunt*, though, just made us all feel icky. It was all about the violence, and it was realistic violence. We all knew there was no way we could explain away that game. There was no way to rationalize it. We were crossing a line.[43]

For Williams, the question of violent video games might not be so much a question of media effects as it is a question of storytelling; that is, not a question of whether or not that media content might cause moral corruption in players, but rather whether or not he was comfortable telling such a dark tale.

Moral panics surrounding gaming are not restricted to violence. Walker talks about widespread fears that gamers would be "a generation of fatties who never left the house" – speaking to assumptions about the social unattractiveness and social awkwardness of gamers.[25] In an infamous – albeit analog – example of the latter point, Fine recounts the story of James Dallas Egbert III, a Michigan State University student who went missing in August 1979.[44] Early fears about Egbert's disappearance centered around his fascination with the role-playing game *Dungeons and Dragons (D&D)*, and many early media reports suggested that he had taken refuge in steam tunnels below the school to re-enact scenarios from the game (it was later discovered that Egbert suffered from severe depression, and had entered the steam tunnels in attempt to commit suicide in seclusion). Following the Egbert story, scores of panics regarding *D&D* players as malcontents incapable of discerning fantasy and reality led to similar allegations in the US and UK. In writing for the BBC, Allison summarizes the fears: "Looking back now, it's possible to see the tendrils of a classic moral panic, and some elements of the slightly esoteric world of role-playing did stir the imaginations of panicked outsiders."[45]

Concerns over gamers being physically fit and socially isolated have been challenged with more recent data. In a survey of 7000 *EverQuest II* players, Williams, Yee and Caplan found players to have lower body mass index scores than the general population, and that a major motivator for their continued play was for social interaction – although the authors also noted that gamers had higher levels of depression than would be expected.[46] Similar work by Kowert and Oldmeadow suggests that not only are gamers social when playing, but that these social skills can be learned in-game and used out-of-game, and work by Banks and Bowman suggests that gamers can even form authentic social relations with their own avatars.[47,48]

The Myopia of Moral Panics

The moral panic over violent video games is doubly harmful. It has led adult authorities to be more suspicious and hostile to many kids who already feel cut off from the system. It also misdirects energy away from eliminating the actual causes of youth violence and allows problems to continue to fester. (para. 4).[49]

The above quote was drawn from an essay by noted technology scholar and sociologist Henry Jenkins, and speaks to the dangers of allowing normative assumptions about psychological principles permeate our research. In speaking specifically about the violent video game debate, Ivory and Elson warn that scholars choosing either side of the debate – powerful effects or null effects – seem to be engaging in an "[increasingly] aggressive academic game" (para. 11) that likely does more to advance individual careers than our societal-level understanding of video games.[4]

Where are the roots of these moral panics? In a 2013 public opinion poll conducted in collaboration with YouGov – a research firm based in the UK – Oxford research fellow Andrew Przybylski found that opinions about the public danger of violent video games differed as a result of a number of different demographic and experience variables; such research suggests that those less experienced with video games are more likely to fear them.[50] In their study, older non-gamers were significantly more likely to feel that games were "a contributing cause in mass shootings" than younger gamers; interestingly, younger gamers were also more likely to agree that "new legislation is needed to restrict the availability of games," which might indicate that gamers are comfortable with labeling and rating the age-appropriateness of games (similar to *Mortal Kombat* creator Ed Boon's comments on his game, earlier in this chapter).

Comments expressed by non-gamers, such as infamous (and now disbarred) US attorney and anti-video game zealot Jack Thompson's dismissal of video games as a form of "mental masturbation" for "knuckleheads" (as cited by Benedetti) reinforces the point that normative perspectives on gaming tend to come from non-gamers.[51] Assuming his masturbation reference is a suggestion that gaming is a self-gratifying leisure activity, one is reminded of perhaps one of the earliest models of mass communication, formulated by sociologist Harold Lasswell in 1948. In his model, Lasswell suggested a three-part function of modern mass media to (a) offer surveillance of societal events, (b) explain the correlation of those events and general public opinion, and (c) to serve as a method for the transmission of cultural heritage.[52] Missing from this definition, of course, is the role of entertainment, which was later added by Wright, along with the notion of political mobilization.[53] Why the differences in perspectives? Lasswell's model was prescriptive (the perspective of a sociologist explaining the ideal role of mass media in society) whereas Wright's model was descriptive (an explanation of his own observations of mass media as it was being used by society). Indeed, nearly 20 years after his original crusade against the morally corrosive content of comic books, Wertram himself wrote a volume, *The World of Fanzines*, that celebrated the creativity that comics books and science fiction novels can foster in children; Gonzalez tells the story of NASA director Charles Bolden nostalgically recalling the role that the space-traveling superhero Flash Gordon played in his eventual career as an astronaut.[54,55]

At the same time, video game scholars (as well as developers and players) are similarly warned about the risk of taking a normative stance in assuming that video games have no capability for negative effects. Huesmann, Debow, and Yang argue that many of the reasons why "intelligent people still doubt the effects [of violent video games on aggression]" are related to the fact that many of the researchers and policy makers are unwilling to accept that an activity that they personally engage in (gaming) could have negative effects.[56] The same article also suggests that a general desensitization to violence as well as a strong third-person effect (subconscious psychological assumptions that others are more affected by content than ourselves) are causing many media psychologists to adopt a normative stance that video games cannot be harmful.

At the 2013 Game Developers Conference meeting, designer Walt Williams was abundantly clear that developers should not claim that games are not violent or that they don't have any influence on gamers – indeed, the point of his presentation was to describe his team's latest game *Spec Ops: The Line*, which makes liberal use of contextualized realistic violence in order to force gamers to question their own acceptance of the atrocities of war (in a more poignant scene from the game, players are confronted with the horrific results of a fatal white phosphoros attack on a group of civilians – an attack which the player perpetrates).[57] Bogost talks about this in terms of the potential for disgust and disinterest reactions to video games, suggesting that when gamers are revolted by interactive on-screen content (such as the active sadism in *The Torture Game*), it is as likely that they will be less rather than more motivated to engage those activities.[58] A pair of recent studies have demonstrated this claim empirically, finding that when a video game presents gamers with moral transgressions, they will actively avoid the anti-normative behavior (such as committing an act of violence) or they will feel a deep sense of guilt if they do commit it.[59,60]

Conclusion

> And I verily do suppose that in the braines and hertes of children, which be membres spirituall, whiles they be tender, and the little slippes of reason begynne in them to bud, ther may happe by evil custome some pestiferous dewe of vice to perse the sayde membres, and infecte and corrupt the soft and tender buddes.[19]

The above is quoted from Sir Thomas Eliot (unedited from the original spelling) as the introductory text for *Seduction of the Innocent*. One interpretation for his choice of words is to frame them as a call to action for his work, providing moral justification for a crusade against corrosive comic book content. Likewise, many have taken similar extracts from centuries of moral philosophy in adopting a defensive and normative stance to understanding the negative impact of mediated communication on the thoughts, feelings, and behaviors of us all – from children through adults. Moreover, as newer interactive technologies, the popularity of video games (especially among children) has re-ignited debates as to the role that mediated fantasies of death and destruction play in the shaping of future generations. As noble as the inspirations of this research are, it is equally important to recognize that moral panics are just that: irrational approaches to observable and quantifiable phenomenon that can be understood separate from subjective evaluation. The current empirical record is by no means invalid but rather, in need of further refinement of research designed to better describe, explain, predict, and eventually control the results of the interaction between mediated content and human interactions with that content. Doing so requires us to better understand our research heritage to seek areas of replication and extension, and this chapter is aimed at providing such an understanding. The legacy of fear of media effects is just that: a fear rooted not in science, but all-too-often in the moral panics of well-meaning researchers less committed to understanding a phenomenon and more committed to stopping it before it is fully understood.

Games References

Custer's Revenge (1982). Published by Mystique.

Death Race (1976). Published by Exidy.

DOOM (1993). Developed by id Software. Published by GT Interactive.

EverQuest II (2004). Developed by Sony Online Entertainment. Published by Sony Online Entertainment.

Grand Theft Auto III (2001). Developed by DMA Design. Published by Rockstar Games.

Manhunt (2003). Developed by Rockstar North. Published by Rockstar Games.

Wolfenstein 3D (1992). Developed by id Software. Published by Apogee Software.

References

1. Rutledge PB. Arguing for media psychology as a distinct field. In: Dill KE, ed. *The Oxford Handbook of Media Psychology*. Oxford, UK: Oxford University Press; 2014: 43–61.
2. Dill KE. Media psychology: Past, present and future. In: Dill KE, ed. *The Oxford Handbook of Media Psychology*. Oxford, UK: Oxford University Press; 2014, 535–545.
3. Wilson TJ. *Strangers to Ourselves: Discovering the Adaptive Unconscious*. Cambridge, MA: Harvard University Press; 2002.
4. Elson M, Ferguson C. Gun violence and media effects: Challenges for science and public policy. *The British Journal of Psychiatry*. 2013; 203: 322–324. doi: 10.1192/bjp.bp.113.128652
5. Graney CM. The Inquisition's semicolon: Punctuation, translation, and science in the 1616 condemnation of the Copernican system. February 2014. Available at: http://arxiv.org/ftp/arxiv/papers/1402/1402.6168.pdf
6. Finocchiaro MA. The Galileo affair: A documentary history. Berkeley, CA: University of California Press; 1989.
7. New Scientist. Vatican admits Galileo was right. *New Scientist*. November 7, 1992: 1846, 5.
8. Thomsett MC. *Heresy in the Roman Catholic Church: A History*. Jefferson, NC: McFarland; 2011.
9. Hoche JG. *Vertraute Briefe über die jetzige abentheuerliche Lesesucht und über den Einfluß derselben auf die Verminderung des häuslichen und öffentlichen Glücks.* [Familiar Letters on the current adventurous reading addiction and about the same influence on the reduction of domestic and public happiness]. Hanover, Germany: Ritscher; 1794.
10. Plato (370 BC). *Phaedrus* (trans. B. Jowett, 1999). Available at: www.gutenberg.org/files/1636/1636.txt
11. Connor A. Crosswords: the meow meow of the 1920s. *The Guardian*. December 15, 2011. Available at: www.theguardian.com/crosswords/crossword-blog/2011/dec/15/crosswords-meow-meow-1920s
12. Zillmann D. The coming of media entertainment. In Zillmann E, Vorderer P, eds. *Media Entertainment: The Psychology of Its Appeal*. Mahwah, NJ: LEA; 2000.
13. Parker S. *Science Discoveries: Alexander Graham Bell*. Philadelphia, PA: Chelsea House Publishers; 1995.

14. Eber DH. *Genius at Work: Images of Alexander Graham Bell*. New York: Viking; 1983.
15. Lowery SL, DeFleur ML. *Milestones in Mass Communication Research* (4th edn). London: Longman; 1995.
16. Charters WW. Chairman's preface. In Charters WW, ed. *Motion Pictures and the Social Attitudes of Children: A Payne Fund Study*. New York: Macmillan & Company; 1933.
17. Sproule JM. *Propaganda and Democracy: The American Experience of Media and Mass Persuasion*. Cambridge, UK: Cambridge University Press, 1997.
18. Crist J. Horror in the nursery. *Collier's Magazine* 121. March 27, 1948: 22–23, 95–97.
19. Wertham F. *Seduction of the Innocent*. New York: Reinhart; 1954.
20. Rogers V. Archie dropping Comics Code Authority seal in February. *NewsARama. com*. January 21, 2011. Available at: www.newsarama.com/6892-archie-dropping-comics-code-authority-seal-in-february.html
21. Tilley CL. Seducing the innocent: Fredric Wertham and the falsifications that helped condemn comics. *Information & Culture: A Journal of History*. 2012: 47(4); 383–413. doi: 10.1353/lac.2012.0024.
22. Klapper J. *The Effects of Mass Communication*. New York: Free Press; 1960.
23. Taylor WL. Cloze procedure: a new tool for measuring readability. *Journalism Quarterly*. 1953: 30; 415–433.
24. Barthes R. *The Death of the Author*. 1967. Available at: www.ubu.com/aspen/aspen5and6/threeEssays.html#barthes
25. Walker J. A short history of game panics. *Reason.com*, May 2014. Available at: http://reason.com/archives/2014/05/07/a-short-history-of-game-panics
26. Blumenthal R. "Death Race" game gains favor, but not with the safety council. *The New York Times*. December 28, 1976. Available at: http://query.nytimes.com/gst/abstract.html?res=9404E1DC133FE334BC4051DFB467838D669EDE
27. Kocurek CA. The agony and the Exidy: A history of video game violence and the legacy of Death Race. *Game Studies*. 2012; 12(1). http://gamestudies.org/1201/articles/carly_kocurek
28. Dworkin A. *Letter from a War Zone*. 1986. Available at: www.nostatusquo.com/ACLU/dworkin/WarZoneChaptIVG2.html
29. Narcisse E. All-time 100 video games: Mortal Kombat. *Time.com*. November 15, 2012. http://techland.time.com/2012/11/15/all-time-100-video-games/slide/mortal-kombat-1992/
30. Gruson L. Video violence: It's hot! It's Mortal! It's Kombat!; teen-agers eagerly await electronic carnage while adults debate message being sent. *The New York Times*. September 16, 1993. Available at: www.nytimes.com/1993/09/16/nyregion/video-violence-it-s-hot-it-s-mortal-it-s-kombat-teen-agers-eagerly-await.html?scp=9&sq=mortal%20kombat&st=cse
31. Elmer-Dewitt P, Dickerson JF. Too violent for kids? *Time*. September 27, 1993; 142(13): 70–72. Available at: http://content.time.com/time/magazine/article/0,9171,979298,00.html
32. Andrews EL. Industry set to issue video game ratings as complaints rise. *The New York Times*. December 9, 1993. Available at: www.nytimes.com/1993/12/09/business/industry-set-to-issue-video-game-ratings-as-complaints-rise.html?scp=18&sq=mortal%20kombat&st=cse
33. Kohler C. July 29, 1994: videogame makers propose ratings board to Congress. *Wired*. July 29, 2009. Available at: www.wired.com/2009/07/dayintech_0729/
34. Entertainment Software Rating Board. *About ESRB*. Available at: www.esrb.org/about/index.jsp
35. Robinson A. Mortal Kombat 1 outrage "had a point," says creator. *Computer and Video Games*. Published 2010. Available at: www.computerandvideogames.com/276782/mortal-kombat-1-outrage-had-a-point-says-creator/
36. Tamborini R, Weber R, Bowman ND, Eden A, Skalski P. "Violence is a many-splintered thing:" the importance of realism, justification, and graphicness in

understanding perceptions of and preferences for violent films and video games. *Projections: The Journal for Movies and Mind*. 2013: 7(1); 100–118. doi: 10.3167/proj. 2013.070108

37. Associated Press. Ashcroft warns about culture, effect of violent video games. *Associated Press*. April 5, 2001.

38. Anderson CA, Bushman BJ. Effects of violent video games on aggressive behavior, aggressive cognition, aggressive affect, physiological arousal, and prosocial behavior: a meta-analytic review of the scientific literature. *Psychol Sci*. 2001; 12(5): 353–359.

39. Ferguson CJ, Rueda S, Cruz A, Ferguson D, Fritz S, Smith S. Violent video games and aggression: Causal relationship or byproduct of family violence and intrinsic violence motivation? *Crim Justice Behav*. 2008; 35: 311–332.

40. *James v. Meow Media, Inc.* United States Court of Appeals, Sixth Circuit, Decided and filed, August 13, 2002. Available at: http://scholar.google.com/scholar_case?case= 2909369074319697416&q=300+F.3d+683&hl=en&as_sdt=2,5

41. Bowman ND. Grand Theft Auto. In: Eastin M, ed. *Encyclopedia of Media Violence*. Thousand Oaks, CA: SAGE; 2014: 189–191.

42. Smith T. Australia bans Manhunt. *The Register*. September 30, 2004. Available at: www.theregister.co.uk/2004/09/30/oz_manhunt_ban/

43. Cundy M. Manhunt nearly caused a "mutiny" at Rockstar. *GamesRadar.com*. July 26, 2007. Available at: www.gamesradar.com/manhunt-nearly-caused-a-mutiny-at-rockstar/

44. Fine GA. *Shared Fantasy: Role-playing Games as Social Worlds*. Chicago, IL: University of Chicago Press; 1983.

45. Allison PR. The great 1980s Dungeons & Dragons panic. *BBC*. April 11, 2014. Available at: www.bbc.com/news/magazine-26328105

46. Williams D, Yee N, Caplan SE. Who plays, how much, and why? Debunking the stereotypical gamer profile. *J Compu-Mediat Comm*. 2008: 13(4); 993–1018. doi: 10.1111/j.1083-6101.2008.00428.x

47. Kowert R, Oldmeadow JA. (A)Social reputation: Exploring the relationship between online video game involvement and social competence. *Comput Hum Behav*. 2013; *29* (4): 1872–1878. doi: 10.1016/.chb.2013.03.003

48. Banks J, Bowman ND. Avatars are (sometimes) people too: Linguistic indicators of parasocial and social ties in player–avatar relationships. *New Media Society* 2014. doi:10.1177/ 1461444814554898

49. Jenkins H. Reality bytes: Eight myths about video games debunked. *PBS.org*. no date. Available at: www.pbs.org/kcts/videogamerevolution/impact/myths.html

50. Przybylski AK. Americans skeptical of link between mass shootings and video games. *YouGov Report*, October 2013. Available at: https://today.yougov.com/news/ 2013/10/17/americans-skeptical-link-between-mass-shootings-an/

51. Benedetti W. Were video games to blame for massacre? *MSNBC*. April 20, 2007. Available at: www.nbcnews.com/id/18220228/#.U-HgNfmSzSY

52. Lasswell HD. The structure and function of communication in society. In Bryson L, ed. *The Communication of Ideas*. New York: Institute for Religious and Social Studies; 1948: 37–51.

53. Wright WR. Functional analysis and mass communication. *Public Opin Quart*. *24*: 610–613; 1960.

54. Wertham F. *The World of Fanzines: A Special Form of Communication*. Carbondale, IL: Southern Illinois University Press; 1973.

55. Gonzalez D. How Flash Gordon inspired Charles Bolden to become the head of NASA. *io9.com*. July 15, 2012. Available at: http://io9.com/5927753/flash-gordon-science-fairs-and-ron-mcnair-how-charles-bolden-became-the-head-of-nasa

56. Huesmann LR, Dubow ER, Yang G. Why is it hard to believe that media violence causes aggression? In Dill KE, ed. *The Oxford Handbook of Media Psychology*. Cambridge, UK: Oxford University Press; 2013: 159–171.

57. Williams W. We are not heroes: Contextualizing violence through narrative. *Game Developers Conference*. March 25–28, San Francisco. March 2013. Available at: www.gdcvault.com/play/1017980/We-Are-Not-Heroes-Contextualizing

58. Bogost I. Disinterest. In Bogost I. *How to Do Things with Video Games*. Minneapolis: University of Minnesota Press; 2012: 134–140.

59. Joeckel S, Bowman ND, Dogruel L. Gut or game: The influence of moral intuitions on decisions in virtual environments. *Media Psychology*. 2012; *15*(4): 460–485. doi: 10.1080/15213269.2012.727218

60. Grizzard M, Tamborini R, Lewis RJ, Wang L, Prabhu S. Being bad in a video game can make us morally sensitive. *CyberPsychol Behav*. 2014; 17(8): 499–504. doi: 10.1089/cyber.2013.0658

3

ARE ELECTRONIC GAMES HEALTH HAZARDS OR HEALTH PROMOTERS?

Cheryl K. Olson

A chapter on health effects of video games may call to mind early news reports of "Nintendonitis," or images of chubby kids on sofas clutching game controllers. Both research studies and media debates tend to focus on ways that video games might damage mental and physical health.

In reality, as electronic games become a routine part of daily life, they are bound to have a wide variety of effects, both trivial and meaningful, on mental and physical health.[1] Commercially available games may have risks and benefits, which vary for different types of players.

Increasingly, researchers and health professionals are modifying games or apps or creating new ones for specific health and medical needs. Educational games help children make healthier eating choices, model how to help someone having a heart attack, or teach someone diagnosed with a chronic illness how to manage their disease. Persuasive games help players set goals and change behaviors, such as quitting smoking. "Exergames" take advantage of motion tracking technologies to allow players to practice dance or sports moves or improve balance.[2]

This chapter will examine the effects video games may have on healthy development, mental health, and physical health – including risky behaviors and exercise habits. Finally, it will introduce the "Games for Health" movement and explore where it may be headed.

The Role of Video Games in Child and Youth Development

Children and teens seem to use video games to meet a wide range of emotional and developmental needs. For example:

Managing feelings. A survey of 1,254 middle-schoolers in two states found that many children use video games for emotional regulation: as an antidote to boredom and loneliness, to relax, and to vent angry feelings.[3] This response, from focus groups with 13-year-old boys, was typical: "If I had a bad day at school, I'll play a violent video game and it just relieves all my stress."[4]

Trying on new identities. Many video games, especially online multi-player games, allow players to safely experiment with new roles and identities. It's perfectly acceptable to play as a character of another age, gender, body shape, or species. Players can test how it feels to not only look different, but to take on a different personality or a new role on a team – and see how others react when they do.[1]

Leadership and teamwork. Researchers have surveyed tens of thousands of people who play MMOGs (massively multi-player online games, such as *EverQuest* and *World of Warcraft*) about their motivations for and experiences with gaming. Online play in mixed-age teams, where no one knows how old or young you are, offers unique opportunities for teens and young adults to observe, learn, and practice leading groups toward shared goals. Online leadership experience has been linked to managing others in "offline" settings, such as voluntary organizations.[5]

Several studies suggest that team video game play encourages real-life helpful behavior. A study of British undergraduate students found that frequent players of computer games were more likely to cooperate for a win-win outcome with other players in "prisoner's dilemma" experiments.[6]

Competition and initiative. In response to a series of questions about why they play video games, more than four in five middle-school boys and almost two-thirds of girls agreed with the statement, "I like to compete with others and win."[3] The challenge and excitement of testing strategies against opponents may promote initiative and healthy youth development.[7] However, there is an ongoing, vigorous debate (addressed elsewhere in this book) about whether aggressive competition in games with violent content might undermine empathy or promote harmful behaviors.

Curiosity, self-expression and testing limits. Video games allow children to escape real-world limitations and let their creativity soar. Boys in focus groups noted that over-the-top, gory games are fun because "I just love the fact that I know it can't happen . . . In a real world, there's [sic] limitations to what you can do."[3] Games that allow "modding" – from customizing characters to designing buildings, maps, and more – let players express themselves in ways that would be costly and difficult in real life, and sometimes to share those mods with others. Players can also test theories or approaches, fail, and try again without real consequences. Suppose you build a *Sim Theme Park* without trash cans or bathrooms? Or erect a *Sim City* and set it on fire?[8]

Practice setting goals and coping with frustration. In the 1970s, psychologist Walter Mischel began a series of now-famous experiments with preschoolers on delay of gratification. A child briefly shared toys in a testing room with the experimenter, then was presented with a "reward object," such as a marshmallow.

She was given the choice to eat the marshmallow now, or wait (usually 15 minutes) until the experimenter came back from an errand, and get *two* marshmallows. This turned out to be a wonderful way to measure frustration tolerance and the ability to wait for a payoff. In longitudinal studies, Mischel's team found that those children who learned ways to distract themselves and earn the second marshmallow had a wide range of advantages over their marshmallow-gobbling peers. For example, they proved better at planning and thinking ahead; were more verbally fluent, resourceful, and attentive; less rattled under stress; and more socially outgoing. These gains persisted into adolescence; seconds of marshmallow-resistance time even statistically predicted higher S.A.T. scores.[9]

Although video games are not designed for this purpose, a challenging, age-appropriate video game is perfectly suited to train children to plan ahead, tolerate failure and frustration, and persist until they meet success.

How Video Games Affect Mental Health

Can Video Games Worsen (or Improve) ADHD?

Children with attention-deficit disorder (ADD) both with and without hyperactivity often struggle to stay focused and pay attention, and are easily distracted – except when it comes to video games. Parents and teachers comment that children with attention problems seem to have no problem concentrating on a video game for long periods.[10]

Given the fast pace of many games, some have wondered if video games might aggravate attention problems. Some studies have linked greater time spent with video games (as well as television) to increased risk for attention-deficit hyperactivity disorder (ADHD) symptoms.[11] There's also evidence that "pathological" gaming – defined as persistent trouble controlling gameplay habits, despite bad consequences – is more common among young people who show signs of ADHD. One study found that teens with attention problems were more likely to go on to develop unhealthy gaming habits.[12]

Of course, the fact that one thing precedes another does not prove cause and effect. Attention problems and video games have a complicated and probably multi-directional relationship. Let's take a closer look.

Children with ADHD tend to have problems with "executive functions," such as working memory and response inhibition, that allow children to focus on what the teacher is saying, wait for their turn to talk, and keep track of assignments. A study comparing children with and without ADHD found that the first group did worse on a standard computer-based test of attention and inhibition (involving clicking on a series of alphabet letters). However, both groups did equally well on *PlayStation* EyeToy games that tapped similar skills.[13] This supports other research suggesting that children with ADHD do better with novel, stimulating tasks that offer immediate rewards, as many video games do.

This may explain why children with ADHD can have trouble tearing themselves away from video games. But it also points to opportunities to improve their skills and performance through wise use of games.[14] For example, researchers compared a standard computer-based working-memory training program for children with ADHD to a program that added game elements (including a story, animation, and rewards). Children who trained with the game version stuck with training longer, improved faster, and made fewer mistakes.[10]

Other studies, which assigned children and adults to play action video games, found that gameplay improved sustained attention and reduced impulsivity. Despite these promising findings, researchers caution that it's too soon to add video games to ADHD treatment plans. Results of studies on normal populations may not translate to people with attention problems, whose brains work a bit differently.[15]

Effects of Videogames on Depression

Compared to attention problems, there are fewer studies looking at whether video games might contribute to depression. Findings vary depending on what researchers were looking for, and who they surveyed. In a large study of urban fifth graders, heavy play of violent video games (two hours-plus per day) was associated with a higher number of depressive symptoms.[16] In a study of Norwegian teens, scoring high on a measure of video game "addiction" was linked to depression, but time spent on games was not.[17] Similarly, young teens who self-report symptoms of depression don't spend more time playing video games (or violent games) compared to their peers, but they *are* more likely to play to cope with feelings and forget problems.[18]

A recent study of nearly 5000 young British teens found that those who kept video game play in balance with other activities (with less than one-third of daily free time devoted to gaming) scored higher on emotional and social wellbeing compared to non-gamers. However, children who spent more than half of their daily free time with video games had *more* emotional and behavioral problems, as well as lower life satisfaction.[19]

More research is needed to tease out the effects (good and bad) of different types of games and patterns of play on different individuals.

Videogames in Psychotherapy

For some therapists working with children, video games fit into a tradition of using toys or board games during counseling sessions to create a nonthreatening ambience and to build rapport. Small studies suggest that video games may help therapists connect with children when traditional approaches have failed.

Therapists can also gain insight into a child's inner world, emotional states, or cognitive skills by playing a video game together, or observing the child's solo play and offering guidance as appropriate. Larger studies of video games in therapy that focus on treatment outcomes are needed.[20]

Games created or modified for therapeutic purposes show promise in helping with mental health issues such as depression,[21] anxiety, phobias, and post-traumatic stress disorder. For example, SPARX is a computer-based fantasy game designed to provide cognitive-behavioral therapy to depressed teens. After choosing an avatar, the player takes on a series of challenges to right a fantasy world overrun by GNATs (Gloomy Negative Automatic Thoughts). After each level, a guide character puts skills learned in the game world into real-life context. A multi-site New Zealand study of 187 adolescents seeking treatment for depression, who were randomized to SPARX or usual care (in this case, a median of four counseling sessions), found that SPARX worked at least as well as usual care. Impressively, 86 percent of subjects finished at least four SPARX levels – with minimal oversight, at their local counseling center or on their home computer – and 60 percent did all seven.[22]

The adventure game *PlayMancer*, funded by the FP7 European Union research program, was designed as a complement to psychotherapy for patients with impulse-related disorders, targeting difficult-to-change emotional regulation and self-control skills. The game uses a Bluetooth wireless mobile monitoring and feedback system (MobiHealth Mobile™) to track players' emotional states by measuring physical signs such as galvanic skin response, heart rate, breathing frequency, facial expressions, and emotion in speech. The island-themed gameplay (plus several mini-games addressing specific skills) reinforces more self-controlled or relaxed reactions, e.g., by making fish easier to catch. Pilot studies found that patients felt comfortable using the game, that it was able to trigger and respond to the necessary emotional states, and that it seemed to increase patients' use of new coping styles in everyday stressful situations.[23]★

A customized version of the video game *Full Spectrum Warrior* has helped treat veterans of Iraq and Afghanistan suffering from post-traumatic stress disorder. This virtual reality therapy, created with input from veterans, uses a head-mounted display along with therapist-controlled multisensory cues (sounds, smells, and vibrations) that call up memories of combat zones.[24] Based on promising results from these studies, researchers are looking for ways to reduce rates of PTSD and depression by using virtual reality pre-deployment to boost soldiers' resilience.

Small, randomized studies of "casual games" such as *Bejeweled* or *Peggle*, funded by game makers, claim that several hours of play per week can reduce symptoms of depression and anxiety.[25] As a form of "self-medication" for

★ A video demo is available at: www.youtube.com/watch?v=osmo9EAClv8.

life's stresses, casual games do have advantages: they are fun, inexpensive, and widely available.

Video Games and Physical Health

What effects might video games have on physical health? How can harmful effects be mitigated, and potential positive effects encouraged? Let's start by looking at medical uses of game technologies.

Both commercially available games and custom-built games have been used to treat or support people coping with a variety of medical problems. For example, a fun game's ability to distract attention can be a liability with homework or chores, but it's invaluable for pediatric cancer patients trying to cope with treatment-related nausea, or children about to undergo surgery.[26]

Video Games and Cancer

Re-Mission, one of the best-known video games used in healthcare settings, began as a PC game for children struggling with cancer. The game was thoughtfully designed to target a set of specific behaviors that increase the odds of treatment success,[27] including sticking to prescribed chemotherapy and antibiotic regimen, using relaxation techniques, and eating despite nausea. Game players guide a nanobot character through 3D environments, destroying cancer cells with chemotherapy ammo and attacking chemotherapy side effects with weapons representing antibiotics, anti-nausea drugs, and stool softeners. In studies, even though most children didn't play the game as much as assigned, there were still differences in cancer knowledge, self-efficacy (feeling confident about participating in their treatment), and sticking with treatment.[28] The *Re-Mission* franchise continues to evolve. In 2013, a *Re-Mission 2* mobile app was launched. Six *Re-Mission 2* games are now available free online, supported by the nonprofit HopeLab (www.re-mission2.org/).

Videogames also have potential to help children manage chronic illnesses, such as diabetes and asthma, that require complex regimens of daily care.[29]

Games for Managing Pain

Severe burns require daily debridement over weeks or months to prevent infection and promote healing; skin grafts require additional care. Burn wound care can be excruciatingly painful. Pain also makes it difficult to complete physical therapy necessary for burn patients to keep the use of affected joints and limbs. Opioid analgesics are somewhat helpful, but patients often develop tolerance to medications, or have problems with side effects. Thus, finding ways to distract burn patients from pain is essential to recovery.

The logic behind this approach is that people have a limited capacity to pay attention (as anyone who's tried to multi-task knows). Distraction means there is less attention available to process incoming signals from pain receptors, so that patients spend less time thinking about pain and actually hurt less.

SnowWorld was a pioneering effort to use virtual reality for healthcare. As pop music plays, patients are immersed in a world among snowmen, penguins, and wooly mammoths, and can even throw virtual snowballs via computer mouse or head tracking. Studies of patients undergoing painful medical procedures (including burn wound care) while using *SnowWorld* found statistically significant and clinically meaningful reductions in pain.[30] These researchers are now investigating whether an inexpensive virtual reality headset (Oculus Rift) could distract patients from pain even more effectively.[31] Other researchers are studying the use of new and relatively inexpensive motion sensing game controllers, such as Kinect for Xbox One and PlayStation Move, to help children recovering from burns manage the physical demands of rehabilitation.[32]

Videogames and Health-Risk Behaviors

Game technologies have potential to increase or discourage behaviors that affect health. Some research has looked at how specific types of video game content might influence risky real-life behaviors, such as reckless driving. A review of studies of "risk-glorifying" media – from video games based on illegal street racing to movies with risk-taking heroes to television shows featuring extreme sports or stunts (such as the TV series *Jackass*) – found an overall correlation between exposure to such content and risk-positive attitudes, feelings, and behaviors.[33] In this set of studies, the link between risk-promoting media and real-life risk-taking was stronger for video games than other media.

The authors suggest this could be due to the active nature of gameplay versus simply watching movies or listening to lyrics. What's not clear is the direction of causality. "Sensation-seeking" personalities may differentially seek out risk-glorifying media; in turn, that media exposure might amplify their natural affinity for risky acts. Experimental studies support the idea that exposure to risk-promoting media content may cue or trigger high-risk behaviors or attitudes. However, we don't know how long those effects last, or whether controlled lab studies are relevant to understanding the influence of risk-glorifying media in the real world, where self-selected games and movies are often group activities, engaged with over months or years.

Just as subtypes of game content may have different effects,[†] some subgroups of people are likely to be at greater risk for problems. A survey of 4,028 high

---

[†] Some health effects of games may have more to do with the screen than its contents. The presence of game consoles in bedrooms has been linked to later sleep times and fewer hours of rest. Bright screens seem to affect melatonin metabolism. Of course, physiologically arousing gameplay may be incompatible with sleep.[34]

school students did not find that video gaming in general was strongly linked to risky or problematic behaviors. Male gamers were significantly less likely to smoke cigarettes than their non-gaming peers. Female gamers were less prone to depression but more likely to get into fights. (In this study and many others, gaming was a mainstream activity for boys but only played by a minority of girls.) About 6 percent of boys reported problems with gaming (i.e., they agreed on the survey that a family member had expressed concern about their video gaming, that they sometimes felt irresistible urges to play video games, *and* that they'd tried to cut back on gaming); this group of boys were more likely to be regular cigarette smokers.[35] (For more on video games and addiction, see Chapter 6.)

Many studies have examined the effects of portrayals of smoking and drinking in movies and television on children's behavior, with some evidence for concern; for example, multiple studies have found that young people heavily exposed to movie smoking were more likely to start smoking themselves.[36] Studies on video games are lacking, but it's not unreasonable to worry that games might "model" substance use and encourage children to copy it. Game ratings organizations have taken note.

The Entertainment Software Rating Board rates virtually all games sold at retail in the US and Canada. Along with age-based ratings, the ESRB may assign any of 30 "content descriptors" to help parents make informed decisions about games. Six of those descriptors address substance use: "use of tobacco," "use of [illegal] drugs," "use of alcohol," "drug reference" (images of or references to illegal drugs), "alcohol reference," and "tobacco reference." The two descriptions alerting parents to questionable lyrics also encompass alcohol/drug use (www.esrb.org/ratings/ratings_guide.jsp). The PEGI rating system, used in 30 countries including most of Europe, features eight icon-like "descriptors" to alert buyers to questionable content. An icon of a syringe signals that the game "refers to or depicts the use of drugs" (www.pegi.info/en/index/id/33/).

Games and Food Choices

The video game equivalent of the television commercial is the online "advergame." Most websites promoted on children's television shows feature advergames, usually with familiar brand characters and logos, and often promoting sugary cereals or other less-healthy foods. Nutritionists worry about the effects of advergames on children's food choices. For example, one study found that young children who played a Froot Loops® advergame were more likely than non-players to say they preferred that cereal. In experimental studies, children who played advergames for sugary snacks chose and ate more of those foods. Children who played fruit-related games chose more healthy snacks, and children playing non-food games fell in between.[37]

Videogames and Obesity

Many researchers (and parents) assume that video games encourage sitting, and that sitting promotes obesity. Some studies see all time spent in front of computer monitors and televisions as equivalent, regardless of what is on the screen or how the watcher may be interacting with it. Based on that logic, dozens of studies have been published of programs intended to reduce children's "screen time."[38]

Some recent studies try to separate out the effects of television watching and game playing. A study of over 9,000 German and American preteens and adolescents, focusing on the relationship between media use and socioeconomic status, found that the relationship between overweight and lower SES was mediated in part by time spent watching TV shows and to TVs in bedrooms – but not by video gaming or movie watching.[39] A meta-analysis combining the results of dozens of studies of media use and physical activity among children aged 3 to 18 found a small but statistically significant link between television viewing and body fatness, but little to support a relationship between electronic game use and excess weight.[40]

Other differences between video game play and TV watching include greater exposure to advertising on television, and the practical difficulties of snacking while using a game controller or keyboard.

Are "Exergames" Good For Your Health?

Since affordable dance games came to home consoles in the late 1990s, dozens of studies have looked at the effects of physically demanding games and their potential to promote health. "Exergames" make use of innovative game controllers such as foot touch pads for dancing, balance boards, and motion sensing cameras. Reviews of the most rigorous exergaming research suggest that under the right circumstances, active games can help children and teens get moving. Another benefit: for children struggling with their weight, exergames may help limit weight gain.[41,42]

Dance games can give players a vigorous workout.[43] In most cases, exergames promote light to moderate activity (akin to brisk walking) rather than working up a sweat, but this varies by the type of game, game controller, and individual motivation. Studies measuring energy expended playing the groundbreaking exergames in Wii Sports (for the Nintendo Wii console) found them less vigorous than real tennis, boxing or bowling; however, Wii Sports did demand 51 percent more energy from players than an ordinary sedentary video game.

Even if Wii Tennis can't match real tennis, it still gets you off the couch.[‡] We now know that time spent sitting is a separate risk factor for obesity and

---

[‡] Exergames have other potential health benefits, such as improving balance and preventing falls – a major cause of injury and death for the elderly.[44]

ill health among adults and children, independent of regular exercise.[45] This has sparked interest in creating games that both reduce sedentary time and break it up with intermittent bursts of light activity – what some researchers call "energames."[46]

One example of promoting intermittent light activity through games is the Pokéwalker – a pedometer accessory for the Nintendo DS. Shaped like the familiar Poké Ball, the pedometer comes with and connects to select Pokémon games via infrared signals. Players earn in-game currency, called "watts," by racking up steps.

Given expanding game technology options and the importance of combating child obesity on multiple fronts, one physician[47] proposed that video games be rated based on energy expenditure, on a four-point scale from "sedentary" to "high intensity," to guide game-buying parents.

Exergames at School

Schools have begun to include exergames in their physical education offerings. West Virginia, a state with high rates of child obesity, was a pioneer in school exergaming. After promising results from at-home tests and a 2004 pilot study at 20 middle schools, the state rolled out *Dance Dance Revolution* to all of its schools, with the help of a grant from its maker, Konami.[48] In *New York Times* interviews, children favorably compared DDR to sometimes hyper-competitive school sports such as baseball or basketball, noting that with DDR, "you don't have to be on a team or go anywhere special to play" and that "you don't have to be good at it to get a good workout."[49]

Encouraging Exergaming

This is surprisingly complicated. One study that tried to assess the effects of exergames in everyday life gave 84 children aged 9 to 12 a Wii console and let them pick one of five popular sports or dance titles such as *Wii Fit Plus*. (A control group got a non-active game.) As in real life, children could use the game console as they wished during the three-month experiment, and received no special instructions on how or when to play the exergame. Children were weighed, and wore an elastic belt with an accelerometer for two non-consecutive weeks to measure activity levels. The result? Children given an exergame were no more physically active than the control group kids.[50] The children's diaries and interviews, as well as Wii console records, suggest that the active games were used. So, what might explain this finding?

The children may have played at lower levels of intensity. Exergaming may have replaced (rather than added to) other everyday physical activity. There was also some "contamination" of the experiment: children in each group acquired and used exergames and non-active games on their own. Interviews with the children hint at other factors, such as confusion about how to play, not having someone to play with, finding a game too hard, or not liking it. It may have been too much to expect fairly young children to try, learn, and make a habit of using an unfamiliar game with no instruction or encouragement from adults, siblings, or peers.

Small studies suggest that children are more likely to stick with exergaming in the context of structured classes and/or multi-player game options.[51] For most children, socializing is a major part of video gaming, and they commonly learn to play new games from siblings and friends.[4]

To encourage young gamers to start and stick with active games, they should ideally be easy to start playing, offer fun short-term challenges that adapt to player skill level to sustain motivation, give feedback on player performance and accomplishments, and allow the option of social play.[46]

Videogames may also have untapped potential to encourage exercise away from the screen. Playing videogames that feature realistic sports (such as basket-ball, soccer, or skateboarding) is correlated with spending more time on real-life exercise, at least for boys.[52] Sports videogames have the potential to introduce players to new sports, increase motivation to practice sports moves or try out for teams, and boost confidence in sports-related abilities. Games that feature real-life athletes as characters allow players to "interact" with people they admire. Personalization of characters can also build motivation; some games even allow players to upload a photo of their own face to create a realistic-looking character.

Using Video Games to Promote Health: The "Games For Health" Movement

After the turn of the century, the idea of using video games for serious purposes, including health promotion and disease management, began attracting researchers and funders. Founders of the Games for Health Project[53] envisioned five areas where games might be used in health or medicine: Preventative (such as "exergames" or games to manage stress), Therapeutic (games to manage diseases or help with rehabilitation), Assessment (games that rank or measure some aspect of health), Educational (teaching skills such as first aid), and Informatics (games that create health records for use by individuals, doctors, or researchers). The Robert Wood Johnson Foundation, Games for Health, Health Games Research, and other groups funded, conducted, or publicized research to see whether games had the potential to improve health, and (if so) how to make them more effective.[§]

[§] The University of Santa Barbara's new Center for Digital Games Research has a database of health games research and information (www.cdgr.ucsb.edu/db).

Improving the Effectiveness of Health Games

"Games for health" have been used everywhere from school classrooms to game consoles and smart phones to medical clinics to Boy Scout gatherings.[54] But video game technology may not be a good fit for all health topics or goals. For example, researchers have created games to promote nutrition knowledge and increase fruit and vegetable consumption. "Escape from Diab" and "Nanoswarm: Invasion from Inner Space" were multipart adventure games designed (at a cost of several million dollars) to match the quality of commercially available video games. After a total of about six hours of gameplay, young players reported eating more fruit and vegetables (about half a serving per day) compared to a control group.[55] In another study, a Xbox Kinect game that let preteens feed nutritious or less-healthy foods to an alien increased nutrition knowledge, especially among a subgroup that did short cardio exercises as part of the game.[56]

Efforts like these help advance our understanding of the potential of game technology. But in future studies, it's important to consider whether custom-created video games are the most effective, or cost-effective, way to teach particular facts and skills.

The goal of a health game should be specific, feasible, and translatable to real life. Food choices are complicated, and many factors influence them. A more modest goal, such as a game that helps parents encourage preschoolers to try new foods, may improve odds of success.

Games may be particularly well suited to health issues that are complicated, emotional, and potentially costly in terms of dollars and disability. For example, a video game that successfully teaches a child newly diagnosed with diabetes to manage technologies for testing blood glucose and administering insulin – *and* helps that child stay motivated to take care of himself – might reduce emergency room visits as well as future health complications. And unlike rushed health care providers, games are endlessly patient; players can repeat content as much as needed, and practice skills at their own pace until they succeed.

Health game designers need to understand behavior change theory. We know, for example, that learning facts is not enough to create change. Even well-thought-out health games need well-designed studies to demonstrate their worth. For example, the Kinect nutrition game mentioned above included just twenty students – not nearly enough to draw conclusions about effects. A review of 149 published studies on health game research found that most studies were done in lab settings, over just five weeks, with players spending less than 100 minutes with the game.[57] Larger studies, conducted under real-world conditions, for longer periods of time are needed to give games a chance to show effects. Similarly, game ideas and prototypes should be tested using focus groups and pilot studies, and final versions assessed in randomized controlled trials.[58]

The best health games are useless if they sit on the shelf. Health game designers need to think about whether their intended game users (or purchasers) are comfortable with game technologies, and feel able to use them properly in clinics or homes. This is particularly challenging given the rapid evolution of game technologies.

Finally, privacy protections will be particularly important when it comes to health games. It's one thing to have companies collect data about your web searches or online shopping habits; it's another to have data on what you eat, how much you exercise, or your use of medicines or devices (such as blood glucose monitors or asthma inhalers) shared with parties unknown.

References

1. Granic I, Lobel A, Engels R. The benefits of playing video games. *Am Psychol.* 2014; 69: 66–78.
2. Brox E, Fernandez-Luque L, Tøllefsen T. Healthy gaming: Video game design to promote health. *Appl Clin Inform.* 2011; 2: 128–142.
3. Olson CK. Children's motivations for video game play in the context of normal development. *Rev Gen Psychol.* 2010; 14: 180–187.
4. Olson CK, Kutner LA, Warner DE. The role of violent video game content in adolescent development: Boys' perspectives. *J Adolescent Res.* 2008; 23: 55–75.
5. Lu L, Shen C, Williams D. Friending your way up the ladder: Connecting massive multi-player online game behaviors with offline leadership. *Comput Hum Behav.* 2014; 35: 54–60.
6. Mengel F. Computer games and prosocial behaviour. *PloS One.* 2014; 9: e94099.
7. Adachi P, Willoughby T. Do video games promote positive youth development? *J Adolescent Res.* 2012; 28: 155–165.
8. Pitts R. New 'Sim City' gives you the power to destroy … and create. *Polygon,* March 29, 2012. Available at: www.polygon.com/gaming/2012/3/29/2909632/sim-city-2013-maxis
9. Mischel W, Shoda Y, Rodriguez ML. Delay of gratification in children. *Science.* 1989; 244: 933–938.
10. Prins P, Dovis S, Ponsioen A, et al. Does computerized working memory training with game elements enhance motivation and training efficacy in children with ADHD? *Cyberpsychol Behav Soc Netw.* 2011; 14: 115–122.
11. Swing EL, Gentile DA, Anderson CA, Walsh DA. Television and video game exposure and the development of attention problems. *Pediatrics.* 2010; 126: 214–221.
12. Ferguson CJ, Ceranoglu TA. Attention problems and pathological gaming: Resolving the "chicken and egg" in a prospective analysis. *Psych Quart.* 2014; 85: 103–110.
13. Bioulac S, Lallemand S, Fabrigoule C, et al. Video game performances are preserved in ADHD children compared with controls. *J Atten Disord.* 2014; 18: 542–550.
14. Durkin K. Videogames and young people with developmental disorders. *Rev Gen Psychol.* 2010; 14: 122–140.
15. Cardoso-Leite P, Bavelier D. Video game play, attention, and learning: How to shape the development of attention and influence learning? *Curr Opin Neurol.* 2014; 27: 185–191.
16. Tortolero SR, Peskin MF, Baumler ER, et al. Daily violent video game playing and depression in preadolescent youth. *Cyberpsychol Behav Soc Netw.* 2014; 17: 609–615.

17. Brunborg GS, Mentzoni RA, Froyland LR. Is video gaming, or video game addiction, associated with depression, academic achievement, heavy episodic drinking, or conduct problems? *J Behav Addict.* 2014; 3: 27–32.

18. Ferguson CJ, Olson CK. Friends, fun, frustration and fantasy: Child motivations for video game play. *Motiv Emotion.* 2013; 37: 154–164.

19. Przybylski AK. Electronic gaming and psychosocial adjustment. *Pediatrics.* 2014; 134: e716–e722.

20. Ceranoglu TA. Video games in psychotherapy. *Rev Gen Psychol.* 2010; 14: 141–146.

21. Li J, Theng YL, Foo S. Game-based digital interventions for depression therapy: A systematic review and meta-analysis. *Cyberpsychol Behav Soc Netw.* 2014; 17: 519–527.

22. Merry SN, Stasiak K, Shepherd M, et al. The effectiveness of SPARX, a computerised self help intervention for adolescents seeking help for depression: a randomised controlled non-inferiority trial. *BMJ.* 2012; 344: e2598.

23. Fernández-Aranda F, Jiménez-Murcia S, Santamaría JJ, et al. Video games as a complementary therapy tool in mental disorders: PlayMancer, a European multicentre study. *JMH.* 2012; 21: 364–374.

24. Rizzo A, John B, Newman B, et al. Virtual reality as a tool for delivering PTSD exposure therapy and stress resilience training. *Mil Behav Health,* 2013; 1: 48–54.

25. Fish MT, Russoniello CV, O'Brien K. The efficacy of prescribed casual videogame play in reducing symptoms of anxiety: A randomized controlled study. *Games Health.* 2014; 3: 291–295.

26. Patel A, Schieble T, Davidson M, et al. Distraction with a hand-held video game reduces pediatric preoperative anxiety. *Paediatr Anaesth.* 2006; 16: 1019–1027.

27. Tate R, Haritatos J, Cole S. HopeLab's approach to Re-Mission. *IJLM.* 2009; 1: 29–35.

28. Kato PM, Cole SW, Bradlyn AS, Pollock BH. A video game improves behavioral outcomes in adolescents and young adults with cancer: A randomized trial. *Pediatrics.* 2008; 122: e305–e317.

29. Lieberman DA. Video games for diabetes self-management: Examples and design strategies. *J Diabetes Sci Technol.* 2012;6:802–806.

30. Hoffman HG, Chambers GT, Meyer WJ III, et al. Virtual reality as an adjunctive non-pharmacologic analgesic for acute burn pain during medical procedures. *Ann Behav Med.* 2011; 41: 183–191.

31. Hoffman HG, Meyer WJ III, Ramirez M, et al. Feasibility of articulated arm mounted Oculus Rift virtual reality goggles for adjunctive pain control during occupational therapy in pediatric burn patients. *Cyberpsychol Behav Soc Netw.* 2014; 17: 397–401.

32. Parry I, Carbullido C, Kawada J, et al. Keeping up with video game technology: Objective analysis of Kinect™ and Playstation 3 Move™ for use in burn rehabilitation. *Burns.* 2014; 40: 852–859.

33. Fischer P, Greitemeyer T, Kastenmüller A, et al. The effects of risk-glorifying media exposure on risk-positive cognitions, emotions, and behaviors: A meta-analytic review. *Psychol Bull.* 2011; 137: 367–390.

34. Ceranoglu TA. Video games and sleep: An overlooked challenge. *Adolesc Psychiatry.* 2014; 4: 104–108.

35. Desai RA, Krishnan-Sarin S, Cavallo D, Potenza MN. (2010). Video-gaming among high school students: Health correlates, gender differences, and problematic gaming. *Pediatrics.* 2010; 126: e1414–e1424.

36. Glantz SA, Titus K, Mitchell S, et al. Smoking in top-grossing movies – United States, 1991–2009. *Morb Mortal Wkly Rep.* 2010; 59: 1014–1017.

37. Harris JL, Speers SE, Schwartz MB, Brownell KD. US food company branded advergames on the Internet: Children's exposure and effects on snack consumption. *J Child Media.* 2012; 6: 51–68.

38. Maniccia DM, Davison KK, Marshall SJ, et al. A meta-analysis of interventions that target children's screen time for reduction. *Pediatrics*. 2011; 128: e193–e210.

39. Morgenstern M, Sargent JD, Hanewinkel R. Relation between socioeconomic status and body mass index: Evidence of an indirect path via television use. *Arch Pediatr Adolesc Med*. 2009; 163: 731–738.

40. Marshall SJ, Biddle SJH, Gorely T, et al. Relationships between media use, body fatness and physical activity in children and youth: a meta-analysis. *Int J Obesity*. 2004; 28: 1238–1246.

41. LeBlanc AG, Chaput JP, McFarlane A et al. Active video games and health indicators in children and youth: A systematic review. *PloS One*. 2013; 8: e65351.

42. Liang Y, Lau P. Effects of active videogames on physical activity and related outcomes among healthy children: A systematic review. *Games Health*. 2014; 3: 122–143.

43. Graves L, Stratton G, Ridgers ND, Cable NT. Energy expenditure in adolescents playing new generation computer games. *Brit J Sport Med*. 2008; 42: 592–594.

44. Mandryk RL, Gerling KM, Stanley KG. Designing games to discourage sedentary behavior. In Nijholt A, ed. *Playful User Interfaces*. Singapore: Springer; 2014: 253–274.

45. Larsen LH, Schou L, Lund HH, Langberg H. The physical effect of exergames in healthy elderly – a systematic review. *Games Health*. 2013; 2: 205–212.

46. Saunders TJ, Tremblay MS, Mathieu ME, et al. Associations of sedentary behavior, sedentary bouts and breaks in sedentary time with cardiometabolic risk in children with a family history of obesity. *PloS One*. 2013; 8: e79143.

47. Ballas P. Opinion: Why videogames need exercise ratings. *Wired* magazine. August 17, 2010.

48. O'Hanlon C. Gaming: Eat breakfast, drink milk, play Xbox. *T.H.E. Journal*. 2007; 34: 34–39.

49. Schiesel S. P.E. classes turn to video game that works legs. *New York Times*, April 30, 2007. Available at: www.nytimes.com/2007/04/30/health/30exer.html

50. Baranowski T, Abdelsamad D, Baranowski J, et al. Impact of an active video game on healthy children's physical activity. *Pediatrics*. 2012; 129: e636–e642.

51. Chin A, Paw MJ, Jacobs WM, Vaessen EP, et al. The motivation of children to play an active video game. *J Sci Med Sport*. 2008; 11: 163–166.

52. Olson CK. Sports videogames and real-world exercise. In: Consalvo M, Mitgutsch K, Stein A, eds. *Sports Videogames*. New York: Routledge; 2013: 278–294.

53. Sawyer B. From cells to cell processors: The integration of health and video games. *IEEE Comput Grap Appl*. 2008; 28: 83–85.

54. Baranowski T, Buday R, Thompson D, et al. Developing games for health behavior change: Getting started. *Games Health*. 2013; 2: 183–190.

55. Baranowski T, Baranowski J, Thompson D, et al. Video game play, child diet, and physical activity behavior change: A randomized clinical trial. *Am J Prev Med*. 2011; 40: 33–38.

56. Johnson-Glenberg MC, Savio-Ramos C, Henry H. "Alien Health": A nutrition instruction exergame using the Kinect sensor. *Games Health*. 2014; 3: 241–251.

57. Kharrazi H, Lu AS, Gharghabi F, Coleman W. A scoping review of health game research: Past, present, and future. *Games Health*. 2012; 1:153–164.

58. Kato PM. Evaluating efficacy and validating games for health. *Games Health*. 2012; 1: 74–76.

4

THE INFLUENCE OF DIGITAL GAMES ON AGGRESSION AND VIOLENT CRIME

Mark Coulson and Christopher J. Ferguson

To an external observer, the events and actions which take place in a video game can appear bewildering. The screen may be covered in luridly colored and fast moving objects. The player (if we can work out who or what that is) dashes frenetically from one place to the next, seemingly without purpose. And all of this is accompanied by explosions, shouting and screaming, and often a thumping soundtrack. Small wonder that such activity sometimes seems alien to the uninitiated, especially when it is chosen in preference to more traditional social, physical, and intellectual pursuits.

This leads us to our first question regarding video games. Why do people, and particularly younger people, like them so much? Section one of this chapter begins by asking this question, which has some interesting and revealing answers. In particular, having established why we like to play games, we will present an account of why violent video games (VVGs) have come to occupy such a dominant position in gaming. In section two we take a close look at these concepts, and consider how to accurately and sensibly measure them so that the conclusions from our research can say useful things about how parents, the media, and society should treat VVGs. In section three, we identify some of the key controversies, and present a 'research evaluation toolkit' which is intended to be a simple set of questions that anyone can use to evaluate new research when it is presented (often uncritically and using provocative and even alarmist language) by media or scholars themselves. Section four asks whether we should be concerned about violence in VVGs, or whether in fact there are other more important things to worry about (spoiler alert: we think violence in games is not the problem, but there might be other problems that are worth investigating and considering). Finally, section five considers the broader implications of the discussion, considering among other issues why politicians and media consistently misrepresent the findings of research on VVGs.

Examining the Motivation to See So Much Violence in Gaming

General: Conan! What is best in life?

Conan: To crush your enemies, to see them driven before you, and to hear the lamentations of their women.

(Conan the Barbarian, 1982, dir. John Milius)

One important point to establish, which has been made many times before but which bears repeating, is that gaming is not a minority activity. Recent evidence[1] suggests that more than half of Americans play games, and have at least one gaming console in their homes. Among children the numbers are even higher, with almost all boys playing video games and a smaller majority of girls playing as well.[2,3] Women are almost as likely to play video games as men, and adults are as likely to play as children and adolescents. A third of American parents play video games with their children at least once a week, and just over half believe that games are a positive part of their children's lives. Games and gamers are ubiquitous. People play alone and together, at home and on the move. All this time spent gaming has largely been at the expense of time previously spent consuming other kinds of media, in particular TV and movies. Nonetheless, people have often worried that gaming has caused serious problems for social interaction and physical activity and health. However, data from gamers themselves question whether such stereotypes apply to the majority of gamers.[4] The socially isolated, physically inactive, teenage gamer certainly exists, but she or he is an endangered species.

So people like video games. In fact people *love* video games. Video games offer us enjoyment, they motivate us to keep playing, and they may be tapping into something quite profound about human nature and what it means to live a fulfilling life. What might these things be?

A helpful place to start is to ask what we mean by a game, and what it is that makes something a game rather than an activity, a sport, or a chore. The game designer and writer Jane McGonigal[5] cites philosopher Bernard Suits, who states that

> To play a game is to engage in activity directed toward bringing about a specific state of affairs, using only means permitted by specific rules, where the means permitted by the rules are more limited in scope than they would be in the absence of the rules, and where the sole reason for accepting such limitation is to make possible such activity.[6]

Abbreviating this somewhat, McGonigal defines a game as 'the voluntary attempt to overcome unnecessary obstacles.' This definition is useful, as it captures the essence of what we are doing when we play. The activity needs to be voluntary, because when we are forced or required to do something, it ceases to be a game and quickly becomes work. Second, the activity is goal oriented, as there is something we are trying to achieve (moving a story arc along, achieving a new high score, advancing our character, killing a dragon). Third, the game places *unnecessary* obstacles in our path. McGonigal observes that walking long distances to drop a ball into a small hole is tedious, trivial, and no fun at all. Introducing an unnecessary obstacle into the activity (trying to get the ball into the hole using only a long stick with a lump of metal at the end) turns the activity into a game, in this case the game of golf. All of a sudden we are playing, and it is fun.

While this definition of a game is attractive, it begs the question of why such activities should be so motivating and enjoyable. To solve this particular problem, what we need is a definition of enjoyment or fun. The economist Edward Castronova,[7,8] who has written extensively on the effects of massively multi-player online games (MMOs) such as *World of Warcraft*, defines fun as *the pleasant experiences associated with co-activation of motivational systems which promote survival, in the context of a person's choices and decisions, in an environment which they know to be a game.* This definition requires some unpacking. First, there is sound neurobiological evidence that we possess two basic motivational systems, one designed to generate behaviors associated with approaching desirable objects (food, friends, magical swords, etc., referred to as the *appetitive* system) and another associated with avoiding undesirable ones (steep cliffs, toxins, dragons, etc., referred to as the *aversive* system). The importance of co-activation is that according to Castronova both systems need to be activated at more or less the same time before anything can be fun. So receiving something appetitive like a kiss from a loved one is nice, and involves activation of the appetitive system, but it is not fun, in the sense of play activity or "having fun." Similarly, wading through cold mud is unpleasant, and activation of the aversive system alone does not result in fun. However when the two are co-active, and we wade through cold mud in order to get a kiss from a loved one, all of a sudden we are having fun. Assuming we know this is a game, and the cold mud was not placed there by a sadistic spouse, but is an unnecessary obstacle between where we start and what our goal is, fun arises.

What is interesting and important about these two definitions, one about what makes a game, and the second about what makes playing games fun, is that they result from biological mechanisms that are common to many species in addition to our own. This observation may offer an explanation for another important feature of video games, the extensive use of violence. In order to arrive at this conclusion we need to examine the functions which play may serve in our own and other species.

There is lots of evidence that the young of many species play with each other, and spend a lot of time engaging in generally fairly rough and tumble activities which seem to serve no obvious purpose. No obvious purpose, perhaps, until we start asking questions about what is being learned during all this play. A highly influential account of why organisms play has been put forward by the psychologist Barbara Fredrickson.[9] Fredrickson argues that when we play, we are actually experimenting with new ways of solving problems, in a safe environment which permits creative experimentation and does not penalise failure. Clearly, experimenting with new ways of escaping from a real predator is not a sensible thing to do, as the risks involved are very high and individuals adopting this strategy would likely end up eaten. In contrast, experimenting with different ways of running away, dodging, and hiding with your brothers and sisters might *broaden* the range of options you have, and *build* physical and psychological resources that could help you survive when the predator is a real one. Fredrickson's *Broaden and Build* theory suggests that play lies at the heart of learning, and those individuals who play stand a greater chance of survival than those who don't precisely because they have greater flexibility in the behavioral responses available to them.

Even seemingly pointless activities such as tickling may actually serve an important function. Psychiatrist Donald Black[10] observed that the places where we are most ticklish (the neck, the sides of the body, the exposed soles of the feet) are also those which we might need to protect in an emergency. Tickling motivates us to escape while simultaneously making us laugh (a signal normally interpreted as meaning 'carry on!') In other words it simulates an emergency situation in that we need to protect vital areas of our bodies from being 'attacked' by an opponent who is not going to give up. As such, tickling co-activates the appetitive and aversive motivational systems, as outlined earlier, and (though sometimes we might not believe it) fits our definition of fun.

So play and fun are inextricably tied up with survival. Like soldiers on the firing range, young organisms engage in safe but violent facsimiles of real world fight or flight, life or death situations. So long as everyone knows it is a game, with punches stopping short and teeth nibbling rather than biting, everyone benefits from the activity.

Games can also be understood as meeting basic psychological needs. For example, Self-Determination Theory[11] suggests that video games can help us to meet basic psychological needs that are not always met through real-life activities, particular needs for socialization, competence, and autonomy. To illustrate this, one need only contrast the drudgery of many people's work lives, filing papers from an inbox into an outbox, with the fictional universe of a video game in which, along with friends, one can seem to have a real and meaningful impact on the game world through one's own actions. This can be powerfully motivating.

Defining and Measuring Violence and Aggression

> I believe that present day civilized man suffers from insufficient discharge of his aggressive drive.
>
> (Konrad Lorenz, *On Aggression*)[12]

The words of Konrad Lorenz, who won the Nobel prize for his work on animal behavior, remind us that aggression is a *drive*, a naturally occurring behavior which helps organisms get what they need. While aggressive behavior may not be appropriate in many situations which face modern humans (and aggressive behavior certainly is an important issue facing society), we should not fall into the trap of believing aggressive responses are *never* appropriate.[13] Aggression motivates us to acquire what we need, achieve our goals, and help defend what we have from others who aggress against us. An individual who lacked aggressive behaviors on which to draw in times of need would not pass its genes on to the next generation.

So there is a natural component to aggression, and aggressive behavior is not necessarily a negative thing although it may be bad overused or used mal-adaptively. What are the effects of repeated experiences of aggression or repeated exposure to the aggression of others?

There are two main responses to this question. Theories which focus on the *desensitizing* effects of violence and exposure to violence state that repeated exposure to violence reduces its emotional impact, and makes violent acts 'normal.' If we live in an environment where, rightly or wrongly, we perceive violence to be normal, then there is nothing wrong with behaving violently ourselves. In this account, exposure to VVGs desensitizes people to violence, making them more likely to be violent in the future.

In contrast, theories which emphasize *catharsis* view aggression and violence in much the same way as Lorenz, as drives which need to be 'discharged.' The principle of catharsis (which originates in the work of the Greek philosopher Aristotle) is seen as a form of purging, or purifying innate emotions and tensions, leaving us in a state of balance. Under these ideas, VVG play represents a psychologically healthy activity, and indeed we might predict that it would lead to a *reduction* rather than an increase in real-life violence.

There is evidence to support both positions, although in general it is rather tenuous. The P3 component of brain activity (called P3 because it is a *positive* electrical change which occurs approximately 300 milliseconds after a stimulus has been presented) is generally regarded as the brain's response to an unexpected event. For people who have little experience of playing VVGs, P3 is reduced when they are exposed to violent images after playing a VVG, relative to a non-violent video game, suggesting they have become desensitized to violence.[14] However, it remains unclear whether they have become desensitized in the sense of being willing to commit violent acts themselves, as opposed to merely becoming bored with repetitive stimuli (we suspect the latter). Other studies have demonstrated that aggressive or hostile tendencies may in fact be reduced after VVG play, providing some support for the catharsis model.[15]

Asking which approach is the 'right' one is a pointless exercise. Like many disagreements, both sides have their strengths and weaknesses, and both desensitization and catharsis play a role in aggression and violence. Rather than ask questions about *which* theory is correct, we should focus our efforts on identifying the circumstances under which *each* exerts its effects. Human behavior is complex, and is determined by many factors interacting together (a fact which should make us realize there is no one answer to questions like 'do violent video games cause violent behavior?'). Most scholars agree that aggression and violence are multi-determined, including influences from biology and genetics, stimuli in the immediate environment (for instance, provocations from others in the social environment), pre-existing tendencies (their personality, aggressive traits and so on), and life history (e.g. exposure to violence in the family or community). No single factor determines whether someone will aggress or not in a given situation. What remains unclear is whether violent video games is, or is not, one of those factors. A risk/resilience approach to understanding violence does not mean "all have won and must have prizes" and some issues people identify for potential concern may ultimately prove to have little value in predicting violence.

In addition to complex relationships between the various factors which might lead to aggression, aggression itself is a complex idea. Aggression can refer to behaviors, or to tendencies and attitudes, and different definitions of aggression lead to difference measurements which present their own advantages and disadvantages. An appreciation of the different kinds of measures which have been used is useful when trying to understand the results of research.

Different researchers choose different measures of aggression, and these relate with differing degrees of effectiveness to the sorts of real-life behavior we are interested in. Sometimes, the measure of aggression is not chosen by the researcher at all, but is simply already available. For instance, if we believed there to be a link between VVG playing and violence, we might conclude that as the availability of VVGs increases, the amount of violent crime also increases. All of these data are publicly available, but in formats over which we have no control (e.g. sales data on VVGs over the past ten years and national data on the incidence of various forms of violent crime over the same time period). Our hypothesis might lead us to predict a strong association between the two. As VVG availability increases, so does violent crime.

When we look at data such as these, the pattern actually appears to be the opposite of what we would expect if there were a link between VVG play and aggression. While sales of VVGs have increased dramatically over the past decade, the incidence of most forms of violent crime has steadily declined. As a society, we experience more virtual violence and less real-life violence than ever before. These observations hold even when we consider sales of violent games specifically.[16] As observed in Figure 4.1, the popularity of

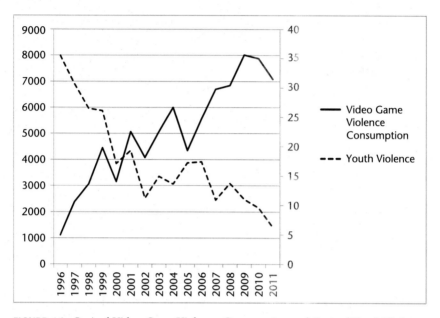

FIGURE 4.1 Societal Video Game Violence Consumption and Societal Youth Violence, 1996–2011

violent video games are inversely related to youth violence rates in the United States (similar results apply to most industrialized nations).

So does this prove that VVGs cause a reduction in real-life violence? No, it doesn't. These data are *correlational*, just two sets of observations, one about the incidence of violent crime, the other about sales of VVGs which when juxtaposed appear to suggest there is no link between the two. We note that these data do not rule out the possibility that video game violence may have some small influence on some types of aggression, particular minor forms of aggression not represented in crime statistics. However, these data do caution us about the types of extreme statements linking video game violence to real-life violence which have become common in the field, such as linking video games to mass shootings, claiming that the effects of violent video games on aggression were as strong as smoking on lung cancer, or that as many as 50 percent of homicides could be attributed to video game or other media violence.[17–19] Data to support such claims simply aren't materializing.

What can we do about this? There are several key issues which include how we draw inferences from data, the kinds of measurements being used, and the nature of the data we are examining as well as the sorts of methods being used to gather those data. We will consider these in the discussion which follows as they are key to understanding how complex these issues are, and how much confidence we should have in the outcomes of research.

When we examine existing data such as VVG sales figures and the incidence of violent crime, we need to recognize that any relationship can be explained in a number of different ways, and the data cannot tell us which if any of these is correct (or even if there is a correct one). The fact that increases in VVG sales are associated with decreases in reported violent crime is just an association – intriguing for sure, but in no sense proof that one factor causes the other. Indeed, with the increasing availability of large datasets, all sorts of intriguing and sometimes amusing associations between data can be found (the interested reader is directed to Tyler Vigen's *Spurious Correlations* website at tylervigen.com). An association between any two factors can be explained in a variety of ways, and the fact that there is an association often offers no clues as to which is the correct explanation. Possible explanations include:

1. The first variable causes the second (in our dataset, playing VVGs makes people less violent).
2. The second variable causes the first (the reduction in real-life violence has made people want to play VVGs).
3. There is an additional factor or factors which explains the association (for instance, people spend more time playing VVGs, and less time going out and being the perpetrators or victims of violent crime).
4. The relationship (or lack of one) is spurious and coincidental (for instance, there is a strong relationship between the number of Somalian pirates and the global temperature, but no one would argue that there is a *causal* relationship at work here).

Thus, advocates for differing views must be cautious in overinterpreting such data. While the data on video game violence and youth violence caution us to be conservative in our statements regarding the impact of video game violence, it would be mistaken to conclude from such data that video game violence is *causing* the reduction in youth violence. This would be an example of an ecological fallacy.

The data discussed above form one end of a continuum of evidence which has been brought to bear on the question of VVGs and violence. Sales and crime data are very large-scale data, but are uncontrolled. They have the advantage of *size* (there are lots of sales and lots of crimes) but the disadvantage of *inference* (we cannot draw any conclusions from them). Other methods sacrifice some of the advantages of size in order to increase the power of inference. For instance, *cross-sectional* studies look at different pre-existing groups (for instance, those who play VVGs and those who don't) and compare them on a variety of measures such as aggression and violent behavior. Such studies tend to be relatively cheap, but their interpretation is often open to question. *Longitudinal* studies measure various factors, including VVG play, over a period of time, perhaps extending over several years, examining how people change as a result of the games they play. Such studies are relatively costly to perform, but yield interesting data although still basically correlational in nature. Finally, *experimental* studies manipulate the experience which participants have, for instance getting people to spend time in a laboratory playing a VVG and then measuring their levels of aggression or violence. Such studies have the advantage of being able to establish causal links (if done properly!), but are costly and time-consuming, and fraught with technical issues, many of which relate to how the experimental manipulation is delivered, and how the resulting behavior is measured.

Cutting across all these methods of investigation is the issue of how to measure and define aggression and violence. A number of different approaches have been taken which can be conveniently categorized into *direct* and *indirect* measures.

Direct measures usually involve an observable act or behavior which is clearly aggressive in nature. Verbal or physical abuse are clear examples, as are the violent crimes from the example considered earlier. While such acts are fairly unambiguous, modern codes of conduct and ethical principles prevent researchers from generating such strong responses in their participants, and less dramatic measures have been developed. Among the most widely used of these is the 'hot sauce' method[20] which involves a participant deciding how much hot sauce another person will be required to consume (the other person rarely has to consume the hot sauce, but the participant believes they will have to). The amount or spiciness of the sauce are taken as direct indicators of how aggressive one person feels about another. A typical experiment might require participants to play either a VVG or a non-violent game, perhaps against another player (who may or may not be visible), and then asked to make up hot sauce which they are informed the other player will have to consume. Hotter or larger portions of sauce are taken as direct indicators of aggression toward the other player. However, it is not clear how much such behavior tells us about aggressive behavior in real life. Is this the sort of minor boost in aggression we might expect from a whole host of situations that involved competition such as playing a board game, watching a sporting event, having a debate, etc.[21] or is such behavior more meaningful? Youth gangs don't chase after each other with vials of Wasabi or Tabasco sauce, after all.

In contrast to direct measures, *indirect* measures eschew observable behavior and instead measure attitudes or beliefs using *self-report* measures. So a participant might play a VVG and then be asked a series of questions about how they feel, or how they are likely to act in a variety of given situations. While such measures are cheap and easy to administer, they suffer from two main weaknesses. The first is that aggressive attitudes do not translate all that well into aggressive behavior, and the second is that the development of reliable questionnaire measures is a science in itself, and requires a great deal of testing and development. Self-report is sometimes the only method which can be used, but we should be wary of drawing strong conclusions from its results. Further, pairing questions about violent video game play with questions about the respondent's own violent or aggressive behavior can create *demand characteristics* in which respondents may feel pressured (consciously or unconsciously) in a particular manner, creating spurious correlations.

So, exactly what is meant by aggression or violence, particularly in the way such constructs are measured in research, remains controversial. Even the concept of *violent video game* is one without clear boundaries. For instance, in a recent murder trial in which a scholar implied a mass homicide might be blamed in part on video games, that scholar had to acknowledge under cross examination that even games such as *Pac-Man* might be considered violent video games in the broad way they are often classified by scholars.[22] Most people would find this to be absurd, of course, but this points to continued issues of poor clarity in the research field regarding the constructs of interest. Indeed the entire concept of "violent video game" may need rethinking. Although such a construct has considerable moral salience, it encapsulates such a broad range of video games under a single heading as to arguably have little conceptual value.

Contradictory Findings and Contradictory Messages

From the discussion above it may now be clear why there are so many conflicting findings and recommendations. It is fairly easy to find what appears to be authoritative guidance which states that VVGs are bad, or good, or neither one nor the other. Dozens of studies have found links between VVG play and aggression, but dozens more have found no links. Even formal methods designed to produce simple answers to questions like this by mathematically combining the results of many studies (i.e. meta-analysis) fail to arrive at the same answer, and lead to yet more technical disagreements.[23–25] How can the non-specialist possibly navigate their way through this morass? In this section we draw upon what has already been discussed, condensing it into a 'research evaluation toolkit' which offers the concerned person a set of questions they can ask about any new piece of evidence which should help them understand its significance and impact.

A Research Evaluation Toolkit

1. Remember that individual studies do not tell us a great deal. A single finding is merely that – a single finding. It is very rare that single findings completely change our understanding of a phenomenon. Always interpret 'groundbreaking' new research not as groundbreaking, but as adding another brick to a slowly enlarging structure whose final form may still be unclear. Be wary of press releases that imply a new study definitively

answers a controversial question . . . such claims often inform us more about researchers' biases that may have influenced their study than they do "truth."

2.   Has the research been published, or is it about to be published, in a reputable peer-reviewed journal (the hallmark or 'gold standard' of academic research)? You can find journals on the internet very easily. If the research has not or is not about to be published in a peer-reviewed journal then it has not been subjected to the scrutiny of experts. While it may indeed be important research, until such time as it has been properly reviewed, it can probably be safely ignored.

3.   How clear is the link between VVG activity and aggression and violence? Referring to our discussion of direct and indirect measures, are the purported links of any importance?

4.   How well have aggression and violence been measured? Good research uses standardized measures which may have taken years to develop and whose utility is well known. Questions which appear to have been made up by the researchers themselves should be treated with caution.

5.   Are the outcomes of clinical or criminal significance? Academic research often focuses on relatively small statistical effects which may be important to theoretical ideas but which may have little if any practical implication. While it may be that playing a particular game makes people more likely to express aggressive thoughts, that does not mean they are bound to act more aggressively. If playing a VVG makes people likely to act aggressively, that does not mean they are bound to be violent. And even acting violently may not be violence directed at another person, or occur in a criminal context. What was the magnitude of the effects? If a study finds evidence for effects, but they change behavior by only 1–2 percent . . . or less . . . are these effects of any practical value in the real world? Would you notice if you were 2 percent more aggressive, or happy, or sad, today as compared to yesterday?

6.   Did the author consider any other possible explanations for their results? As we will see later, VVGs are not purely about violence. They may include competition and frustration, both of which may contribute to aggressive thoughts or behaviors.

7.   Were there any pre-existing facts about the participants in the research which might have influenced the outcomes? Were the participants representative of the population, or unusual in some way (e.g. college students, the most popular source of data for research)? Was the study design set up in a way to make it obvious to participants what the researchers' hypothesis was (which can cause spurious results)?

8.   Does the study engage in "citation bias?" Citation bias is when study authors don't cite any studies that conflict with their personal beliefs. Typically authors do this to make it sound like the evidence against video games is more conclusive than it actually is. Such behavior is considered

unscientific practice.[26] It also alerts the reader to significant researcher biases which can have an influence on the results of their study.

A final point to bear in mind when evaluating evidence concerns one's own personal beliefs. For reasons which we develop in section 5, many people have a pre-conceived notion that new media are dangerous. We don't doubt that there are potential dangers in any new media (and indeed in any new technology), but we think it is sensible to adopt a neutral stance on new technologies, neither loving nor hating them. Assume new media can be used for both good and bad, and evaluate the evidence which arises from careful investigation of these effects.

Video Game Violence and Real World Violence

Sometimes, the focus on the effects of VVGs on people seems to ignore the very thing social science research is concerned about – people. People respond very differently to different media, and these individual differences might mediate any relationship between exposure to VVGs and violent behaviors. Our personalities constitute an excellent and informative example of where individual differences may be at least if not more important as the kinds of games we play in determining what happens to us.

Psychologists believe that personality is best described in terms of five underlying factors, or dimensions, all of which are possessed by everyone to a lesser or greater degree. In effect, everyone's personality can be described in terms of where they lie along five measurements, where each measurement is completely independent from all the others.

The five dimensions can be summarized by the acronym OCEAN, which stands for Openness to experience, Conscientiousness, Extraversion, Agreeableness, and Neuroticism. Like most measures, people tend to cluster around the average (for instance being neither extraverted nor its opposite, introverted), with decreasing proportions of people scoring toward the extremes (this is the well-known 'bell shaped curve' which describes the distribution of scores in a very large variety of measures). While our personalities may change a little over time, they are pretty fixed, and there is some evidence that they are partially determined by genetics.[27]

As outlined above, the five personality dimensions are independent. So, knowing whether someone is agreeable or not (that is, they place a high importance on getting along with other people) tells you nothing about how conscientious they are (that is, the degree to which they do or do not value order and attention to detail). Each of us is a mix of the five dimensions, so our personality might be average on openness, high on conscientiousness, low on extraversion, average on agreeableness, and high on neuroticism. This is how a simple five factor model, which on the surface might appear rather simplistic, is actually capable of describing a very large number of different personalities.*

So is there a personality 'type' or profile which might make people especially vulnerable to VVGs? While there is not a great deal of evidence which either supports or challenges this idea, there is every reason to suspect that people will respond differently to VVGs (indeed, it would be astounding if they didn't) and that personality might hold the key to discovering what these relationships might be. The key lies in looking not just at a single dimension, but how particular patterns of scores on different dimensions might relate to psychological vulnerability.

Just such a question was asked by researchers Patrick and Charlotte Markey and published in 2010.[28] They argued that no one personality dimension makes a person vulnerable, but that certain levels in three of the Big 5 dimensions, when present in the same individual, might be critical. Their conclusion is that people who score low on conscientiousness, low on agreeableness, and high on neuroticism may possess a pre-existing disposition to be negatively affected by VVGs. Such people tend to be fairly unconcerned about the feelings of others, are likely to break rules and not worry about convention, and experience strong emotional reactions to events. When exposed to violence or frustration, people who have this 'vulnerable' personality may respond strongly, and without concern for social rules or the feelings of others.

While fascinating, these ideas are far from conclusive, and have only been subject to a small amount of experimental investigation. It is important to note that Markey and Markey say only that predisposed individuals become a bit more hostile after playing VVGs, not that they engage in violent acts, or commit mass shootings. Other evidence has found a lack of relationship between VVG playing and pre-existing mental health symptoms in children,[29] so it's important not to generalize these results too far. However, the emphasis on an interaction between VVGs and individual differences is important, and this general notion has received a great deal of attention from researchers interested in asking the broader question about whether we can predict the type of person who will commit acts of violence. The developing field of *behavioral genetics*, for instance, looks at both the genetics and the environment of a person, and seeks to identify how the two interact in order to affect behavior. For instance, a gene referred to, somewhat unintelligently, as the 'warrior' gene, affects the levels of an enzyme, monoamine oxidase A (MAOA) which is responsible for breaking down some of the chemicals affecting transmission of information in the brain. About a third of the population has a version of the MAOA gene which means they produce lower levels of the enzyme. Such people are indistinguishable

---

* If you are interested in measuring your own personality, a good place to head is https://personality-testing.info/tests/BIG5.php which is a 50-item assessment of the Big 5 personality traits.

from those who produce normal levels of the enzyme except when certain environmental conditions hold. In one piece of research, which examined the effects of MAOA levels and childhood maltreatment on violent criminal behavior, neither MAOA level nor a history of childhood maltreatment had an effect in isolation, but in combination the two accounted for a significant proportion of violent crime, i.e. those who had the 'low' form of the MAOA gene *and* were mistreated as children.[30] In a second paper,[31] those with low levels of MAOA tended to respond more aggressively when severely provoked (notably there was no effect for mild forms of provocation), in that they administered more hot sauce to their opponent than participants with normal levels of MAOA.

What this all means is that there is fairly clear and increasing evidence that VVGs do not 'cause' aggression, but may interact with biological and psychological characteristics of individual people, making some more vulnerable individuals more likely to respond aggressively than before. However, how we interact with media is often complex and individualized. Playing VVGs may make one person a little angrier . . . but playing a non-violent game might make a different person a little angrier. We've all seen people who respond to losing a game of checkers or cards by throwing the game pieces across the room. It's difficult to definitively predict how media will influence any one person. Does this still mean we ought to be worried about violence in games? One more factor casts doubt on this conclusion.

When we play a VVG, it is typically the violence which we first notice. Many games are built around continuous violence on a scale no living person would ever realistically expect to encounter. As such, the salience of all this violence grabs our attention and focuses it. It is hardly surprising that when asked to identify what it is about VVGs which is 'the problem,' we tend to focus on the violence.

But games, even extremely violent ones, contain much more than just violence. They require planning, and timing, and coordination. They typically involve some degree of competition, whether it is against other (human) players, or computer controlled enemies, obstacles, or challenges. So there is an element of winning and losing involved. All of these activities make demands on our *cognitive* faculties, those parts of the brain responsible for thinking, problem solving, planning, and decision making. As anyone who has seen a carefully developed strategy or plan fail (whether in the virtual world of a video game or in the real world) will know, such frustrations can generate significant levels of aggression. Games, even the most violent ones, involve a great deal more than just violence.

A serious challenge of research which aims to investigate the relationship between VVGs and violent behavior is that when a person plays a VVG, they are also planning, and competing, and problem solving, and coordinating their movements. Just because the violence is salient does not mean that any behavioral or psychological effects of play are being caused by the violence in the game. We might imagine two games, one of which is principally based around violence, the other not, with both involving the same amount of competition and/or frustration. Any differences between how people behave or think before and after playing this pair of games has probably been caused by the violent content, as this is effectively the only difference between them. If on the other hand we take two VVGs with the same violent content, but one is frustrating while the other is not, and we still observe differences between people before and after playing the games, then clearly the violent content is not having an effect.

When researchers examine what happens when the violent content of a VVG is extracted or matched in some way, interesting findings emerge. For instance, a violent game can be 'modded' to remove a lot of the violent content while leaving the game otherwise unchanged. A team of researchers headed by Malte Elson[32] changed the normal blood and gore content of a game, replacing the gun used by the player with something that looked and sounded like a tennis racquet, and freezing enemies in place rather than have them die graphically and noisily. All the other game mechanics remained the same, but the change in violence levels had no effect on players' levels of aggression.

In a separate series of studies, Paul Adachi and Teena Willoughby examined two situations where aspects of games were matched.[21] In the first, participants played games matched in competitiveness, where one was violent and the other non-violent. Using the (by now familiar) hot sauce paradigm, they found that levels of aggression were not elevated in those who played the violent competitive game compared with those who played the non-violent competitive game. In the second study, the authors used four different games matched in terms of both competitiveness and violence, so participants played either a non-violent non-competitive game, a non-violent competitive game, a violent non-competitive game, or a violent competitive game. Consistent with the idea that it is competition, not violence, which leads to aggression, participants who played competitive games used more hot sauce than those who played non-competitive games, but those who played violent games used no more hot sauce than those who played non-violent games. Andrew Przybylski and colleagues[33] found similar results when controlling carefully for levels of frustration in video games. Frustration, but not violent content, was causally associated with aggressive behavior.

Increasingly we are seeing that it is difficult to conclusively link VVG exposure to aggressive behavior or certainly violent behavior in society. Research studies have produced conflicting results and even those that do find results produce very small effects. A good question is, if the research has been inconsistent and tended to produce such weak results, why do some scholars persist in proclaiming VVGs as an imminent public health threat? It is to this issue that we next turn.

The Sociology of Media Violence Research

Perhaps part of the challenge for the general public as they watch the sometimes acrimonious debates on media violence is the assumption that science always works objectively toward a desire to seek "truth." This is, of course, the ideal of science, but we often forget that science is a human endeavor, part of human society, and in many ways influenced by that society. Scientists need to secure grant funding and tend to enjoy news coverage of their studies, professional and societal prestige, and even political influence. Generally, these goals are more easily met by proclaiming something to be a problem that can be fixed by scientists, rather than deciding no problem exists at all. This does not mean that scientists are not acting in good faith, only that they are human and are not immune to societal pressures.

To understand those societal pressures we can turn to a sociological theory known as Moral Panic Theory.[34] Put briefly, Moral Panic Theory (see Chapter 2) states that people try to explain distressing social circumstances (real or imagined) by seeking "folk devils" to blame them on. Blaming mass shootings on VVGs is a perfect example. Mass shootings make us anxious, and we seek out answers for why they happen that give us an illusion of control. If only we get rid of the VVGs, we might prevent mass shootings! This is, of course, false, but it gives people a sense of control over something uncontrollable. Historically all manner of media, from dime novels, to waltzes, jazz, rock and rap, to comic books, to *Dungeons and Dragons*, Harry Potter and now VVGs have been the subject of moral panics. Very often scholars participate in and fuel these moral panics. Most famously, Frederic Wertham, a prominent psychiatrist, testified before congress in the 1950s that comic books caused not only juvenile delinquency but homosexuality (because, it was said, characters such as Batman and Robin were secretly gay). In retrospect, Wertham is typically perceived as an overzealous advocate who may have falsified his data.[35] Scholars have participated in other moral panics, such as that over *Dungeons and Dragons*, as well as the congressional hearings in the 1980s over rock and pop music (which targeted bands ranging from AC/DC to Twisted Sister to Cyndi Lauper!).

It would undoubtedly help us to understand how the scientific community responds to moral panics, and how moral panics and political pressure can do damage to the objectivity of scientific research. Whatever one may think about VVGs having some minor influence on aggression, it is now clear that some of the extreme statements of scholars[17-19] were misguided and accomplished little other than to damage the reputation of social science as an objective enterprise.[36,37]

Understanding why this occurred can be helpful in preventing further cycles of moral panic among scholars in the future. For instance, although it was not uncommon to hear proponents of the causal position claim near universal agreement among scholars on the issue of media or VVG effects, recent data

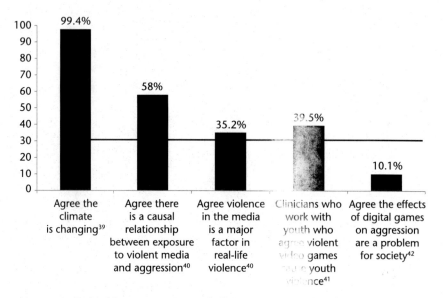

FIGURE 4.2   Lack of Consensus among Scholars on Violent Media Effects

have put paid to such claims (see Figure 4.2). Rather than a clear consensus, across studies, it appears that a minority of about 30–40 percent of scholars agree that violent media is a societal problem. This is not to say that such a substantial minority should be ignored, rather it is time to dispense with the myth of a universal consensus among scholars and return the academic culture to one in which open dialogue and discussion, rather than quasi-religious insistence on particular "truths," has become the norm. Indeed, some causationist scholars have taken to smearing their opponents as "industry apologists" despite the absence of industry funding in aggression research,[38] and this aggressive culture among scholars themselves is unlikely to be productive for scientific objectivity. Only by opening the field to scholars of all opinions can the reputation of the field as an objective science be salvaged.

Given that scholars have varied opinions about what influences VVGs might have (for both good and bad) it would be valuable to examine scholars themselves. For instance, work with the general public[43] demonstrates that fears of video games tend to resonate along generational lines. That is, older adults who don't play video games tend to fear them more than younger adults who do. It may very well be that a similar pattern holds for scholars. Or perhaps certain fears of youth (i.e. juvenoia) or personality traits also predict certain types of opinions about video games, which may, in turn influence research findings through researcher expectancy effects.

It may also be helpful to examine how well-known sociological processes such as group-think, confirmation bias, and cognitive dissonance (i.e. scholars producing research to support their own parenting practices) may influence research fields. Furthermore, how do *warning bias* (the bias to warn the general public about potential problems even if the evidence isn't clear) and *sanctimony bias* (the bias involving warning of dangers created by other people, such as the video game industry, which by contrast make oneself appear morally superior) influence scientific research fields, particularly on morally valenced issues such as violence? Understanding this sociology of media effects research may help us to be more cautious as we inevitably approach questions of yet newer media in coming decades. It would be beneficial to learn from history rather than to simply repeat it.

Concluding Statements

People generally want to know a simple answer as to whether VVGs cause aggression or societal violence. As we can see here, the likelihood that VVGs cause societal violence is minimal. Even in the heyday of panic over VVGs in the mid-2000s, the American Medical Association came to this conclusion[44] despite worrying over more minor short-term aggression. However, as we've seen, even the research on short-term, minor aggressive behaviors is unclear. It may be that other features such as frustration or competition are more important than violent content when it comes to aggressive behavior.

Understanding the influences of VVGs or other media can only be done with a fuller understanding of societal moral panics over media and how these moral panics influence the scientific process. Without such an understanding, we are unlikely to exit a repetitive cycle of exaggerated fears followed by public ridicule (e.g. Fredric Wertham). And before we are able, as a scientific field, to produce reliable answers, we must change the scientific culture from one in which adherence to particular "truths" is rejected in favor of a culture of open inquiry in which scholars of all conclusions are welcomed.

References

1. Entertainment Software Association. *2015 Sales, Demographic and Usage Data*. 2015. Available at: www.theesa.com/wp-content/uploads/2015/04/ESA-Essential-Facts-2015.pdf. Accessed November 19, 2014.
2. Kutner L, Olson C. *Grand Theft Childhood: The Surprising Truth about Violent Video Games and What Parents Can Do*. New York: Simon and Schuster; 2008.
3. Lenhart A, Kahne J, Middaugh E, Macgill AR, Evans C, Vitak J. Teens, video games, and civics: Teens' gaming experiences are diverse and include significant social interaction and civic engagement. *Pew Internet & American Life Project*. 2008. Available at: http://eric.ed.gov/?id=ED525058. Accessed November 19, 2014.
4. Kowert R, Festl R, Quandt T. Unpopular, overweight, and socially inept: Reconsidering the stereotype of online gamers. *Cyberpsychol Behav Soc Netw.* 2014; 17(3): 141–146.
5. McGonigal J. *Reality Is Broken: Why Games Make Us Better and How They Can Change the World*. Reprint edition. New York: Penguin Books; 2011.

6. Suits B. What is a game? *Philos Sci.* 1967; 34(2): 148–156.
7. Castronova E. *Synthetic Worlds.* Chicago: University of Chicago Press; 2005.
8. Castronova E. *Exodus to the Virtual World: How Online Fun Is Changing Reality.* New York: Palgrave Macmillan; 2007.
9. Fredrickson BL. The role of positive emotions in positive psychology: The broaden-and-build theory of positive emotions. *Am Psychol.* 2001; 56(3): 218.
10. Black DW. Laughter. *JAMA* 1984; 252(21): 2995–2998.
11. Przybylski AK, Rigby CS, Ryan RM. A motivational model of video game engagement. *Rev Gen Psychol.* 2010; 14(2): 154–166. doi:10.1037/a0019440
12. Lorenz K. *On Aggression.* New York: Harcourt, Brace and World; 1963.
13. Smith P. Why has aggression been thought of as maladaptive. In: Hawley PH, Little TD, Rodkin PC eds. *Aggression and Adaptation: The Bright Side To Bad Behavior.* Mahwah, NJ: Lawrence Erlbaum Associates; 2007: 65–83.
14. Engelhardt CR, Bartholow BD, Kerr GT, Bushman BJ. This is your brain on violent video games: Neural desensitization to violence predicts increased aggression following violent video game exposure. *J Exp Soc Psychol.* 2011; 47(5): 1033–1036. doi:10.1016/j.jesp.2011.03.027
15. Markey PM, Markey CN, French JE. *Violent Video Games and Real-World Violence: Rhetoric Versus Data.* 2014. Available at: http://psycnet.apa.org/psycinfo/2014-33466-001. Accessed November 19, 2014.
16. Ferguson CJ. Does media violence predict societal violence? It depends on what you look at and when. *J Commun.* 2014. doi:10.1111/jcom.12129
17. Bushman BJ, Anderson CA. Media violence and the American public: Scientific facts versus media misinformation. *Am Psychol.* 2001; 56(6–7): 477–489. doi: 10.1037//0003-066X.56.6-7.477
18. Cook DE. Media violence. *Testimony of the American Academy of Pediatrics before the US Senate Commerce Committee.* 2000.
19. Strasburger VC. Go ahead punk, make my day: It's time for pediatricians to take action against media violence. *Pediatrics* 2007; 119(6): e1398–e1399. doi:10.1542/peds.2007-0083
20. Lieberman JD, Solomon S, Greenberg J, McGregor HA. A hot new way to measure aggression: Hot sauce allocation. *Aggr. Behav.* 1999; 25(5): 331–348. doi:10.1002/(SICI)1098-2337(1999)25:5<331::AID-AB2>3.0.CO;2-1
21. Adachi PJC, Willoughby T. The effect of video game competition and violence on aggressive behavior: Which characteristic has the greatest influence? *Psychol Viol.* 2011; 1(4): 259–274. doi:10.1037/a0024908
22. Rushton B. Backdooring it: Defense maneuvers around setback. 2013. Available at: www.illinoistimes.com/Springfield/article-11440-backdooring-it.html. Accessed November 19, 2014.
23. Anderson CA, Shibuya A, Ihori N, et al. Violent video game effects on aggression, empathy, and prosocial behavior in Eastern and Western countries: A meta-analytic review. *Psychol Bull.* 2010; 136(2): 151–173. doi:10.1037/a0018251
24. Ferguson CJ. Does media violence predict societal violence? It depends on what you look at and when. *J Comm.* 2015; 65(1); E1–E22. doi:10.1111/jcom.12129
25. Sherry JL. Violent video games and aggression: Why can't we find effects? In: Preiss RW, Gayle BM, Burrell N, et al. eds. *Mass Media Effects Research: Advances through Meta-Analysis.* Mahwah, NJ: Lawrence Erlbaum Associates; 2007: 245–262.
26. Babor TF, McGovern T, Alighieri D. Dante's inferno: Seven deadly sins in scientific publishing and how to avoid them. *Publishing Addiction Science: A Guide for the Perplexed* (2nd edition). International Society of Addiction Journal Editors, London 2008. Available at: http://cdrwww.who.int/entity/substance_abuse/publications/publishing_addiction_science_chapter7.pdf. Accessed November 19, 2014.
27. McCrae RR, Costa PT Jr. Personality trait structure as a human universal. *Am Psychol.* 1997; 52(5): 509–516. doi:10.1037//0003-066X.52.5.509

behavioral addiction and consisted of a compulsive behavioral involvement, a lack of interest in other activities, association mainly with other addicts, and physical and mental symptoms when attempting to stop the behavior (e.g., the shakes). Some credence was given to these claims that video game addiction existed following papers on the seemingly successful treatment of video game addiction using cognitive behavioral therapy.[6,7] However, all of these studies were somewhat observational, anecdotal, and/or case studies, primarily based on teenage males, and all based on a particular type of video game in a particular medium (i.e., 'pay-to-play' arcade video games).

Shotton[8] carried out the first empirical study specifically on gaming addiction on a relatively small sample of 127 people (almost all teenage or young adult males) who described themselves as "hooked" on home video games for at least five years. Shotton's conceptualization of game addiction was more positive than negative, and she reported that her 'addicts' were on the whole highly intelligent, motivated, and achieving people but often misunderstood by others in society. In relation to gaming addiction, the main problem with the study was that no standardized measure of addiction was actually used. The only criterion for being 'addicted' was the individual's own admission that they were 'hooked' on computer games. Despite this major shortcoming, recent research by Widyanto, Griffiths and Brunsden[9] reported that a person's self-diagnosis of whether they were addicted to the Internet or not was correlated highly with more standardized measures of Internet addiction.

Gaming Addiction in the 1990s

The 1990s saw a small but significant increase of research into video game addiction with almost all of these studies being carried out in the UK and on adolescents typically surveying children in school settings.[10–16] In contrast to the early 1980s studies, these studies mainly examined non-arcade video game playing (i.e., home console games, handheld games, PC gaming). However, all of these studies were self-report surveys, relatively small scale and the main problem was that all of them assessed video game addiction using adapted versions of the DSM-III-R[17] or DSM-IV[18] criteria for pathological gambling. Based on further analysis of the adapted DSM criteria used, these studies were later criticized as being more likely to be assessing video game preoccupation rather than video game addiction.[19]

Gaming Addiction in the 2000s

The 2000s saw a substantial growth in the number of studies on video game addiction particularly as gaming expanded into the new online medium where games could be played as part of a gaming community (i.e., Massively Multiplayer Online Role-Playing Games [MMORPGs] such as *World of Warcraft* and *Everquest*). Approximately sixty studies were published on gaming addiction between 2000 and 2010[20] and a vast majority of these examined MMORPG addiction and was not limited to the study of adolescent males. Furthermore, many of these studies collected their data online and a significant minority of studies examined various other aspects of video game addiction using non-self-report methodologies. These include studies using polysomnographic measures and visual and verbal memory tests,[21] medical examinations including the patient's history, and physical, radiologic, intraoperative, and pathologic findings,[22] functional Magnetic Resonance Imaging,[23–25] electroencephalography,[26] and genotyping.[27] Given the methodological shortcomings of the studies published prior to 2000, and the fact that gaming has evolved substantially over the last decade, the remainder of this chapter will mainly focus on studies published in the last decade (i.e., post-2000 papers) with the exception of those concerning the health and medical consequences of excessive video game play.

Features of Gaming Addiction

There are a multitude of psychological perspectives on addiction, which has led to addiction being defined in many different ways. However, most models of addictive behavior refer to a persistent and uncontrollable urge to consume a substance, or engage in an activity, that results in significant personal harm and interpersonal conflict for the user.[28] Thus, gaming addiction is often said to be present when an individual has completely lost control over their game playing and their excessive playing behavior has had a detrimental effect on all aspects of their life, and compromises their job and/or educational activities, interpersonal relationships, hobbies, general health, and psychological well-being.[28] These two criteria (impaired control and harmful consequences) are regarded as fundamentally important criteria for addiction. An alternative model of addictive behavior has proposed six features or *components* of gaming addiction.[29] To indicate addiction, it is thought that these criteria must be sustained for a period of between three to six months. Otherwise, they may simply indicate a temporary absorption in video games. These criteria are:

- *Salience.* This occurs when gaming becomes the most important activity in a person's life, dominating their thoughts (preoccupation and cognitive distortions), emotions (cravings), and behavior (deterioration of normal behaviors). An addicted gamer is obsessed with all aspects of video games and, when not playing, will be anticipating or planning the next playing session.
- *Mood modification.* This refers to changes in a person's mood state that occur as a result of gaming. Mood change may involve a subjective feeling of euphoria as well as an increase in physiological arousal (increased heart rate, muscle tension, or shaky hands) or, alternatively, a tranquilizing feeling of calm or numbing sensation.

- *Tolerance.* This refers to the process whereby increasing amounts of gaming are required to achieve the former mood-modifying effects. This means that players gradually increase the amount of time they spend engaged in gaming. It could be argued that addicted gamers build up their tolerance to the point that they will end a playing session only when they have become mentally or physically exhausted.
- *Withdrawal.* These are the aversive mood states and/or physical effects that occur when gaming is suddenly discontinued or reduced. Psychological withdrawal symptoms include feelings of frustration, irritability, and flattened affect. Withdrawal motivates the individual to play video games on a regular basis, and to minimize periods of absence from a video game, in order to alleviate these unpleasant feeling states.
- *Relapse.* This refers to the tendency for the player to make repeated reversions to earlier patterns of gaming, and for even the most extreme patterns typical of the height of excessive gaming to be quickly restored after periods of abstinence or moderation. Relapse usually indicates that the individual has lost personal agency over their behavior.
- *Conflict (Harm).* This refers to the negative consequences of excessive gaming. Harm includes conflicts between the addicted video game player and other people (family members and friends), other activities (job, school, social life, hobbies and interests), and from within the addict themselves (psychological distress).

Charlton[19] suggests that three of these features may not be reliable indicators of video game addiction. His research suggests that cognitive salience (pre-occupation), euphoria (mood modification), and tolerance also indicate *high engagement,* or a type of healthy obsession, with gaming. Therefore, studies may overestimate the prevalence of problem video game play if high engagement with gaming is not properly distinguished from gaming addiction. Given these issues of reliability, many addiction specialists maintain that impaired control and harmful effects are the most appropriate criteria for identifying gaming addiction.

Prevalence of Problematic Video Game Use and Gaming Addiction

At present, it is quite difficult to estimate the prevalence of problematic online gaming due to the lack of a clear definition, the application of measures without proper psychometric characteristics and studies using different samples and different research methodologies. Large sample studies generally report prevalence values below 10 percent. A study conducted in the US on a national representative sample of teenagers,[30] as well as a large sample of Singaporean children,[31] both reported a problematic game use of approximately 9 percent. Results of another representative study in Germany showed that 3 percent of the male and 0.3 percent of the female students were diagnosed as dependent on video games, while another 4.7 percent of male and 0.5 percent of female students were at risk of becoming dependent.[32] In a large Hungarian online gamer sample 3.4 percent of gamers belonged to the high-risk group of problematic gaming and another 15.2 percent to the medium-risk group.[33] A proportion of 4.6 percent of Hungarian adolescents (approx. 16 years old) belonging to a national sample were classified as high-risk users[34] (see Table 5.1).

Demographics and Gaming Addiction

According to an online survey examining all types of online gamers[35] (N=4374), the mean age was 21 years, and participants were mostly male (91 percent) and single (66 percent). Their average weekly game time varied between less than 7 hours (10 percent) and more than 42 hours (also 10 percent) with most of the gamers playing 15–27 hours weekly (35 percent). Furthermore, 16 percent of all gamers were playing professionally (i.e., they participate in competitions and earn money if they win). The majority of the sample (79 percent) had a clear gaming preference, namely they played one single game type most of the time.

Data regarding the three main game types give a more nuanced view. The proportion of female gamers is the lowest in the case of Massively Multi-player Online First Person Shooter (MMOFPS) games (1–2 percent)[35] and the highest in Massively Multi-player Online Role-Playing Game (MMORPG) users (15–30 percent).[35–37] MMOFPS users are the youngest (18–19.8 years),[35] while both Massively Multi-player Online Real-Time Strategy (MMORTS) (22 years)[35] and MMORPG players (21–27 years)[34,36] are significantly older. Among the three main groups, MMORPG gamers spend the most time playing.[35] Since MMORPGs are the most researched games (most likely because they allow players to interact to form friendships, create communities, and work together to accomplish a variety of goals,[38] there is additional information regarding such players that is still unknown in the case of other game types. For instance, half of MMORPG players work full time, 22.2 percent are students, and 14.8 percent are homemakers (89.9 percent of whom were female). Furthermore, 36 percent of the gamers are married and 22 percent of them have children.[37] Overall, the demographic composition of MMORPG users is quite varied, and probably more diverse than the composition of MMORTS and MMOFPS users (although this needs to be empirically established).

From a substantive perspective, there are some generalizations that can be made with regard to the demographic characteristics of gamers and problem gamers. The literature, to date, suggests that adolescent males and young male adults appear to be at greater risk of experiencing problematic video game play. However, the course and severity of these problems is not well known[39] and

TABLE 5.1 Prevalence of Problematic Online Gaming Involving Large Samples

Author(s) (reference)	Location	Research subjects (mean age (M), standard deviation (SD))	Method	Measure	Criteria of problematic use	Life-prevalence value
Yee (2006)[37]	USA, Canada	3,166 persons, MMORPG gamers	online survey	Direct question ("Do you consider yourself addicted to MMORPGs?" yes/no question)	yes to the direct question	50%
Grüsser, Thalemann, and Griffiths (2007)[105]	Germany	7,069 gamers (M: 21,1 years, SD: 6,4)	online survey	6 criteria of key symptoms of a dependence syndrome as outlined in WHO's ICD-10	3 or more criteria fulfilled	11,9%
Gentile (2009)[30]	USA	1,178 persons (adolescents aged 8–18 years)	national representative survey (online)	Pathological Video-Game Use	6 or more yes answers	8,5%
Porter et al. (2010)[84]	USA, Canada, Europe, Australia, New Zealand, Asia, Central and South America	1,945 persons, gamers older than 14 years	online survey	Video Game Use Questionnaire, (VGUQ), 10 criteria: 3 (preoccupation), 7 (adverse consequences), yes/no answers	2 or more criteria (preoccupation) + 3 or more criteria (adverse consequences)	8%

(continued)

(Table 5.1 Continued)

Author(s) (reference)	Location	Research subjects (mean age (M), standard deviation (SD))	Method	Measure	Criteria of problematic use	Life-prevalence value
Van Rooij et al. (2011)[107]	Netherlands	4,559 persons (M: 14.4 years, SD: 1.2) (T1) and 3,740 persons (M: 14.3 years SD: 1.0) (T2)	pen-and-pencil survey	Compulsive Internet Use Scale (CIUS) + weekly hours online gaming	latent profile analysis	1,6% (T1), 1,5% (T2) ~ 1,5%
Gentile et al. (2011)[31]	Singapore	3,034 persons (elementary and secondary school students)	2 years longitudinal study, pen-and-paper survey	Pathological Video-Game Use	5 or more yes answer	7,6% – 9,9%
Lemmens, Valkenburg, and Peters (2011)[48]	Netherlands	543 adolescent gamers (M: 13.9 years, SD: 1.4)	Longitudinal pen-and pencil survey	Game Addiction Scale	score of 3 or higher	6% (T1), 4% (T2)
Rehbein et al. (2010)[32]	Germany	15,168 ninth graders (15.3 years, SD: 0.69)	nationally representative survey	Video Game Dependency Scale (KFN-CSAS–II)	score higher than 42 dependent players; score between 35 and 41: players at risk	dependent: boys 3%, girls 0,3%; at risk: boys 4,7%, girls 0,5%
Thomas and Martin (2010)[106]	Australia	2,031 persons (705 university students, 1,326 secondary and college students)	pen-and-paper survey	Adaptation of YDQ (Young's Diagnostic Questionnaire) to computer games	score of 5 or higher	5%

Author	Country	Sample	Survey type	Instrument	Method	Prevalence
Jeong and Kim (2011)[52]	South Korea	600 persons (12–18 years)	Nationally representative pen-and-pencil survey	Young's internet Addiction Test (IAT) modified by replacing the word "Internet" with "gaming"	score above 80	2.2%
Demetrovics et al. (2012)[33]	Hungary	3,415 persons, online gamers (M: 21 years, SD: 5,9)	online survey	POGQ	latent profile analysis	high risk problematic online gamers: 3,4%; medium risk of problematic use: 15,2%
Pápay et al. (2013)[34]	Hungary	5,045 students from secondary general and secondary vocational schools (M: 16.4, SD: 0.9)	nationally representative survey (pen-and-pencil)	POGQ-SF	latent profile analysis	4.6%

the finding that this group is more at risk may be a consequence of sampling bias and the fact that this group plays video games more frequently than other socio-demographic groups. It has also been suggested that university students may be vulnerable to developing problematic video gaming. Reasons for this include their flexible tuition and study hours, ready access to high-speed broadband on a 24/7 basis, and multiple stressors associated with adjusting to new social obligations and/or living out-of-home for the first time.[39,40]

Negative Consequences of Excessive Video Game Use

Irrespective of whether problematic video game play can be classed as an addiction, there is now a relatively large number of studies all indicating that excessive video game play can lead to a wide variety of negative psychosocial consequences for a minority of affected individuals. These include sacrificing work, education, hobbies, socializing, time with partner/family, and sleep,[32, 37, 41–46] increased stress,[41] an absence of real life relationships,[47] lower psychosocial well-being and loneliness,[48] poorer social skills,[49–50] decreased academic achievement,[32,51–53] increased inattention,[41,54] aggressive/oppositional behavior and hostility,[51,54] maladaptive coping,[41,55,56] decreases in verbal memory performance,[21] maladaptive cognitions,[45] and suicidal ideation.[32]

In addition to the reported negative psychosocial consequences, there are also many reported health and medical consequences that may result from excessive video game playing. These include epileptic seizures,[57–62] auditory hallucinations,[63,64] visual hallucinations,[65] enuresis,[66] encoprisis,[67] obesity,[68–71] wrist pain,[72] neck pain,[73] elbow pain,[73] tenosynovitis – also called "Nintendinitis,"[74–77] blisters, calluses, sore tendons, and numbness of fingers,[78] hand-arm vibration syndrome,[79] sleep abnormalities,[21,47] psychosomatic challenges,[41] and repetitive strain injuries.[80] Taken together, this relatively long list of potential psychosocial and medical negative consequences clearly indicates that excessive gaming is an issue irrespective of whether it is an addiction. It also suggests that more extensive recognition is needed of the wide range of potential negative and life-limiting consequences of excessive video play.

Factors Associated with Problematic Video Game Use and Video Game Addiction

A number of studies have examined the role of different personality factors, comorbidity factors, and biological factors, and their association with gaming addiction. In relation to personality traits, gaming addiction has been shown to have associations with neuroticism,[46,81] aggression and hostility,[51,81–83] avoidant and schizoid interpersonal tendencies,[47] loneliness and introversion,[82] social inhibition,[84] boredom inclination,[51] sensation-seeking,[51,81] diminished agreeableness,[46] diminished self-control and narcissistic personality traits,[82] low self-esteem,[85] state and trait anxiety,[81] and low emotional intelligence.[86] It is hard to assess the etiological significance of these associations with gaming addiction, as they may not be unique to the disorder. Further research is therefore needed.

Research has also shown gaming addiction to be associated with a variety of comorbid disorders. This includes attention deficit hyperactivity disorder,[41,47,54,87] symptoms of generalized anxiety disorder, panic disorder, depression, social phobia,[47] school phobia,[41] and various psychosomatic symptoms.[41] Through use of fMRI, biological research has shown that gaming addicts show similar neural processes and increased activity in brain areas associated with substance-related addictions and other behavioral addictions, such as pathological gambling (significant activation in the left occipital lobe, parahippocampal gyrus, dorsolateral prefrontal cortex, nucleus accumbens, right orbitofrontal cortex, bilateral anterior cingulate, medial frontal cortex, and the caudate nucleus).[23–25] It has also been reported that gaming addicts (like substance addicts) have a higher prevalence of two specific polymorphisms of the dopaminergic system (i.e., Taq1A1 allele of the dopamine D2 receptor and the Val158Met in the Catecholamine-O-Methyltransferase).[27]

Internet Gaming Disorder and the DSM-5

Prior to the publication of the latest DSM-5,[2] there had been some debate as to whether 'Internet addiction' should be introduced into the text as a separate disorder.[88,89] Alongside this, there was debate as to whether those researching in the online addiction field should be researching generalized Internet use and/or the potentially addictive activities that can be engaged in on the Internet (e.g., gambling, video gaming, sex, shopping, etc.).[90,91] Following these debates, the Substance Use Disorder Work Group (SUDWG) recommended that the DSM-5 include a sub-type of problematic Internet use (i.e., internet gaming disorder [IGD]) in Section 3 ('Emerging Measures and Models') as an area that needed future research before being included in future editions of the DSM.[89] According to Petry and O'Brien,[89] IGD will not be included as a separate mental disorder until the (i) defining features of IGD have been identified, (ii) reliability and validity of specific IGD criteria have been obtained cross-culturally, (iii) prevalence rates have been determined in representative epidemiological samples across the world, and (iv) etiology and associated biological features have been evaluated.

One of the key reasons that IGD was not included in the main text of the DSM-5 was that the SUDWG concluded that no standard diagnostic criteria were used to assess gaming addiction across these many studies.[90] A review of instruments assessing problematic, pathological and/or addictive gaming by

King and colleagues[91] reported that 18 different screening instruments had been developed, and that these had been used in 63 quantitative studies comprising 58,415 participants. This comprehensive review identified both strengths and weaknesses of these instruments. The main strengths of the instrumentation included: (i) the brevity and ease of scoring, (ii) excellent psychometric properties such as convergent validity and internal consistency, and (iii) robust data that will aid the development of standardized norms for adolescent populations. However, the main weaknesses identified in the instrumentation included: (i) core addiction indicators being inconsistent across studies, (ii) a general lack of any temporal dimension, (iii) inconsistent cut-off scores relating to clinical status, (iv) poor and/or inadequate inter-rater reliability and predictive validity, and (v) untested or inconsistent dimensionality. It has also been noted by a number of authors that the criteria for IGD assessment tools are theoretically based on a variety of different potentially problematic activities including substance use disorders, pathological gambling, and/or other behavioral addiction criteria.[89,91] There are also issues surrounding the settings in which diagnostic screens are used as those used in clinical practice settings may require a different emphasis than those used in epidemiological, experimental and neurobiological research settings.[91,92]

A recent review by Király and colleagues[93] argued that some researchers consider video games as the starting point for examining the characteristics of this specific disorder, while others consider the Internet as the main platform that unites different addictive Internet activities, including online games. Recent studies[32,94] have made an effort to integrate both approaches. Consequently, IGD can either be viewed as a specific type of video game addiction, or as a variant of Internet addiction, or as an independent diagnosis.[90]

Griffiths[29] has argued that although all addictions have particular and idiosyncratic characteristics, they share more commonalities than differences (i.e., salience, mood modification, tolerance, withdrawal symptoms, conflict, and relapse), and this likely reflects a common etiology of addictive behavior. Consequently, online game addiction is viewed as a specific type of video game addiction. Similarly, Porter and colleagues[84] do not differentiate between problematic video game use and problematic online game use. They conceptualized problematic video game use as excessive use of one or more video games resulting in a preoccupation with and a loss of control over playing video games, and various negative psychosocial and/or physical consequences. However, unlike Griffiths,[29] their criteria for problematic video game use does not include other features usually associated with dependence or addiction, (e.g., tolerance, physical symptoms of withdrawal), as they say there is no clear evidence that problematic gaming is associated with such phenomena. Researchers such as Young[95] view online gaming addiction as a sub-type of Internet addiction and that the Internet itself provides situation-specific characteristics that facilitate gaming becoming problematic and/or addictive.

Kim and Kim's[94] Problematic Online Game Use (POGU) model takes a more integrative approach and claims that neither of the approaches outlined above adequately capture the unique features of online games such as Massively Multi-player Online Role-Playing Games (MMORPGs). They argue that the Internet is just one channel where people may access the content they want (e.g., gambling, shopping, sex, etc.) and that such users may become addicted to the particular content rather than the channel itself. This is analogous to the argument by Griffiths[96] that there is a fundamental difference between addiction *to* the Internet, and addictions *on* the Internet. However MMORPGs differ from traditional standalone video games as there are social and/or role-playing dimension that allow interaction with other gamers.

The POGU model resulted in five underlying dimensions of addictive gameplay (i.e., euphoria, health problems, conflict, failure of self-control, and preference of virtual relationship). Demetrovics and colleagues[33] also support the integrative approach and stress the need to include all types of online games in addiction models in order to make comparisons between genres and gamer populations possible (such as those who play online Real-Time Strategy (RTS) games and online First Person Shooter (FPS) games in addition to the widely researched MMORPG players). Their model comprises six dimensions (i.e., preoccupation, overuse, immersion, social isolation, interpersonal conflicts, and withdrawal).

Irrespective of approach or model, the components and dimensions that comprise online gaming addiction outlined above are very similar to the IGD criteria in Section 3 of the DSM-5. For instance, Griffiths'[29] six addiction components directly map onto the nine proposed criteria for IGD (of which five or more need to be endorsed and resulting in clinically significant impairment). More specifically: (1) *preoccupation with Internet games* [salience]; (2) *withdrawal symptoms when Internet gaming is taken away* [withdrawal]; (3) *the need to spend increasing amounts of time engaged in Internet gaming* [tolerance], (4) *unsuccessful attempts to control participation in Internet gaming* [relapse/loss of control]; (5) *loss of interest in hobbies and entertainment as a result of, and with the exception of, Internet gaming* [conflict]; (6) *continued excessive use of Internet games despite knowledge of psychosocial problems* [conflict]; (7) *deception of family members, therapists, or others regarding the amount of Internet gaming* [conflict]; (8) *use of the Internet gaming to escape or relieve a negative mood* [mood modification]; and (9) *loss of a significant relationship, job, or educational or career opportunity because of participation in Internet games* [conflict].

Treatment of Gaming Addiction

Clinical interventions and treatment for problematic and/or addictive gaming vary considerably in the literature, with most of the very few published studies employing some type of cognitive-behavioral therapy (CBT), pharmacotherapy, and/or self-devised psychological interventions.[30,87,97–99] Han et al.[23,100] presented some successful case studies regarding pharmacotherapeutic treatment. After a six-week[23] and a twelve-week[100] period of bupropion sustained release treatment, problematic gamers showed significant improvement both in decreased problem behavior and decreased depression scores. The researchers' pharmacological choice had been driven by the similarities in neurological activity of different behavioral addictions.[20,23,85]

Currently, the evidence base on the treatment of problematic and/or addictive gaming is limited. Furthermore, the lack of consistent approaches to treating problematic video game playing and video game addiction makes it difficult to produce any definitive conclusions as to the efficacy of treatment, although at this stage CBT (as with the treatment efficacy of other addictions) appears to show good preliminary support.[39] There remains a need for controlled, comparative studies of psychological and pharmacological treatments, administered individually and in combination with each other, to determine the optimal treatment approach.

The lack of comparative treatment studies might suggest that there is a general lack of demand for psychological services for problematic video game play and/or video game addiction.[28] However, this may not necessarily be the case. For instance, Woog[101] surveyed a random sample of 5,000 US mental health professionals. Although only 229 participants completed the questionnaire, two-thirds had treated someone with excessive computer use problems in the year prior to the survey. Woog also reported that problematic gaming was most common among 11- to 17-year-old clients. However, this client group may be more likely to present in therapy as anecdotal evidence suggests they are typically forced by concerned parents to attend treatment. Adult gaming addicts may not seek treatment, or seek treatment at a later stage for other psychological problems (e.g., depression) that develop after experiencing the severe negative consequences of gaming.

In South East Asia there appears to be significant demand for treatment for online-related problems including gaming addiction. The South Korean government has reportedly established a network of over 140 counseling centers for treatment of online addiction.[99] In Western countries, gaming addiction clinics have also started to emerge in places such as Holland and the UK.[97,99] There are also treatment groups that are modeled on 12-step self-help treatment (e.g., Online Gamers Anonymous).[97] However, little detail is known about the treatment protocols or their efficacy.

Block[88] suggested that the diagnosis for online problems (including excessive gaming) should be included in the DSM-5 as a compulsive-impulsive spectrum disorder. Publication of clinical criteria in a future DSM would facilitate and enhance standardization of research and treatment in the gaming studies field. It may also help minimize the potential for inappropriate clustering of clinical behaviors within an overly broad classification of problematic online behavior.[88]

Conclusions

Based on the published empirical studies, and particularly those published over the last decade, it appears that in extreme cases, excessive gaming can have potentially damaging effects upon individuals who appear to display compulsive and/or addictive behavior similar to other more traditional addictions. However, the field has been hindered by the use of inconsistent and non-standardized criteria to assess and identify problematic and/or addictive video game use. Furthermore, most studies' recruitment methods have serious sampling biases with an over-reliance on self-selected samples.

Despite these shortcomings, there are several noticeable trends that can be drawn from this review of problematic video game play and gaming addiction.

- There has been a significant increase in empirical research decade by decade since the early 1980s.
- There has been a noticeable (and arguably strategic) shift in researching the mode of video game play. In the 1980s, research mainly concerned 'pay-to-play' arcade video games. In the 1990s, research mainly concerned standalone (offline) video games played at home on consoles, PCs or hand-held devices. In the 2000s, research mainly concerned online massively multi-player video games.
- There has been a noticeable shift in how data are collected. Up until the early 2000s, data about video game behavior was typically collected face-to-face, whereas contemporary studies collect data online, strategically targeting online forums where gamers are known to (virtually) congregate. These samples are typically self-selecting and (by default) unrepresentative of the general population. Therefore, generalization is almost always one of the methodological shortcomings of this data collection approach.
- Survey study sample sizes have generally increased. In the 1980s and 1990s, sample sizes were typically in the low hundreds. In the 2000s, sample sizes in their thousands – even if unrepresentative – are not uncommon.
- There has been a diversification in the way data are collected including experiments, physiological investigations, secondary analysis of existing data (such as that collected from online forums), and behavioral tracking studies.
- There has been increased research on adult (i.e., non-child and non-adolescent) samples reflecting the fact that the demographics of gaming have changed.
- There has been increasing sophistication in relation to issues concerning assessment and measurement of problematic video game play and video game addiction. In the last few years, instruments have been developed that have more robust psychometric properties in terms of reliability and validity. However, there are still some concerns as many of the most widely

used screening instruments were adapted from adult screens and much of the video game literature has examined children and adolescents. King et al.[28] assert that to enable future advances in the development and testing of interventions for video game-related problems, there must be some consensus among clinicians and researchers as to the precise classification of these problems.

The fact that IGD was included in Section 3 of the DSM-5 appears to have been well received by researchers and clinicians in the gaming addiction field (and by those individuals that have sought treatment for such disorders and had their experiences psychiatrically validated and feel less stigmatized). However, for IGD to be included in the section on 'Substance-Related and Addictive Disorders' along with 'Gambling Disorder', the gaming addiction field must unite and start using the same assessment measures so that comparisons can be made across different demographic groups and different cultures. For epidemiological purposes, Koronczai and colleagues[92] asserted that the most appropriate measures in assessing problematic online use (including Internet gaming) should meet six requirements. Such an instrument should have: (i) brevity (to make surveys as short as possible and help overcome question fatigue); (ii) comprehensiveness (to examine all core aspects of PAP gaming as possible); (iii) reliability and validity across age groups (e.g., adolescents vs. adults); (iv) reliability and validity across data collection methods (e.g., online, face-to-face interview, paper-and-pencil); (v) cross-cultural reliability and validity; and (vi) clinical validation. It was also noted that an ideal assessment instrument should serve as the basis for defining adequate cut-off scores in terms of both specificity and sensitivity.

Clearly, there exist a number of gaps in the current understanding of problematic video game play and gaming addiction. King and colleagues[28] note there is a need for epidemiological research to determine the incidence and prevalence of clinically significant problems associated with video game play in the broader population. There are too few clinical studies that describe the unique features and symptoms of problematic video game play and/or video game addiction. Most of the studies tend to examine problematic video play from the perspective of the individual. However, there is a small body of research suggesting that the characteristics of the video games themselves may have a role in the acquisition, development and maintenance of video game addiction. These studies have investigated the role of structural characteristics of video games in maintaining problem playing behavior,[102–104] but there is little empirical research that examines why some individuals may be protected from developing excessive playing habits, or simply mature out of their problem playing behavior.

Another growing concern is the recent explosion of online and mobile gaming although, as yet, little research has been done. There are also strong links between online gaming, gambling, non-gambling fantasy games, role-playing games, board games and card games. These may be an additional cause for concern as youth migrate from free gaming sites to online gambling sites. It should also be noted that video game playing does not occur in a vacuum, but is a single behavior engaged in alongside many others. To date, very few studies have been used to examine links between video games and other risk behaviors (e.g., gambling, drug and alcohol use, seatbelt use, poor school performance, conduct problems, truancy, delinquency, violence and sexual activity).

References

1. Pontes H, Griffiths MD. The assessment of internet gaming disorder in clinical research. *Clin Res and Regul Aff.* 2014. doi: 10.3109/10601333.2014.962748
2. American Psychiatric Association. *Diagnostic and Statistical Manual of Mental Disorders – Text Revision (Fifth Edition).* Washington, D.C.: Author; 2013.
3. Ross DR, Finestone DH, Lavin GK. Space Invaders obsession. *J Am Med Ass.* 1982; 248: 1117.
4. Nilles JM. *Exploring the World of the Personal Computer.* Englewood Cliffs, NJ: Prentice Hall; 1982.
5. Soper WB, Miller MJ. Junk time junkies: An emerging addiction among students. *School Counsellor.* 1983; 31: 40–43.
6. Kuczmierczyk AR, Walley PB, Calhoun KS. Relaxation training, in vivo exposure and response-prevention in the treatment of compulsive video-game playing. *Scand J Behav Ther.* 1987; 16: 185–190.
7. Keepers GA. Pathological preoccupation with video games. *J Am Acad Child Psy.* 1990; 29: 49–50.
8. Shotton M. *Computer Addiction? A Study of Computer Dependency.* London: Taylor and Francis; 1989.
9. Widyanto L, Griffiths MD, Brunsden, V. A psychometric comparison of the Internet Addiction Test, the Internet Related Problem Scale, and Self-Diagnosis. *Cyberpsychol Beh Soc Networking.* 2011; 14: 141–≠149.
10. Brown RIF, Robertson S. Home computer and video game addictions in relation to adolescent gambling: Conceptual and developmental aspects. In: Eadington WR, Cornelius JA, eds. *Gambling Behavior and Problem Gambling.* Reno: University of Nevada Press; 1993: 451–471.
11. Fisher SE. Identifying video game addiction in children and adolescents. *Addict Behav.* 1994; 19: 545–553.
12. Griffiths MD. Computer game playing in early adolescence. *Youth Soc.* 1997; 29: 223–237.
13. Griffiths MD, Hunt N. Computer game playing in adolescence: Prevalence and demographic indicators. *J Community Appl Soc Psychol.* 1995; 5: 189–193.
14. Griffiths MD, Hunt N. Dependence on computer games by adolescents. *Psychol Rep* 1998; 82: 475–480.
15. Parsons K. Educational places or terminal cases: Young people and the attraction of computer games. Paper presented at the British Sociological Association Annual Conference, University of Leicester; April 1995.
16. Phillips CA, Rolls S, Rouse A, Griffiths MD. Home video game playing in schoolchildren: A study of incidence and pattern of play. *J Adolescence.* 1995; 18: 687–691.
17. American Psychiatric Association. *Diagnostic and Statistical Manual of Mental Disorders – Text Revision (Third Edition, Revised).* Washington, D.C.: Author; 1987.

18. American Psychiatric Association. *Diagnostic and Statistical Manual of Mental Disorders – Text Revision (Fourth Edition).* Washington, D.C.: Author; 1994.
19. Charlton JP. A factor-analytic investigation of computer 'addiction' and engagement. *Brit J Psychol.* 2002; 93: 329–344.
20. Kuss DJ, Griffiths MD. Online gaming addiction: A systematic review. *Int J Ment Health Addict.* 2012; 10: 278–296.
21. Dworak M, Schierl T, Bruns T, Struder HK. Impact of singular excessive computer game and television exposure on sleep patterns and memory performance of school-aged children. *Pediatrics.* 2007; 120: 978–985.
22. Cultrara A, Har-El G. Hyperactivity-induced suprahyoid muscular hypertrophy secondary to excessive video game play: a case report. *J Oral Maxil Surg.* 2002; 60: 326–327.
23. Han DH, Hwang JW, Renshaw PF. Bupropion sustained release treatment decreases craving for video games and cue-induced brain activity in patients with Internet video game addiction. *Exp Clin Psychopharm,* 2010; 18: 297–304.
24. Hoeft F, Watson CL, Kesler SR, Bettinger KE, Reiss AL. Gender differences in the mesocorticolimbic system during computer game-play. *J Psychiat Res.* 2008; 42: 253–258.
25. Ko CH, Liu GC, Hsiao SM, Yen JY, Yang MJ, Lin WC, et al. Brain activities associated with gaming urge of online gaming addiction. *J Psychiat Res.* 2009; 43: 739–747.
26. Thalemann R, Wölfling K, Grüsser SM. Specific cue reactivity on computer game-related cues in excessive gamers. *Behav Neurosci.* 2007; 12: 614–618.
27. Han DH, Lee YS, Yang KC, Kim EY, Lyoo IK, & Renshaw PF. Dopamine genes and reward dependence in adolescents with excessive Internet video game play. *J Addict Med.* 2007; 1: 133–138.
28. King DL, Delfabbro PH, Griffiths MD. Video game addiction. In: Miller P, ed. *Principles of Addiction: Comprehensive Addictive Behaviors and Disorders.* Vol. 1. San Diego: Academic Press; 2013: 819–825.
29. Griffiths MD. A 'components' model of addiction within a biopsychosocial framework. *J Substance Use,* 2005; 10: 191–197.
30. Gentile DA. Pathological video-game use among youth ages 8 to 18: A national study. *Psychol Sci.* 2009; 20: 594–602.
31. Gentile DA, Choo H, Liau, A, Sim T, Li DD, Fung D, Khoo A. Pathological video game use among youths: a two-year longitudinal study. *Pediatrics.* 2011; 127: 319–329.
32. Rehbein F, Kleimann M, Mossle T. Prevalence and risk factors of video game dependency in adolescence: results of a German nationwide survey. *Cyberpsychol Beh Soc Networking.* 2010; 13: 269–277.
33. Demetrovics Z, Urbán R, Nagygyörgy K, et al. The development of the Problematic Online Gaming Questionnaire (POGQ). *PLoS ONE.* 2012; 7(5): e36417.
34. Pápay, O., Urbán, R., Griffiths, M. D., et al. (2013). Psychometric properties of the Problematic Online Gaming Questionnaire Short-Form (POGQ-SF) and prevalence of problematic online gaming in a national sample of adolescents. *Cyberpsychol Beh Soc Networking.* 2013;16: 340–348.
35. Nagygyörgy K, Urbán R, Farkas J, et al. Typology and socio-demographic characteristics of Massively Multi-player Online Game players. *Int J Hum-Comput Int.* 2013; 29(3): 192–200.
36. Cole H, Griffiths MD. Social interactions in Massively Multiplayer Online Role-Playing gamers. *CyberPsychol Behav.* 2007; 10: 575–583.
37. Yee N. The demographics, motivations and derived experiences of users of massively-multiuser online graphical environments. *PRESENCE: Teleoperators and Virtual Environments.* 2006; 15: 309–329.

38. Barnett J, Coulson M. Virtually real: A psychological perspective on massively multiplayer online games. *Rev Gen Psychol.* 2010; 4: 167–179.
39. King DL, Delfabbro PH, Griffiths, MD. Clinical interventions for technology-based problems: Excessive Internet and video game use. *J Cog Psychotherapy.* 2012; 26: 43–56.
40. Young K. *Caught in the Net.* Chichester: Wiley; 1998.
41. Batthyány D, Müller KW, Benker F, Wölfling K. Computer game playing: Clinical characteristics of dependence and abuse among adolescents. *Wiener Klinische Wochenschrift.* 2009; 121: 502–509.
42. Griffiths MD, Davies MNO, Chappell D. Demographic factors and playing variables in online computer gaming. *CyberPsychol Behav.* 2004; 7: 479–487.
43. King DL, Delfabbro P. Understanding and assisting excessive players of video games: a community psychology perspective. *Aust Community Psychol.* 2009; 21(1): 62–74.
44. Liu M, Peng W. Cognitive and psychological predictors of the negative outcomes associated with playing MMOGs (massively multiplayer online games). *Comput Hum Behav.* 2009; 25: 1306–1311.
45. Peng W, Liu M. Online gaming dependency: a preliminary study in China. *Cyberpsychol Beh Soc Networking.* 2010; 13: 329–333.
46. Peters CS, Malesky LA. Problematic usage among highly-engaged players of massively multiplayer online role playing games. *CyberPsychol Behav.* 2008; 11: 480–483.
47. Allison SE, von Wahlde L, Shockley T, Gabbard GO. The development of the self in the era of the Internet and role-playing fantasy games. *Am J Psychiat.* 2006; 163: 381–385.
48. Lemmens, JS, Valkenburg PM, Peter J. Psychosocial causes and consequences of pathological gaming. *Comput Hum Behav.* 2011; 27: 144–152.
49. Griffiths MD. Computer game playing and social skills: A pilot study. *Aloma: Revista de Psicologia, Ciències de l'Educació i de l'Esport.* 2010; 27: 301–310.
50. Zamani E, Kheradmand A, Cheshmi M, Abedi A, Hedayati N. Comparing the social skills of students addicted to computer games with normal students. *J Addict Health.* 2010; 2: 59–69.
51. Chiu SI, Lee JZ, Huang DH. Video game addiction in children and teenagers in Taiwan. *CyberPsychol Behav.* 2004; 7: 571–581.
52. Jeong EJ, Kim DW. Social activities, self-efficacy, game attitudes, and game addiction. *Cyberpsychol Beh Soc Networking,* 2011; 14: 213–221.
53. Skoric MM, Teo LLC, Neo RL. Children and video games: addiction, engagement, and scholastic achievement. *CyberPsychol Behav.* 2009; 12: 567–572.
54. Chan PA, Rabinowitz T. A cross-sectional analysis of video games and attention deficit hyperactivity disorder symptoms in adolescents. *Ann Gen Psychiat.* 2006; 5(1): 16–26.
55. Hussain Z, Griffiths MD. The attitudes, feelings, and experiences of online gamers: a qualitative analysis. *CyberPsychol Behav.* 2009; 12: 747–753.
56. Hussain Z, Griffiths MD. Excessive use of massively-multi-player online role-playing games: a pilot study. *Int J Ment Health Addict.* 2009; 7: 563–571.
57. Maeda Y, Kurokawa T, Sakamoto K, Kitamoto I, Kohji U, Tashima S. Electroclinical study of video-game epilepsy. *Dev Med Child Neurol.* 1990; 32: 493–500.
58. Graf WD, Chatrian GE, Glass ST, Knauss TA. Video-game related seizures: A report on 10 patients and a review of the literature. *Pediatrics.* 1994; 3: 551–556.
59. Harding GFA, Jeavons PM. *Photosensitive Epilepsy.* London: Mac Keith Press; 1994.
60. Quirk JA, Fish DR, Smith SJM, Sander JW, Shorvon SD, Allen PJ. First seizures associated with playing electronic screen games: A community based study in Great Britain. *Ann Neurol.* 1995; 37: 110–124.

61. Millett CJ, Fish DR, Thompson PJ. A survey of epilepsy-patient perceptions of video-game material/electronic screens and other factors as seizure precipitants. *Seizure*. 1997; 6: 457–459.

62. Chuang YC. Massively multiplayer online role-playing game-induced seizures: A neglected health problem in Internet addiction. *CyberPsychol Behav*. 2006; 9: 451–456.

63. Ortiz de Gortari AB, Griffiths MD. Auditory experiences in Game Transfer Phenomena: An empirical self-report study. *Int J Cyber Beh Psychol Learning*. 2014; 4(1): 59–75.

64. Spence SA. Nintendo hallucinations: A new phenomenological entity. *Irish J Psychol Med*. 1993; 10: 98–99.

65. Ortiz de Gortari AB, Griffiths MD. Altered visual perception in Game Transfer Phenomena: An empirical self-report study. *Int J Hum-Comput Int*. 2014; 30: 95–105.

66. Schink JC. Nintendo enuresis. *Am J Dis Child*. 1991; 145: 1094.

67. Corkery JC. Nintendo power. *Am J Dis Child*. 1990; 144: 959.

68. Shimai S, Yamada F, Masuda K, Tada M. TV game play and obesity in Japanese school children. *Percept Motor Skill*. 1993; 76: 1121–1122.

69. Deheger M, Rolland-Cachera MF, Fontvieille AM. Physical activity and body composition in 10 year old French children: Linkages with nutritional intake? *Int J Obesity*. 1997; 21: 372– 379.

70. Johnson B, Hackett AF. Eating habits of 11–14-year-old schoolchildren living in less affluent areas of Liverpool, UK. *J Hum Nutr Diet*. 1997; 10: 135–144.

71. Vandewater EA, Shim M, Caplovitz AG. Linking obesity and activity level with children's television and game use. *J Adolescence*. 2004; 27: 71–85.

72. McCowan TC. Space Invaders wrist. *New Engl J Med*. 1981; 304: 1368.

73. Miller DLG. Nintendo neck. *Can Med Assoc J*. 1991; 145: 1202.

74. Reinstein L. De Quervain's stenosing tenosynovitis in a video games player. *Arch Physical Med Rehab*. 1983; 64: 434–435.

75. Brasington R. Nintendinitis. *New Engl J Med*. 1990; 322: 1473–1474.

76. Casanova J, Casanova J. Nintendinitis. *J Hand Surg*. 1991; 16: 181.

77. Siegal IM. Nintendonitis. *Orthopedics*. 1991; 14: 745.

78. Loftus GA, Loftus EF. *Mind at Play: The Psychology of Video Games*. New York: Basic Books; 1983.

79. Cleary AG, McKendrick H, Sills JA. Hand-arm vibration syndrome may be associated with prolonged use of vibrating computer games. *Brit Med J*. 2002; 324: 301.

80. Mirman MJ, Bonian VG. "Mouse elbow": A new repetitive stress injury. *J Am Osteopath Assoc*. 1992; 92: 701.

81. Mehroof M, Griffiths MD. Online gaming addiction: the role of sensation seeking, self-control, neuroticism, aggression, state anxiety, and trait anxiety. *CyberPsychol Behav*. 2010; 13: 313–316.

82. Caplan SE, Williams D, Yee N. Problematic internet use and psychosocial well-being among MMO players. *Comput Hum Behav*. 2009; 25: 1312–1319.

83. Kim EJ, Namkoong K, Ku T, Kim SJ. The relationship between online game addiction and aggression, self-control and narcissistic personality traits. *European Psychiatry*. 2008; 23: 12–218.

84. Porter G, Starcevic V, Berle D, Fenech P. Recognizing problem video game use. *Aust NZ J Psychiat*. 2010; 44(2): 120–128.

85. Ko CH, Yen JY, Chen CC, Chen SH, Yen CF. Gender differences and related factors affecting online gaming addiction among Taiwanese adolescents. *J Nerv Ment Dis*. 2005; 193: 273–277.

86. Parker JDA, Taylor RN, Eastabrook JM, Schell SL, Wood LM. Problem gambling in adolescence: relationships with internet misuse, gaming abuse and emotional intelligence. *Pers Indiv Differ*. 2008; 45(2): 174–180.

87. Han DH, Lee YS, Na C, et al. The effect of methylphenidate on Internet video game play in children with attention-deficit/hyperactivity disorder. *Compr Psychiat*. 2009; 50: 251–256.

88. Block JJ. Issues for DSM-V: Internet addiction [Editorial]. *Am J Psychiatr*. 2008; 165: 306.

89. Petry NM, O'Brien CP. Internet gaming disorder and the DSM-5. *Addiction*. 2013; 108: 1186–1187.

90. Griffiths MD, King DL, Demetrovics Z. DSM-5 Internet Gaming Disorder needs a unified approach to assessment. *Neuropsychiatry*. 2014; 4(1): 1–4.

91. King DL, Haagsma MC, Delfabbro PH, Gradisar MS, Griffiths MD. Toward a consensus definition of pathological video-gaming: A systematic review of psychometric assessment tools. *Clin Psychol Rev*. 2013; 33: 331–342.

92. Koronczai B, Urban R, Kokonyei G, et al. Confirmation of the three-factor model of problematic internet use on off-line adolescent and adult samples. *Cyberpsychol Beh Soc Networking*. 2011; 14: 657–664.

93. Király O, Nagygyörgy K, Griffiths MD, Demetrovics Z. Problematic online gaming. In: Rosenberg K, Feder L, eds. *Behavioral Addictions: Criteria, Evidence and Treatment*. New York: Elsevier; 2014: 61–95.

94. Kim MG, Kim J. Cross-validation of reliability, convergent and discriminant validity for the problematic online game use scale. *Comput Hum Behav*. 2010; 26: 389–398.

95. Young KS. Internet addiction: The emergence of a new clinical disorder. *CyberPsychol Behav*. 1998; 1: 237–244.

96. Griffiths MD. Internet addiction – Time to be taken seriously? *Addict Res*. 2000; 8: 413–418.

97. Griffiths MD, Meredith A. Videogame addiction and treatment. *J Contemporary Psychotherapy*. 2009; 39(4): 47–53.

98. King DL, Delfabbro PH, Griffiths MD. Cognitive behavioural therapy for problematic video game players: Conceptual considerations and practice issues. *J CyberTherapy and Rehabilitation*. 2010; 3: 261–273.

99. King DL, Delfabbro PH, Griffiths MD, Gradisar M. Assessing clinical trials of Internet addiction treatment: A systematic review and CONSORT evaluation. *Clin Psychol Rev*. 2011; 31: 1110–1116.

100. Han DH, Renshaw PF. Bupropion in the treatment of problematic online game play in patients with major depressive disorder. *J Psychopharmacol*. 2012; 26: 689–696.

101. Woog K. A survey of mental health professionals' clinical exposure to problematic computer use. 2004. Located at: www.wooglabs.com/. Accessed August 18, 2011.

102. Wood RTA, Griffiths MD, Chappell D, Davies MNO. The structural characteristics of video games: A psycho-structural analysis. *CyberPsychol Behav*. 2004; 7: 1–10.

103. Westwood D, Griffiths MD. The role of structural characteristics in video game play motivation: A Q-Methodology Study. *Cyberpsychol Beh Soc Networking*. 2010; 13: 581–585.

104. King DL, Delfabbro PH, Griffiths MD. The role of structural characteristics in problematic video game play: An empirical study. *Int J Ment Health Addict*. 2011; 9: 320–333.

105. Grüsser SM, Thalemann R, Griffiths MD. Excessive computer game playing: Evidence for addiction and aggression? *CyberPsychol Behav*. 2007; 10: 290–292.

106. Thomas NJ, Martin FH. Video-arcade game, computer game and Internet activities of Australian students: Participation habits and prevalence of addiction. *Aust J Psychol*. 2010; 62: 59–66.

107. Van Rooij AJ, Schoenmakers TM, Vermulst AA, Van den Eijnden RJ, Van de Mheen D. Online video game addiction: identification of addicted adolescent gamers. *Addiction*. 2011; 106(1): 205–212.

6

SOCIAL OUTCOMES: ONLINE GAME PLAY, SOCIAL CURRENCY, AND SOCIAL ABILITY

Rachel Kowert

Introduction

Since the popularization of e-mail and online chat rooms, researchers have noted concern over the potential consequences of utilizing the Internet for social purposes. Much of the concern stems from the fact that Internet-based social services, such as those mentioned above, are believed to displace the time allocated for offline social activities[1] and, consequently, disrupt offline relationships.[1-3] The rising popularity of online gaming has revived many of these concerns. Branded as pseudo-communities, these Internet-based social spaces are believed to provide a superficial sense of social support and displace the time that could be spent fostering more "meaningful" offline relationships.[4,5] Online games are of particular concern as displacement effects could potentially be greater within these spaces than with other mediated environments as they provide a social space characterized by shared, playful, and often novel activities. This difference is key, as the shared activities between co-players can contribute to the formation of long-lasting, highly intimate friendship bonds with sustainable levels of self-disclosure and intimacy not traditionally found in other mediated spaces.[6-9] Thus, it is feared that the formation of in-game friendship bonds will contribute to a preference for online interaction that is potentially greater than other mediated outlets and lead to a variety of negative consequences for the player.

This chapter will examine the veracity of these claims by examining the theoretical and empirical relationships between online video game involvement and social outcomes. However, prior to this, a brief overview of online games will be presented, focusing on how their unique integration of play within a social space has created a distinct social environment that converges and diverges from other Internet-based social spaces. Following this, an overview of two predominant theoretical viewpoints that attempt to explain how and why online video game play may be associated with poorer social outcomes (i.e., Social Displacement and Social Compensation Hypotheses) will be discussed. While these hypotheses differ in their proposed origin of the social impact of online games (i.e., media effects versus social compensation motivations) they both argue that there is an inverse relationship between online video game play and social outcomes among users of the medium. A proposal for a Cycle Model of Use, which integrates the tenets of the Social Displacement and Social Compensation hypotheses, is also briefly discussed. The chapter will conclude with an examination of the empirical work that has assessed the impact of online video game involvement on players' "social currency" (i.e., size and quality of friendship networks) and "social ability" (i.e., social effectiveness).

Online Games: Playful, Social Spaces

Online video games are digital games played over the Internet. The integration of the Internet within video game technologies has expanded video games' multi-player functionality by allowing players to connect with others in a shared gaming space beyond one's geographical boundaries. This has transformed video game play from a solitary or small group activity to a large, thriving social network.[10] In 2013, it was reported that over 700 million people, or 44 percent of the world's online population, play online games.[11] Online games have become the second most popular online activity, behind watching videos (such as those hosted on *YouTube*), but ahead of watching television programs, movies, and listening to the radio.[12] Like traditional video games, online video games are playful activities that one engages in for the primary purpose of entertainment. However, unlike traditional video games, online games integrate playful activities within an Internet-based, social context. This has created a distinctive environment, reminiscent of both traditional video games and other mediated social spaces, but unique in their enabling of *social play*.

Like other mediated social spaces (e.g., chat rooms, online forums, social networking websites, etc.), online video games are social environments where friendships often develop.[7,13,14] Up to 75 percent of online game players report making "good friends" within their gaming communities,[7] and of these, between 40 percent[7] and 70 percent[13] report regularly discussing "offline" issues online, including concerns that they have not discussed with their offline friends. Researchers have also found the social aspects of play (e.g., socializing with other players, developing friendships, achieving collective goals, etc.) to be one of the primary motivators for initial and continued engagement within these environments, as well a key contributor to the enjoyment of the activity.[13,15,16] In this sense, online games converge with other Internet-based social outlets, where the development of acquaintances, friendships, and romantic relationships has been well documented.[17-19]

However, online video games are also communities centered on playful activities. Thus, unlike other mediated social spaces, online video game play is both instrumental and social, with its primary purpose, and strongest motivator of game play, being to achieve in-game objectives rather than to socialize.[7,20,21] Although, as in-game goals can be more easily accomplished with the assistance of others, players often form collectives and work together. The shared, playful activities experienced by co-players then helps to stimulate the formation of intimate bonds between them, more so than socialization itself,[22-24] and promote the formation of close and long-standing friendship bonds between a player and the other members of their online community that are not traditionally found in other mediated channels.[6-8]

In addition to participating in shared activities, the key features of the social environment of online games also contributes to the formation of close friendships between co-players. For example, a primary reliance on a text-based chat system★ within these environments means that there are few non-verbal cues. A lack of such cues promotes dissociative anonymity (i.e., "You don't know me") and invisibility (i.e., "You can't see me"), which, taken together, generates a unique combination of trust and anonymity, often referred to as the Online Disinhibition Effect.[25] This unique combination of features stimulates open and intimate conversations by removing the fear of any social repercussions.[25-27] Consequently, individuals become inclined to self-disclose at a quicker rate than is found in non-visually anonymous relationships[17,25,28-30] and to be more honest and open.[31]

While these features of online games have been linked to the promotion of close, intimate friendships, and increased self-disclosure, they are also believed to contribute to the potential for one's in-game friendship bonds to displace one's offline relationships. That is, at least partially due to the range of social affordances provided by online games, players may begin to offset, or *displace*, the time dedicated to offline social activities in order to spend more time online. This displacement of offline for online contacts is believed to lead to a range of consequences, such as declines in the quantity and quality of offline communication and the size of one's social circle.[6,7,32-36] Prolonged online video game involvement has also been linked to more long-term social consequences, such as an exacerbation of pre-existing social difficulties

---

★ Some players choose to augment the text-based chat within online games with voice-over technologies, such as *Teamspeak*. When using these technologies players are able to verbally engage with other players and the element of asynchronicity is lost. However, as it is unknown how many individuals use these kinds of technologies and text-based communication is a standard feature, and the default modality of socialization between players within most online gaming environments, voice-over technologies will not be discussed further.

(e.g., social anxiety, depression, etc.),[16,20,34–37] a hindered ability to develop and maintain traditional "offline" social skills,[8,37–39] and an inability to form and maintain reciprocal offline relationships.[7,34,36,40]

Social Implications of Online Video Game Involvement

The rise of affordable and accessible Internet connectivity has changed the way video games are being played by allowing individuals to connect worldwide in shared gaming spaces. While these highly social environments hold the potential for players to connect, interact with, and learn from each other, there is growing concern that these social environments also have the potential to displace real-world connections and interactions, contributing to a variety of losses in "offline" sociability.[7,8,34,36,40] While the belief in the association between online video game play, social isolation, and social ineptitude remains widespread, so much so that it has evolved into a core component of the cultural perception of those who participate within these spaces,[41,42] the empirical evidence illustrating this relationship has been conflicting and the potential mechanisms that underlie these associations remain unclear.

To clarify the relationships between online video game play and social outcomes, the following sections will overview the theoretical and empirical links between online video game involvement and social outcomes. The theoretical links will first be reviewed, focusing on the Social Displacement and Social Compensation hypotheses. While proponents of these theories contend that inverse relationships exist between social outcomes and online video game play, they differ in their proposed foundation of these differences. Displacement theorists highlight the potential for social atrophy over time due to online video game engagement.[26,32,34–36,38] This is a classic "media effects" perspective, as it is use of the media itself that is believed to contribute to any negative outcomes. Conversely, compensation theorists focus on the motivational role of pre-exiting social dispositions (e.g., loneliness, social anxiety) in online video game involvement.[6,7] After presenting an overview of the theoretical links, the empirical links between social competence and online video game involvement will be discussed. The focus of this section will be on outcomes related to the size and quality of friendship networks (i.e., social currency) and social effectiveness (i.e., social ability) as these are the primary facets of sociability that are believed to be negatively influenced by increased online video game play.

Theoretical Links: Social Displacement and Social Compensation

The Social Displacement and Social Compensation hypotheses (originally developed for research on excessive use of the Internet)[43] are the most commonly enlisted theoretical frameworks used to explain any inverse relationships between online video game involvement and social outcomes. While these two theories differ in the proposed origin of social differences among the online game playing community, they both contend that social differences do exist, which either originate from or are exacerbated by a general increase in time spent within online gaming environments. An examination of these two theoretical perspectives is presented in more detail below. This section will conclude with a brief presentation of an alternative perspective, which suggests that displacement and compensation mechanisms may actually work together, rather than being mutually exclusive, in a Cycle Model of Use.[44]

Social Displacement

Interaction within Internet-based social spaces can be "a socially liberating experience."[43(p332)] Freed from the rules and pressures of traditional socialization, users may begin to perceive themselves as "safer, more efficacious, more confident, and more comfortable with online interpersonal interactions and relationships than traditional face-to-face social activities."[45(p629)] However, largely due to the "*inelasticity of time*"[1(p42)] (i.e., there are a finite number of hours that one can dedicate to socialization), one's online social community may begin to thrive at the expense of face-to-face interactions[2,6,16,26,40,46] and lead to the displacement, or exchange, of offline social contacts for online ones.[2,33,43,47]

The exchange of offline for online contacts is believed to be socially problematic due to a reduced sense of social presence online[48] as well as the production of bridging, rather than bonding, social capital within online relationships.[49] Taken together, these differences are believed to limit the capability of Internet-based relationships to provide feelings of social support and closeness, thereby making the displacement of offline for online social contacts a disproportionate exchange. Thus, rather than replacing one's offline friends with a virtual substitute, players are supplanting valuable sources of social and emotional support for less intimate and diffuse online relationships.[5,49,50] An examination of these arguments, as supported by social presence and social capital theorists, is briefly presented below.

Social Presence

The relative weakness of online interpersonal contacts, as compared to their offline counterparts, is often discussed in relation to differences in social presence across contexts. Social presence refers to the degree of awareness of the *other* person in a communication interaction.[48] This idea developed from Mehrabian's[51] concept of "Immediacy," which refers to the mutual exchange of specific "communication behaviors that enhance closeness to, and non-verbal interaction with, another" (p. 77). Typically, a sense of immediacy is promoted through the exchange of non-verbal cues, such as facial expressions, gestures, and eye contact. When these cues are present, more intense and affective social interactions will ensue (see Williams[52] for a review of the research). The impact of these cues was first documented in Mehrabian's[51,53] work, where communicators who displayed more immediacy cues (e.g., close physical proximity, eye contact, orientation towards their communication partner, etc.) were rated as being more liked than disliked. The general social impact of immediacy cues can also be seen in Milgram's[54] obedience study, as the rate of obedience for the experimenter's request to continue the administration of more painful shocks to a confederate participate (i.e., an actor hired by the experimenter to pretend that they were receiving the imposed electrical shocks) declined from 66 percent to 40 percent when participants were face to face. Furthermore, three times as many participants obeyed the authority's instructions in the face-to-face condition than when the cues were given via telephone. Reductions in the experimenter's physical proximity, and consequently the number of immediacy cues, reduced the overall sense of social presence, the intimacy of the interaction, and the sense of realism, all of which led to greater dissent.

However, Social Presence Theory[48] was not developed to explain differences in individual social interactions but across social systems. The fewer immediacy cues that are available within a particular system (e.g., face-to-face, telephone, computer mediated, etc.), the less attention one will give to the presence of other social participants and the less likely the other participants will be perceived as "real."[48] Thus, social interactions are believed to become less intimate as the rate of social presence decreases.

While some offline, non-verbal norms have transferred into online gaming communities (e.g., interpersonal distance),[55] online gaming environments generally provide few non-verbal cues. As such, it is believed to be particularly low in social presence[5,56,57] and, therefore, is believed to generate more impersonal, and less intimate, communication than those supported by immediacy cues.[5,58] Some game developers have attempted to increase the sense of social presence by integrating in-game gesturing systems and adopting a variety of text-based emoticons, both of which can be used to express emotional cues that are typically only expressed non-verbally in face-to-face interactions.[59] While research suggests that the adoption of emoticons can accommodate for a substantial proportion of non-verbal cues that are missing in text-based communication,[60] in order to provide these cues, players must explicitly communicate the information through in-game commands or text-based messages. Thus, rather than simulating face-to-face interactions, this non-verbal cue system simulates a world in which verbal and non-verbal cues are disjointed.[61] This is in contrast to face-to-face socialization, whereby one can emanate a range of information even when not intending to communicate.[62] For example, both static (e.g., clothing) and dynamic (e.g., posture, facial expressions) cues have been found to provide information about an individual, and that this information is used to form judgments about a person's personality, such as their level of agreeableness or self-esteem.[63]

Although, some researchers are beginning to consider the possibility that the absence of social cues found online may actually be beneficial, by providing a level of social accommodation not found in traditional interpersonal interactions.[17,21,29,31,64,65] For example, the lack of non-verbal cues can promote the Online Disinhibition Effect,[25] which can positively influence the social perceptions and behaviors of others, including the promotion of greater self-disclosure.[17,25,28–30] Thus, while a lack of non-verbal may limit the quality of communication within online games in some ways, researchers are beginning to suggest that this lack of immediacy cues may actually be more socially beneficial than harmful.

Social Capital

While the impact of social presence on the quality of mediated communication remains debatable, face-to-face and Internet-based friendships remain significantly different in terms of the social capital they generate. Broadly speaking, social capital refers to the resources that are accumulated within interpersonal relationships.[66] As defined by Bourdieu and Wacquant,[67] social capital is "the sum of the resources, actual or virtual, that accrue to an individual or group by virtue of possessing a durable network of more or less institutionalized relationships of mutual acquaintance and recognition" (p. 14). The particular resources that can be gained vary across social relationships but it can include intellectual resources (e.g., new information), social and emotional resources (e.g., social and emotional support), and/or physical resources (e.g., tangible favors). The successful accumulation of social capital has been linked to a range of positive outcomes, including career success,[68] increased life satisfaction,[69–71] enhanced self-esteem, and general physical and psychosocial well-being.[72,73]

The kind of social capital that can be generated within interpersonal relationships can be further differentiated into two subtypes: bridging and bonding.[70] Individuals are believed to generate bridging social capital through their inclusive and diffuse networks, such as a community choir or bowling club. These kinds of social networks form from loose connections between individuals (often of different backgrounds) and are seen to be valuable tools in helping to expand one's social and worldviews[70] but typically do not provide substantial emotional support.[74] Conversely, bonding social capital is generated among close interpersonal bonds that provide substantial emotional support for one another.[70] These friendship bonds are more exclusive and tend to form among individuals who are from similar backgrounds, such as close family members and friends.

While many researchers have questioned if and how mediated relationships support the production of bridging and/or bonding social capital (for a review see Bargh and McKenna),[75] few have examined these links empirically. Perhaps the most comprehensive evaluation of social capital across offline and online contexts comes from Williams.[49] In a large-scale survey study, members of an online gaming community were asked to complete social capital scales for both offline and online social contexts. After controlling for demographics, time online was found to be negatively associated with offline bridging and bonding social capital. Additionally, significantly more bridging social capital and less bonding social capital was found to be generated online than offline. Williams[49] concluded that the social connections that are established within online video games are related to increases in bridging and decreases in bonding social capital, illustrating the lack of equivalency between online and offline interpersonal relationships. Similar trends have been noted in cross-sectional research examining social capital and Internet-based social networking.[76,77] The production of bridging, rather than bonding, social capital in online relationships has been attributed to a combination of the low entry and exit costs of online communities,[50] which encourages broad membership, and a diminished sense of social presence.[27,51,53]

Social Displacement: Summary

Displacement theorists contend that online video game players suffer significant social consequences due to the displacement of offline contacts. As the social freedoms granted by online video gaming spaces generate highly intimate and sustainable bonds with one's co-players, offline social contacts may quickly be replaced with online ones.[7,26,32,35,36] Over time, this displacement is feared to lead to "offline" social disengagement[7,26,32,35,36] and the exchange of valuable sources of social and emotional support provided by offline social ties for less intimate and more diffuse online relationships.

Social Compensation

Unlike Social Displacement theorists, proponents of the Social Compensation hypothesis believe that the inverse relationships between social outcomes and online video game play are reflective of inherent qualities of the game players themselves rather than direct social consequences due to engagement. Researchers have long suggested that mediated social environments, particularly online video games, appeal to those who are socially unskilled, have an unmet need for sociability in their lives, and feel anxious over establishing real-world relationships.[29,78-80] The distinctive characteristics of online video games have generated a highly desirable social space, as the combination of greater communicative flexibility, enhanced social presentation strategies, and shared experiences, diminishes the possibility of social rejection while stimulating the formation of intimate friendships.[21,25,28,49,81,82] As such, individuals who have experienced difficulties in forming interpersonal relationships in traditional contexts are likely to be drawn to engage within online video games as an alternative social outlet. While displacement effects may exacerbate these relationships, a certain degree of social inadequacy is believed to exist among those who are motivated to engage within online video gaming spaces. Supporting this contention, researchers have found that more involved online video game players display poorer social resources, in terms of higher rates of the symptoms associated with loneliness, depression, and social anxiety[16,20,34-37,83] and poorer social skills[8,37-40] (for a more detailed discussion of Social Displacement and Social Compensation theories see Kowert[44]).

Alternative Perspectives: The Cycle Model of Use

The Social Displacement and Social Compensation hypotheses both attempt to clarify why online game players may exhibit poorer social outcomes. Even though these theories differ in the proposed origin of social differences among the online game playing community, they both contend that a general increase in time spent in these environments detrimentally impacts a user's sociability in some way. While displacement theorists believe that social differences within the online gaming population are attributable to the direct displacement of offline social interactions due to increased participation within online video game environments and the "*inelasticity of time*," social compensation theorists maintain that they are reflective of an pre-existing condition, such as loneliness, depression, social anxiety, or poor social skills.

However, it is possible that these theories are not mutually exclusive. That is, it may be that pre-existing conditions (e.g., loneliness, depression, social anxiety, poor social skills) motivate the initial engagement within online video gaming environments and, over time, become exacerbated through the displacement of offline for online contacts. As discussed by Kowert,[44] there are empirical links to support the possibility of a "Cycle Model of Use" (see Figure 6.1), as increased online video game play has been found to be associated with a range of social outcomes indicative of both social displacement and compensation effects, including declines in the quantity and quality of offline communication and the size of one's social circle,[6,7,32-36] a failure to develop and maintain effective social and emotional skills,[8,34,38-40] and higher rates of the symptoms associated with loneliness, depression, and social anxiety.[16,20,34-37]

Preliminary empirical support for the cyclical nature of this model can also be seen in the longitudinal work (i.e., research following the same users over time) of Lemmens and colleagues,[37] who found loneliness to be both a cause and a consequence of problematic play over a six-month period. While a follow up study by Kowert and colleagues[83] found no such reciprocal links, this was likely due to differences in assessment techniques and sampling measures between these studies rather than being representative of an inconsistency in

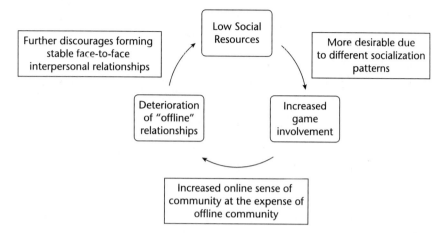

FIGURE 6.1   The Cycle Model of Use as Outlined by Kowert[44]

the validity of the model itself. For example, while Lemmens and colleagues[37] examined the psychosocial causal and consequential relationships within a problematic playing adolescent sample over a six-month period, Kowert et al.[83] drew from a representative, adult sample of video game players and evaluated the relationships over a one- and two-year time span. Thus, it may be that the Cycle Model of Use is applicable only in relation to short-term effects or specific populations, such as problematic, adolescent players. Additional analyses are needed to examine the fluctuation of social resources (e.g., low social skills, low social opportunity, social anxiety, depression, etc.) over time among varied game playing groups (problematic, non-problematic, adolescent, adult) before definitive conclusions as to the empirical validity of this model can be drawn.

It should also be noted that there is also a recent wave of research that has suggested that online video game involvement does not actively contribute to negative social outcomes, but rather is socially beneficial by providing an easily accessible social outlet as well as ideal space for social learning.[84–87] A more detailed discussion of this topic is presented in Chapter 7.

Empirical Links: Online Video Game Play, Social Currency, and Social Ability

The empirical relationships between video game involvement and social outcomes were first explored in the 1980s when researchers found that high frequency arcade players displayed lower self-esteem[88] than low frequency players, and were more likely to report that arcade machines provide them with companionship that was preferable to interaction with their peers.[89] Coining the term "electronic friendship," Senlow[89] believed that these findings suggested that arcade machines could be emerging as substitutes for social engagement. However, with the advent of affordable and accessible Internet access, Senlow's ideas were expanded to propose that one's online, in-game friends have the potential to replace one's "offline" friends.[85,90,91] There is preliminary evidence to support this possibility, as a large percentage of online game players report that their in-game friends are equivalent or superior to their offline ones[92] and that their online friends satisfy some social needs that are not satisfied by pre-existing offline relationships.[32,93] While causal links have not been firmly established, increased online video game involvement has been associated with a variety of negative social consequences for online players, such as hindered ability to form and maintain reciprocal offline relationships[7,36] or develop effective social and emotional skills.[8,34,36,40]

The following section will outline the scientific research that has examined the relationship between social outcomes and online video game involvement. The focus will be placed on outcomes related to social currency (i.e., relationship quality and quantity) and social ability (i.e., psychosocial dispositions related to social effectiveness and social skills) as these are the primary aspects of sociability that are believed to be negatively influenced due to increased online video game play.

Social Currency: Relationship Quality and Quantity

Kraut and colleagues[2] were among the first to examine the potential impact of social Internet use on pre-existing interpersonal relationships. Utilizing a longitudinal design, the researchers evaluated the social displacement effects of social Internet use during individuals' first one to two years online. Supporting their hypotheses, greater Internet use was found to be associated with significant declines in social involvement, including decreased family communication, and the size of one's local and distant social networks. Similar results were uncovered in a large-scale survey conducted by Bessierie et al.,[47] whereby social uses of the Internet (i.e., to meet others) was found to significantly predict declines in community involvement and reduced participation in organized groups such as churches and clubs.

Parallel relationships have been uncovered when evaluating the specific social impact of online video game play. For example, Lo and colleagues[35] found heavier users of online games (30+ hours a week of play) reported a poorer quality of offline interpersonal relationships than light users (2–7 hours a week of play) or non-playing participants. Similarly, Shen and Williams[36] uncovered a negative linear association between online video game play frequency and family communication quality, indicating a poorer quality of communication for those who did not play online games with family members. Meeting new people online was pinpointed as a particularly strong predictor of shorter family communication and of a worse quality. Additionally, online game players who were primarily motivated to play for social reasons (i.e., to meet new people) were the only group to retain a negative linear relationship between play frequency and family communication time when play motivations were controlled. Researchers have also found significant negative correlations between online game addiction scores and offline social relationship scores,[34] suggesting that addicted online game players also experience social difficulties and stress in offline interpersonal relationships.

In the only known experimental study evaluating the potential social effects of engagement across gaming modalities, Smyth[10] randomly assigned participants to play offline, single-player video games (i.e., arcade, console, or computer games) or a massively multi-player online role-playing game (MMORPG). After one month of play, online game players reported a greater play frequency, a greater reduction in the time spent socializing with "offline friends," and a greater interest in continuing to play than players of single-player offline games. These results illustrate the desirability of online games in relation to the more traditional video game playing activities. As players grew closer to their in-game contacts, offline activities were displaced and online game play was reported as more desirable. Researchers have also found the more active online game players to display patterns of cocooning (i.e., retreating into the seclusion of one's home during leisure time) over time, as they begin to place a higher value on their in-game social contacts at the expense of pre-existing relationships.[6] The players themselves have also noted this particular shift in social behavior that corresponds with increased use, as online game players have actively discussed the breakdown of friendships and relationships due to play and linked being social online to being anti-social offline.[32]

While the breakdown of offline relationships due to online game play has been found, the relationship between online video game play and social outcomes have been predominantly examined, and found, among the most active online game players rather than the average user. For example, Lo and colleagues[35] found differences among those who reported playing 30+ hours a week or more, Cole and Griffiths[7] found players of MMORPGs (i.e., one of the most time-consuming genres of online games as it is a persistent and perpetual gaming environment),[94] to discuss the breakdown of friendships due to play, while Kim et al.[34] found a significant, negative correlation between online game addiction scores and offline social relationship scores. The emergence of linear relationships between social outcomes and online video game addiction scores and broad differences between the most and least involved players suggests that that the variation in relationship quality and quantity among online game players may be limited to those who are most involved in the activity. This contention is supported by the work of Kowert, Festl, and Quandt[95] as they found a linear relationship between the quality and quantity of friendships and online video game play time among a large representative sample of online players, but no broad differences between online, offline, or non-game players. This suggests that the variation in social outcomes attributable to online video game play is evident only among the *most* involved players.

Taken together, it can be concluded that the average online game player unlikely suffers significant social disruptions to their social circle due to online video game play. However, significant differences have been found between high- and low-involved opportunity samples, as well as inverse linear relationships between online video game play and the size and quality of a players' social circle, indicating that more involved online game players may experience variation in their social circles due to game play. These findings refute the contention that online game players have smaller, lower-quality, friendship circles, but support the notion that more involved and addicted online game players may experience variation in their social circles due to game play. Although, it is difficult to determine causality between online video game play and social currency outcomes from these findings as the presence of linear relationships does not indicate a direct cause and effect relationship but rather a linear correspondence between outcomes.

Social Ability: Psychosocial Predispositions and Social Skills

Psychosocial Dispositions

Individuals with a history of poor interpersonal relationships are believed to be drawn to online video game environments as an alternative social space as it provides easily accessible and less risky friendships.[7,25,96] This may be particularly the case for those with low social resources, such as less perceived social support, lower interpersonal activity, and fewer group memberships, as using the Internet for social purposes can reduce negative feelings and bolster one's social network. For example, individuals who are lonely have been found to be more likely than non-lonely individuals to prefer online to offline communication.[26] Additionally, lonely individuals report that the sense of anonymity offered by online spaces is socially liberating, and that they feel "more themselves" online, display a greater propensity to self-disclose while online, and find it easier to make friends and generate a social network online than offline.

Online game players have also been found to display higher rates of the symptoms associated with loneliness and social anxiety.[16,34–37] For example, Caplan and colleagues[16] found loneliness to be the single most influential psychosocial predictor of increased online video game use, with lonelier participants reporting increased involvement. Positive linear relationships between loneliness and time spent in online gaming environments have also been uncovered.[36] Game players who report a social motivation to play (i.e., to socialize and develop supportive friendships) rather than any other motivation to play (e.g., achievement or immersion) have also been found to report higher levels of loneliness, indicating that more involved and socially motivated game players display higher rates of loneliness than less involved, or non-socially motivated, game players.

The links between social anxiety and online video game involvement have been less extensively examined; however, research has found that increased time spent playing online games also coincides with higher levels of social anxiety.[35] A positive, linear relationship between social anxiety and online video game addiction has also been found.[34] However, a lack of comparison measures (e.g., assessment of relationship quality or quantity) makes it difficult to determine the magnitude of these effects on users' everyday social life.

Although it is clear that there are significant links between loneliness, social anxiety, and online video game play, a general lack of longitudinal research in this area has made it difficult to determine whether these links are representative of use motivations (i.e., they are driving online video game use) or if they are indicative of an exacerbation of pre-existing difficulties (i.e., they worsen due to use). There are two exceptions to this, as Lemmens et al.[37] and Kowert et al.[83] have attempted to uncover the causal or consequential nature of these relationships using longitudinal research designs. Lemmens et al.[37] were the first to examine the psychosocial causes and consequences of problematic video game play over time. They found loneliness to be both a cause and a consequence of increased problematic play among adolescent players, as loneliness predicted increased pathological play and pathological play was found to predict loneliness over a six-month period. While it is curious that loneliness was not found to be alleviated through engagement, but rather become exacerbated through use, this may be due to the fact that the researchers were focusing on problematic game players rather than the general game playing community. This seems particularly likely, as a follow up study by Kowert et al.[83] found that these same relationships do not hold among a general game playing population. Instead, they found positive links between online video game play and self-esteem among adolescent players, suggesting a positive influence of online video game use on adolescent players. Additionally, among young adults (i.e., 19–39 years old), evidence for social compensation mechanisms was discovered, as lower life satisfaction was found to predict online video game play.

Social Skills

In addition to exacerbating pre-existing conditions in ways that may negatively influence effective socialization, prolonged online video game play is feared to negatively impact one's ability to form and maintain reciprocal offline relationships through an attenuation of the development or maintenance of effective 'offline' social and emotional skills,[7,8,34,36,40] such as the ability to verbally engage others or manage one's social self-presentation in real time.[7,8,26,32,35,36] As stated by Kim et al.,[34(p215)]

> the [use of] online games is associated with a decline in participants' communication with family members in the household and a decline in the size of their social circles, and because of this they become socially isolated and are no longer able to socialize in a normal way.

This concern has spurred numerous examinations into the associations between video game involvement and social skills.[37–40,87,95] In one of the first examinations, Chiu and colleagues[40] examined the relationship between video game addiction and social skills among child and teenage video game users. While social skills did not emerge as a significant predictor of video game addiction, lower rates of boredom and greater family functioning did emerge as significant predictors of effective social skills. The researchers suggested that these results indicate the potential for video game playing to replace the development of immediate social relationships, and subsequently, negatively influence social skills, particularly among younger players. Liu and Peng[38] uncovered similar results, as they found play frequency to be a positive predictor of psychological dependency on MMORPG playing, preference for a virtual life, and personal life problems, one of which was low social engagement. Lower social control (i.e., the ability to manage one's self-presentation in real time) also emerged as a significant individual predictor of an increased preference for a virtual life, which, in turn, was a significant individual predictor of psychological dependency on MMORPGs. While the link between social control and MMORPG dependency was not a direct one, these results indicate an indirect relationship between lower social control and problematic play in the form of preference for a virtual life. In a longitudinal assessment, Lemmens et al.[37] confirmed a direct linear relationship between social skills and pathological gaming, with lower social skills predicting increased pathological gaming six months later. However, this relationship was not reciprocal, as pathological gaming did not predict later social skill outcomes, suggesting that lower social skills are more likely to be a cause, rather than a consequence, of video game involvement. Kowert et al.[83] found similar associations as significant inverse links were found between social competence and online video game play, and play of a greater frequency, among young adult players (i.e., 19–39 years old). In line with the conclusions of Lemmens and colleagues,[37] the particular pattern of findings were indicative of social compensation rather than displacement mechanisms.

While these assessments indicate that there are relationships between social ability and online video game play, which is most likely motivational rather than a consequence of engagement, they have primarily focused on the relationship with problematic and addicted play (with the exception of Kowert and colleagues[83] who enlisted a representative sample of game players), leaving little to be known about the relationship among the general population of game players. Addressing this issue, Kowert and Oldmeadow[8] assessed the relationship between social skills and video game involvement among a broad sample of game players. Confirming previous findings, the researchers uncovered significant linear relationships between social skills and online video game involvement, indicating that more involved video game players report higher ability to express and control emotions, but a lower ability to verbally engage others. However, broad differences between online, offline, and online and offline game players were not found. The researchers concluded that more involved game players display different social profiles than their less involved counterparts, however, the lack of broad differences between online players and other gaming groups dispute the all-encompassing, maladaptive social skills that are anecdotally attributed to online video game players.[20,41,42]

Taken together, it can be concluded that significant inverse relationships between social skills and online video game involvement do exist; more involved online game players perceive themselves as lacking self-presentation skills, and report being less comfortable in social situations, and less verbally controlled, and emotionally expressive.[8,37–39,95] More involved online players have been found to show different social profiles than their less involved counterparts, in the sense that they exhibit linear relationships between video game involvement and a range of social skills, including greater sensitivity to non-verbal cues and greater social hesitancy.[8] More involved players have also demonstrated lower overall social competency on global assessments.[39] The presence of linear relationships between social skill outcomes and online video game involvement, rather than broad differences, suggests that these relationships are more likely driven by displacement, rather than compensatory, mechanisms. However, this has not been supported by longitudinal research, as social skill outcomes have been found to be causal rather than consequential. Additional research is needed to explore these relationships among large, broad samples of online video game players in order to determine the mechanisms underlying these relationships, whether they are indicative of displacement mechanisms, compensatory motivations, or a cyclical interaction between the two.

Even though the mechanisms underlying the relationships between online video game play and social outcomes are unclear, it can be concluded that the findings of the empirical research in the field highlight the unreliability of the claims that increased online video game involvement inevitably leads to decline in one's ability to socialize effectively in offline socialization. Just as the relationships between friendship outcomes and OVG involvement seem limited to the most involved and/or addicted players, a lack of broad differences between game players, offline players, and non-players indicate the same patterns in relation to social skill outcomes.

Conclusion

The incorporation of 'real-time' social services within a shared interactive environment has furthered the scope of video games by providing an Internet-based, shared gaming space in which millions of individuals across the globe regularly participate. Despite their popularity, online video games have been met with suspicion by the popular media and academic community as the potential consequences of engagement within these spaces continue to be given considerable attention. In particular, researchers are concerned about the potential social consequences of online game play, as fears about the medium's ability to produce a generation of socially inept, reclusive individuals, continues to rise. While online communities may be thriving, it appears to be at the expense of offline relationships and activities, as online game players themselves link being social online to being anti-social offline and report that participation within these environments has contributed to the breakdown of offline relationships.[7,32] Online games seem to have created a "communication paradox," as increased participation within these environments, which promote interaction and sociability, has been found to be associated with a range of negative social outcomes.[36]

In support of these claims, lonely,[16,26,37] socially anxious,[34,35] and socially unskilled[8,37-39,95] individuals have been found to engage in increased amounts of online video game play, presumably to modulate their negative moods and gain companionship. Additionally, the social profile of the most involved and addicted users has been found to vary significantly from less involved or non-playing samples, with more involved players reporting to be overly concerned with social norms and their public appearance, and less verbally fluent and able to engage others in conversation, effectively express their emotions, and adapt to social situations. Together, these findings indicate that the most involved and addicted players may have a social self-consciousness that could inhibit social participation and be indicative of a certain degree of social hesitancy.[97-99]

While it cannot be concluded whether these relationships are attributable to social displacement effects or compensation motivations (or a combination of the two), the consistent emergence of linear relationships between social outcomes and game play, rather than broad differences between different game playing groups, suggests that the impact of online video game play on a player's sociability can be attributed to compensation motivations. Even though longitudinal research does not support these claims, this is likely due to the limitations of the longitudinal research in this area rather than a lack of an effect. There are only two known longitudinal assessments in this area (Lemmens et al.[37] and Kowert et al.[83]) and both enlisted abridged measures (i.e., shortened versions of validated scales) of sociability, which could have limited the ability to detect any significant changes over time. Thus, while significant cross-sectional relationships have been consistently found, it remains unclear what, if any, impact online video game involvement has on a user's daily social functioning.

Taken together, it can be concluded that the online game playing community is not a population of reclusive, socially inept, individuals who have turned to online video gaming environments for social refuge. It can also be concluded that increased online video game involvement does not inevitably lead to worse social outcomes as more involved online players do not demonstrate the all-encompassing, maladaptive social skills that are anecdotally attributed to them.[20,41,42] A general lack of broad differences between online and non-online game playing groups, as well as a minimal magnitude of linear relationships between OVG involvement and social outcomes, largely disputes the all-encompassing, social ineptitude anecdotally attributed to online video game players and instead indicates that online game play may displace pre-existing offline friendships only among the most involved players. In turn, this could negatively impact one's social ability over time; however, these effects have yet to be causally attributed to increased (non-pathological) online video game play.

References

1. Nie N. Sociability, interpersonal relations, and the Internet: Reconciling conflicting findings. *Am Behav Sci.* 2001; 45: 420–435.
2. Kraut R, Patterson M, Lundmark V, Kiesler S, Mukopadhyay T, Scherlis W. Internet paradox: A social technology that reduces social involvement and psychological well-being? *Am Psychol.* 1998; 53(9): 1017–1031.
3. Sanders CE, Field TM, Diego M, Kaplan M. The relationship of Internet use to depression and social isolation among adolescents. *Adolescence.* 2000; 35(158): 237–242.
4. Beniger J. Personalization of mass media and the growth of pseudo-community. *Communic Res.* 1987; 14(3): 352–371.
5. Slouka M. *War of the Worlds: Cyberspace and the High-tech Assault on Reality.* New York: Basic Books; 1995.
6. Williams D. Groups and goblins: The social and civic impact of online games. *J Broadcast Electron Media.* 2006; 50: 651–681. doi:10.1207/s15506878jobem5004_5
7. Cole H, Griffiths MD. Social interactions in massively multi-player online role-playing games. *Cyberpsychology Behav.* 2007; 10(4): 575–583. doi:10.1089/cpb.2007.9988
8. Kowert R, Oldmeadow JA. (A)Social reputation: Exploring the relationship between online video game involvement and social competence. *Comput Human Behav.* 2013; 29(4): 1872–1878. doi:10.1016/j.chb.2010.07.015
9. Yee N. Befriending ogres and wood-elves – understanding relationship formation in MMORPGs. *nickyee.com.* 2002. Available at: www.nickyee.com/hub/relationships/home.html
10. Smyth J. Beyond self-selection in video game play. *Cyberpsychology Behav.* 2007; 10(5): 717–721.
11. SpilGames. State of online gaming report. *SpilGames.* 2013. Available at: http://auth-83051f68-ec6c-44e0-afe5-bd8902acff57.cdn.spilcloud.com/v1/archives/1384952861.25_State_of_Gaming_2013_US_FINAL.pdf
12. eMarketer. How mobile is shaping global digital behavior. *eMarketer.* 2013. Available at: www.emarketer.com/Article/How-Mobile-Shaping-Global-Digital-Behavior/1009995

13. Williams D, Ducheneaut N, Xiong L, Yee N, Nickell E. From tree house to barracks. *Games Cult.* 2006; 1(4): 338–361.
14. Domahidi E, Kowert R, Quandt T. Friends with benefits? Assessing the relationship between social skills, gaming-related friendships, and social capital among social online game players. *Under review.*
15. Ducheneaut N, Yee N, Nickell E, Moore R. "Alone together?": exploring the social dynamics of massively multi-player online games. In: *SIGCHI Conference on Human Factors in Computing Systems.* New York, NY: ACM; 2006.
16. Caplan S, Williams D, Yee N. Problematic Internet use and psychosocial well-being among MMO players. *Comput Human Behav.* 2009; 25(6): 1312–1319. doi:10.1016/j.chb.2009.06.006
17. Parks MR, Floyd K. Making friends in cyberspace. *J Commun.* 1996; 46: 80–97.
18. Peris R, Gimeno MA, Pinazo D, et al. Online chat rooms: Virtual spaces of interaction for socially oriented people. *Cyberpsychology Behav.* 2004; 5(1): 43–51.
19. Ridings C, Gefen D. Virtual community attraction: Why people hang out online. *J Comput Commun.* 2004; 10(1).
20. Williams D, Yee N, Caplan S. Who plays, how much, and why? Debunking the stereotypical gamer profile. *J Comput Commun Monogr.* 2008; 13(4): 993–1018. doi:10.1111/j.1083-6101.2008.00428.x
21. Yee N. Motivations of play in online games. *CyberPsychology Behav.* 2007; 9(6): 772–775.
22. Hill MS. Marital stability and spouses' shared time: A multidisciplinary hypothesis. *J Fam Issues.* 1988; 9(4): 427–451.
23. Holman TB, Jacquart M. Leisure-activity patterns and marital satisfaction: A further test. *J Marriage Fam.* 1988; (50): 69–77.
24. Orthner DK. Leisure-activity patterns and marital satisfaction over the marital career. *J Marriage Fam.* 1975; (37): 91–101.
25. Suler J. The Online Disinhibition Effect. *Cyberpsychology Behav.* 2004; 7(3): 321–326.
26. Morahan-Martin J, Schumacher P. Loneliness and social uses of the Internet. *Comput Human Behav.* 2003; 19: 659–671.
27. Walther J. Computer-mediated communication: Impersonal, interpersonal, and hyperpersonal interaction. *Communic Res.* 1996; 23(1): 3–43.
28. Joinson A. Self-disclosure in computer-mediated communication: the role of self-awareness and visual anonymity. *Eur J Soc Psychol.* 2001; 31: 177–192.
29. McKenna K, Bargh J. Plan 9 from cyberspace: The implications of the Internet for personality and social psychology. *Personal Soc Psychol Rev.* 2000; 4(1): 57–75. doi:10.1207/S15327957PSPR0401_6
30. Parks MR, Roberts LD. Making MOOsic': The development of personal relationships on line and a comparison to their offline counterparts. *J Soc Pers Relat.* 1998; 15(4): 517–537.
31. Whitty M, Gavin J. Age/sex/location: Uncovering the social cues in the development of online relationships. *Cyberpsychology Behav.* 2001; 4(5): 623–630.
32. Hussain Z, Griffiths M. The attitudes, feelings, and experiences of online gamers: A qualitative analysis. *Cyberpsychology Behav.* 2009; 12(6): 747–753.
33. Blais J, Craig WM, Pepler D, Connolly J. Adolescents online: The importance of Internet activity choices on salient relationships. *J Youth Adolesc.* 2008; 37: 522–536. doi:10.1007/s10964-007-9262-7
34. Kim E, Namkoong K, Ku T, Kim S. The relationship between online game addiction and aggression, self-control, and narcissistic personality traits. *Eur Psychiatry.* 2008; 23(3): 212–218. doi:10.1016/j.eurpsy.2007.10.010
35. Lo S, Wang C, Fang W. Physical interpersonal relationships and social anxiety among online game players. *Cyberpsychology Behav.* 2005; 8(1): 15–20. doi:10.1089/cpb.2005.8.15

36. Shen C, Williams D. Unpacking time online: Connecting Internet and massively multiplayer online game use with psychological well-being. *Communic Res.* 2010; 20(10): 1–27. doi:10.1177/0093650210377196

37. Lemmens J, Valkenburg P, Peter J. Psychological causes and consequences of pathological gaming. *Comput Human Behav.* 2011; 27(1): 144–152. doi:10.1016/j.chb.2010.07.015

38. Liu M, Peng W. Cognitive and psychological predictors of the negative outcomes associated with playing MMOGs (massively multiplayer online games). *Comput Human Behav.* 2009; 25(6): 1306–1311. doi:10.1016/j.chb.2009.06.002

39. Griffiths MD. Computer game playing and social skills: a pilot study. *Aloma.* 2010; 27: 301–310.

40. Chiu S, Lee J, Huang D. Video game addiction in children and teenagers in Taiwan. *Cyberpsychology Behav.* 2004; 7(5): 571–581.

41. Kowert R, Oldmeadow JA. The stereotype of online gamers: New characterization or recycled prototype. In: *Nordic DiGRA: Games in Culture and Society Conference Proceedings.* Tampere, Finland: DiGRA; 2012.

42. Kowert R, Griffiths MD, Oldmeadow JA. Geek or chic? Emerging stereotypes of online gamers. *Bull Sci Technol Soc.* 2012; 32(6): 471–479. doi:10.1177/0270467612469078

43. Davis RA. A cognitive behavioral model of pathologial Internet use. *Comput Human Behav.* 2001; 17(2): 187–195.

44. Kowert R. *Video Games and Social Competence.* New York: Routledge; 2014.

45. Caplan S. Preference for online social interaction: A theory of problematic Internet use and psychosocial well-being. *Communic Res.* 2003; 30: 625–648.

46. Nie N, Erbring L. Internet and mass media: A preliminary report. *IT Soc.* 2002; 1(2): 134–141.

47. Bessiere K, Kiesler S, Kraut R, Boneva B. Longitudinal effects of internet uses on depressive affect: A social resources approach. In: *American Sociological Association.* Philadelphia, PA; 2012.

48. Short J, Williams E, Christie B. *The Social Psychology of Telecommunications.* London: Wiley; 1976.

49. Williams D. The impact of time online: Social capital and Cyberbalkanization. *Cyberpsychology Behav.* 2007; 10(3): 398–406.

50. Galston WA. Does the Internet strengthen community. *Natl Civ Rev.* 2000; 89(3): 193–202.

51. Mehrabian A. Some referents and measures of non-verbal behavior. *Behav Research Methods Instrum.* 1969; 1: 203–207.

52. Williams E. Experimental comparisons of face-to-face and mediated communication: A review. *Psychol Bull.* 1977; 84(5): 963–976.

53. Mehrabian A. Significance of posture and position in the communication of attitude and status relationships. *Psychol Bull.* 1969; 71: 359–372.

54. Milgram S. Some conditions of obedience and disobedience to authority. *Hum Relations.* 1965; 18(57): 57–76.

55. Yee N, Bailenson J. A method for longitudinal behavioral data collection in second life. *Presence Teleoperators Virtual Environ.* 2008; 17(6): 594–596.

56. Rice RE, Love G. Electronic emotion. *Communic Res.* 1987; 14(1): 85–108.

57. Rice RE. Media appropriateness: Using social presence theory to compare traditional and new organization media. *Hum Commun Res.* 1993; 19(4): 451–484.

58. Sproull L, Kiesler S. Reducing social context cues: Electronic mail in organizational communication. *Manage Sci.* 1986; (32):1492–1512.

59. Wilkins H. Computer talk: Long-distance conversations by computer. *Writ Commun.* 1991; 8: 56–78.

60. Gunawardena C, Zittle F. Social presence as a predictor of satisfaction within a computer-mediated conferencing environment. *Am J Distance Educ.* 1997; 11(3): 8–26.

61. Moore R, Ducheneaut N, Nickell E. Doing virtually nothing: Awareness and accountability in massively multiplayer online worlds. *Comput Support Coop Work.* 2007; 16(3): 265–305.
62. Goffman E. *The Presentation of Self in Everyday Life.* New York, NY: The Overlook Press; 1959.
63. Naumann L, Vazire S, Rentfrow P, Gosling S. Personality judgments based on physical appearance. *Personal Soc Psychol Bull.* 2009; (35): 1661–1671.
64. Kiesler S, Sproull L. Group decision making and communication technology. *Organ Behav Hum Decis Process.* 1992; (52): 96–123.
65. Lea M, Spears R. Love at first byte? Building personal relationships over computer networks. In: Wood JT, Duck SW, eds. *Understudied Relationships: Off the Beaten Track.* Newbury Park, CA: Sage; 1995: 197–233.
66. Coleman JS. Social capital in the creation of human capital. *Am J Sociol.* 1988; (94): 95–120.
67. Bourdieu P, Wacquant L. *An Invitation to Reflexive Sociology.* Chicago: The University of Chicago Press; 1992.
68. Gabbay SM, Zuckerman EW. Social Capital and opportunity in coporate R&D: The contingent effect of contact density on mobility expectations. *Soc Sci Res.* 1998; 27: 189–217.
69. Bjornskov C. The happy few: Cross-country evidence on social capital and life satisfaction. *Kyklos.* 2003; 56: 3–16.
70. Putnam R. *Bowling Alone: The Collapse and Revival of American Community.* New York: Simon & Schuster; 2000.
71. Winkelmann R. Unemployment, social capital, and subjective well-being. *J Happiness Stud.* 2009; 101(1): 1–24.
72. Helliwell JF, Putnam R. The social context of well-being. *Philos Trans R Soc.* 2004; 359(1149): 1435–1446.
73. Helliwell JF. Well-being, social capital and public policy: What's new? *Econ J.* 2006; 16(510): 34–45.
74. Granovetter MS. The strength of weak ties: A network theory revisited. In: Mardsen PV, Lin N, eds. *Social Structure and Network Analysis.* Thousand Oaks, CA: Sage Publications; 1982: 105–130.
75. Bargh J, McKenna K. The Internet and social life. *Annu Rev Psychol.* 2004; 55(1): 573–590.
76. Ellison N, Steinfield C, Lampe C. The benefits of Facebook "Friends:" Social capital and college students' use of online social network sites. *J Comput Commun.* 2007; (12): 1143–1168.
77. Steinfield C, Ellison N, Lampe C. Social capital, self-esteem, and use of online social network sites: A longitudinal analysis. *J Appl Dev Psychol.* 2008; 29: 434–445.
78. Chak K, Leung L. Shyness and locus of control as predictors of Internet addiction and Internet use. *Cyberpsychology Behav.* 2004; 7(5): 559–570. doi:10.1089/cpb.2004.7.559
79. Whitty M, Carr A. Cyberspace as potential space: Considering the web as a playground to cyber-flirt. *Hum Relations.* 2003; 56: 861–891.
80. Whitty M. Cyber-flirting: Playing at love on the internet. *Theory Psychol.* 2003; 13: 339–357.
81. Chan D, Cheng G. A comparison of offline and online friendship qualities at different stages of relationship development. *J Soc Pers Relat.* 2004; 21(3): 305–320.
82. Pena J, Hancock JT. An analysis of socioemotional and task communication in online multi-player video games. *Communic Res.* 2006; 33(1): 92–109.
83. Kowert R, Vogelgesang J, Festl R, Quandt T. Psychosocial causes and consequences of online video game play. *Comput Human Behav.* 2015: 45: 51–58. doi: 10.1016/j.chb.2014.11.074

84. Ducheneaut N, Moore R. More than just "XP": Learning social skills in massively multiplayer online games. *Interact Technol Smart Educ.* 2005; 2(2): 89–100.
85. Steinkuehler C, Williams D. Where everybody knows your (screen) name: Online games as "third places." *J Comput Commun.* 2006; 11(4): 885–909.
86. Kowert R, Domahidi E, Quandt T. The relationship between online video game involvement and gaming-related friendships among emotionally sensitive individuals. *Cyberpsychol Behav Soc Netw.* 2014. doi:10.1089/cyber.2013.0656
87. Kowert R, Oldmeadow JA. Seeking social comfort online: Video game play as a social accommodator for the insecurely attached. *Comput Human Behav.* 2014. doi:10.1016/j.chb.2014.05.004
88. Dominick JR. Video games, television violence, and aggression in teenagers. *J Commun.* 1984; 34(2): 136–147. doi:10.1111/j.1460-2466.1984.tb02165.x
89. Senlow G. Playing videogames: The electronic friend. *J Commun.* 1984; 34(2): 148–156.
90. Brightman J. Study: Video games can promote sociability. *gamedaily.com.* 2006. Available at: www.gamedaily.com/articles/features/study-video-games-can-promote-sociability/69323/?biz=1
91. Colwell J, Kato M. Investigation of the relationship between social isolation, self-esteem, aggression and computer game play in Japanese adolescents. *Asian J Soc Psychol.* 2003; 9: 149–158.
92. Yee N. The demographics, motivations, and derived experiences of users of massively-multi-user online graphical environments. *Teleoperators Virtual Environ.* 2006; 15(3): 309–329.
93. Hussain Z, Griffiths M. Gender swapping and socializing in cyberspace: an exploratory study. *Cyberpsychology Behav.* 2008; 11(1): 47–53.
94. Barnett J, Coulson M. Virtually real: A psychological perspective on massively multiplayer online games. *Rev Gen Psychol.* 2010; 14(2): 167–179.
95. Kowert R, Festl R, Quandt T. Unpopular, overweight, and socially inept: Reconsidering the stereotype of online gamers. *Cyberpsych Behav Soc Netw.* 2013; 17(3): 141–146. doi:10.1089/cyber.2013.0118
96. Jakobsson M, Taylor TL. The Sopranos meets EverQuest: Social networking in massively multiplayer online games. In: *2003 Digital Arts and Culture (DAC) Conference.* Melbourne, Australia; 2003: 90–91.
97. Riggio R, Carney D. *Manual for the Social Skills Inventory.* Palo Alto, CA: Research ed. Consulting Psychologists Pr.; 1989.
98. Riggio R, Carney DC. *Manual for the Social Skills Inventory.* 2nd edn. Mountain View, CA: Mind Garden; 2003.
99. Riggio R, Throckmorton B, DePaola S. Social skills and self-esteem. *Personal Individual Differ.* 1990; 11(8): 799–804.

7

DEBATING HOW TO LEARN FROM VIDEO GAMES

John L. Sherry

In 1971, a student teacher hoping to stimulate learning in his eighth-grade American history class wrote what was to become the most famous educational game of all time: *Oregon Trail*. Several generations of middle school students across the United States and Canada experienced the difficulties of the western expansion of the United States through *Oregon Trail*, a simulation game that allowed players to face pioneer decisions and learn the consequences of those decisions. The original version of the game was entirely text-based; later versions added a few very simple graphics. As of 2011, the game has sold an estimated 65 million copies[1] and exposed unknown millions of American history students to digital dysentery.

There's strong consensus that digital games have the potential to transform education.[2,3] In fact, the promise of digital games for promoting learning has been cited in a diverse range of societal sectors ranging from the President of the United States and the US National Academies of Science[4] to public school classrooms and education researchers around the world. Recent years have seen an increase in government support for learning games in Europe, Asia, and North America; foundation funding opportunities; academic societies and conferences; and undergraduate and graduate degree specializations. An expanding roster of books, journal articles, and scholarly reports continues to address this topic. Scholars in fields ranging from learning sciences (e.g., Gee, Kafai, Squire, Steinkuhler), developmental psychology (e.g., Blumberg, Calvert, Fisch, Greenfield), media effects (e.g., Bryant, Lieberman, Sherry, Wartella), and humanities (e.g., Jenkins, Consalvo), as well as game designers (e.g., Prensky, Salen, Sawyer, Zimmerman), private foundations (e.g., Robert Wood Johnson, MacArthur, Spencer, Kauffman), and research centers (e.g., Joan Ganz Cooney Center, Sesame Workshop) all believe that video games can be a powerful tool for learning.

At first glance, this conclusion is a no-brainer. One need only talk to a teenage *Call of Duty: Black Ops* player with an encyclopedic knowledge of the latest munitions or a *FIFA Manager* gamer who knows the statistics of hundreds of professional football players to realize that individuals can learn a tremendous amount of information from games. In order to master any complex game (e.g., shooter, adventure, role-playing game, multi-player online game, etc.), a gamer must learn the components, rules and affordances of that game world.[5] Beyond basic knowledge learning, a player must be able to analyze the components of that new virtual world in order to understand how it works, draw tentative conclusions about relationships in the world, manipulate the environment to test those relationships and then solve the tasks provided by the game designer to beat each level. A typical first-person shooter game requires all six levels of Bloom's famous hierarchy of learning.[6] Players will voluntarily commit to 50 hours of struggle to master the game. What if we could get school children to dedicate 50 hours of struggle to learning, analyzing, understanding, and manipulating school material? The broad cross-section of scholars and game designers is excited about such a possibility.

The reasons for this optimism are compelling. Games are reward-based logic puzzles that oblige players to actively learn content. In order to conquer each level, the player must learn the basic rules of the game universe and apply those rules to puzzles presented. As such, games provide an opportunity for inductive and deductive reasoning in real time. A well-designed game gradually ratchets up the difficulty as the player acquires greater knowledge and skills, enhancing engagement and making sure each game is tailored to the individual learner's knowledge and style. Games can provide the types of learning environments that education researchers dream about, where children can interactively explore the world individually or in groups. They can simulate just about any phenomenon a teacher might want students to understand. In fact, computer games can be used to do many things in a classroom that are not otherwise possible (e.g., simulate a billion years of geophysical development). A well-designed game engages players in a highly rewarding flow experience by gradually increasing cognitive challenges as the skill level of the player increases.[7] Unlike traditional classroom instruction, every game experience is customized to the individual's prior knowledge and learning rate.

Importantly, well-designed games have the potential to play an important role in children's informal learning because digital game play accounts for a significant amount of children's time outside of school.[8,9,10] Enthusiasm for informal games can also be attributed to the growing body of empirical research linking digital game play to enhancement of learning[3] and cognitive skills such as inductive reasoning and problem solving;[11,12,13] metacognition;[14] spatial skills;[15,16,17,18] and visual attention skills.[19,20] To what extent might informal development of these skills enhance classroom learning?

The Debate

While it is difficult to find a reasonable, open-minded person who cannot be readily convinced of the potential of games for formal and informal education, there remains no "killer app" educational game. Where is the *Sesame Street* equivalent of learning games? It has been four decades since the introduction of *Oregon Trail*; it took slightly over one decade for educational television in the United States to debut *Sesame Street*. A much larger financial and academic investment has been made for educational games than was made for *Sesame Street*, but there remains no shining star of the educational game world. One of the primary reasons for this state of affairs is that the large amount of research that has been conducted has not provided the types of guidance that were found in the work done by the Children's Television Workshop when creating *Sesame Street*. Instead, the dominant paradigm in learning game research fails to provide much useful insight. Additionally, there are at least three separate camps that can't agree what insight should look like. In this section, I will describe and critique the dominant paradigm and then discuss the intellectual commitments of each of the three camps.

The Dominant Paradigm

The field of games for learning has developed across many disciplines, each with their own strengths and insights. Education scholars have attempted to build strong pedagogical principles into games while communication researchers have focused on how learners relate to the medium. Scientists have built games that are strong on content accuracy and computer science/game design scholars and developers have captured the fun aspects in truly interactional games. In the end, we have a large and growing catalog of games that are pedagogically or scientifically sound but lack fun, or games that are fun to play, but lack necessary content or pedagogy. Few games appear to combine the best input of all scholarly worlds. While some scholars have argued for the multidisciplinary approach,[21,22] there is seldom cooperation across disciplines. Despite remarkable efforts, progress has been slow in developing empirically proven principles for designing effective computer games for STEM education. Research to date can be characterized as disconnected and unfocused. According to Hays,[21] "The empirical research on the instructional effectiveness of games is fragmented, filled with ill defined terms, and plagued with methodological flaws." Each game team designs and tests in isolation from others, with little commonly defined terminology and no unified sense of what is known as a result of all the efforts. Science is a cumulative process but to build on the work of others, we must know what they have learned.

Despite working in separate silos, educational game designers share an affection for experimental demonstration of learning from games they design or commercial games they adopt for use in the classroom. Typically, a team working on developing a game designs it based on a general pedagogical principle (e.g., scaffolding, active learning, inquiry-based learning), social science theory (e.g., flow, capacity model, schema theory) or experience-based intuition. Another approach is to repurpose an existing commercial game, such as *Sim City*, to realize a defined educational goal. The game intervention is then evaluated using a pretest/posttest design, with or without a control group. For example, the evaluation of the game may consist of measuring learners' focal knowledge before and after game play to determine whether there was an increase in learning. Often, the posttest analysis also includes questions about whether the learner enjoyed the experience and would use the game more often. Occasionally, a control group is used. In control group designs, the learning group plays the game while an equivalent control group does not. The expectation is that the group that played the game will show greater knowledge gain and liking for the educational game than the control group. For example, a researcher may be testing the efficacy of a game that is designed to teach a basic math skill. He directs one second-grade class to play the math game for an entire week, while the other second-grade class has no access to the game (control group). At the end of the week, he administers a test of the content covered in the game. If the average score for the group of kids who played the game is significantly higher than the group who didn't play the game, the researcher could claim an effect on learning. The most frequently used methodology is to conduct qualitative interviews with participants to gauge their enjoyment of and preference for the game, as well as to determine how the game might be designed to play better.[23,24] To the cynical eye, these evaluations appear designed more to convince readers that a particular game is effective rather than to test whether it really is. Results from a few positive evaluations are often generalized to support the claim that games, in general, are effective for most any type of content.

Critique of the Dominant Paradigm

What can be gleaned from these experiments? There are currently hundreds of books, journal articles, conference papers, white papers, and other academic writings describing the outcomes of these educational interventions. These include qualitative and quantitative empirical studies testing the use of games to enact a specific learning principle, empirical qualitative and quantitative studies evaluating the efficacy of a specific game on a specific learning outcome (typically content knowledge), and aesthetic analyses of games for learning. A number of reviews,[21–27] and even a special section of *Science*[28] dedicated to games for learning conclude there is not much to learn from this literature because the results are often too general. There is little attention to the role of formal game features, nor is it clear how a genre's game mechanics are necessary for a particular outcome, and there is almost no acknowledgement of individual differences.

Non-Generalizable Findings

The Children's Television Workshop produced empirical principles of television formal features that promoted children's attention to the screen and subsequent learning.[29,30] These studies laid out the fundamentals for the production of effective educational television that are still being used today. These principles have been used in programs for a range of age groups and learning content (e.g., *Electric Company, Blue's Clues, Dora the Explorer*, etc.). However, it is not possible to derive similar principles in the educational game literature because an entire game containing numerous visual, auditory, and interaction techniques is tested as a whole. Which game features led to learning? Was it the theoretical ideas in the initial proposal or was it something else? Even if we could parse out the technique that facilitated learning, would that technique work for other types of learning? Can that technique be separated from the game genre it is instantiated within?

Another problem is rooted in the types of evidence presented in the field. There are three general categories of scholarship in this literature: 1) theory/review articles that argue for the efficacy of games for learning and advocate learning mechanisms in games; 2) empirical studies that take an experimental approach to measuring the effects of gaming on standard measures of cognitive skills or learning; and 3) studies for which idiosyncratic measures of game specific learning outcomes are reported qualitatively.[21] By far, the most frequently published articles advocate for a particular approach to games for learning, based on a theory, mechanism, or experience and provide no empirical data. It is impossible to determine whether the author's approach might be efficacious because the assertions are not tested in the article. However, these articles are often cited in warranting design decisions when making an educational game. Empirical research with standard or idiosyncratic measures is not much help because they often test the entire game experience rather than a specified mechanism. As a result, the results often don't generalize beyond the specific game or idiosyncratic measure. For example, consider a game intended to teach fractions. One group of children is allowed to play the game for 30 minutes and the other group (the control) receives the standard lecture. Subsequently, children are asked whether they enjoyed the lesson, if they would like to have similar sessions, and are measured on their knowledge of fractions. What can we learn from such a study? Should we be surprised that children prefer the unusual experience of playing an animated game to a traditional lecture? If they evidence a greater knowledge of fractions, why? Did they pay more attention because the game play was novel in their school day? What features of the game lead to greater learning? What if the human teacher was better or worse? These questions reveal a number of areas that currently lack research attention.

Formal Features

The Children's Television Workshop performed repeated experiments to determine which formal features of television draw attention and lead to learning in the target audience of pre-school children. Formal features for television include use of color, shot scale, editing, sound effects, length of program segments, type and sex of characters, and other factors. No equivalent work exists in the game literature. Occasionally, knowledge of formal features from the television literature is used for games, under the assumption that the media are similar. Is this the case? What about formal features that are particular to games, such as game mechanics, type of interactivity, controller complexity, point of view, or game genre? We simply don't know which features attract the attention of gamers of different ages and might lead to learning.

Matching Games with Learning

Video games come in a variety of genres, each demanding different skills and types of problem solving. A simple puzzle game like Tetris may only require color recognition and 2D mental rotation, while a 3D shooter game might require multiple cognitive skills (e.g., 3D mental rotation, disembedding, object location memory, etc.) as well as planning and analytic abilities. The literature about matching games with learning is almost entirely from theory/review articles.[6] When designers choose a particular game genre for a particular learning outcome, they may or may not give any consideration to the fit of the genre.

Individual Differences

What impact do individual differences make on the enjoyment and learning from games? If a student is poor at 3D mental rotation, and thus has a problem playing a 3D game, what happens to his/her learning? Research has shown that individual differences in a range of cognitive skills affect both performance and liking of video games.[31] Because experiments do not focus on how children interact with specific formal features in educational games, it is impossible to say the role that individual differences might play. Instead, advocates of games for learning repeat the bromide that every gamer's experience is individualized. In the case of the low 3D rotation skilled child playing a 3D game, that individualized experience may be repeated failure while his/her classmates move quickly through higher levels. There may be ways to remediate these differences but few researchers have focused on this. For example, one unpublished study found that the disorientation experienced by players with low 3D mental rotation ability navigating a 3D game could be eliminated by providing navigational markers.

Alternative Visions

A number of competing visions have emerged for moving forward in the design and evaluation of effective digital games for learning (see Table 7.1). These visions have different assumptions about how knowledge of educational games should proceed, how learning occurs, and what the relationship is between scholarship and educational game design. Scholars from each faction typically publish in different journals and to different audiences and have built separate networks for collaboration and seeking funding. There is little interaction among these groups (see Table 7.1).

Traditional Science

The traditional scientific approach for understanding the effect of media on learning is the most similar to the Children's Television Workshop's design and evaluation of *Sesame Street*. CTW researchers examined how production processes related to learning processes in an ongoing series of experiments. They divided the learning process into a series of variables including learning processes (symbolic, cognitive, environment, and social self), individual differences in viewers, and effect of parental co-viewing. Similarly, the television production process consisted of a set of variables including shot scale, editing pace, visual clutter, program length, character types, and others. For example, an experiment may look at the relationship between program length and audience attention by manipulating the length of program segments and looking for differences in audience attention to the screen. The principles developed by researchers at CTW continue to inform production and research of new educational television to this day.[32]

These scholars are typically trained in behavioral science or in cognitive science and often subscribe to an information processing approach. Information processing refers to the mechanisms involved when people extract

TABLE 7.1 Summary Comparison of Three Separate Camps

	Traditional Science	Situative Learning	Design Thinking
Strength	Specific recommendations	Learning in context	Professional quality
Weaknesses	Artificial research settings	Lack of generalizable results	Lack of pedagogical knowledge
Challenges	Create stimulus materials	Account for vast complexity	Communicate with academics

information from the environment and use available brain systems to transform and make sense of that information. Hence, learning is the appropriation of information from the environment (classroom, game, book, etc.) and the transformation of that information into a storehouse of facts and mechanisms for manipulating those facts (ways of thinking). Topics of interest include attention, perception, motivation/reward, memory, controller affordances, and effects of virtual or collocated others. The largest problem is that of transfer, defined as the degree to which learning "that occurs when learning in one context affects one's learning or ability to carry out a task in another context."[33]

Following the example of the CTW and the methods of their respective fields, information processing researchers believe that educational games need to undergo fine-grained examination of how formal features are related to desired learning outcomes for a variety of audiences. Hence, they are in favor of dividing the process into sets of focal constructs to examine through comparative empirical manipulation. The commitment to this approach slows traditional science research on games for learning for two reasons. First, scholars in these fields are often reliant on off-the-shelf games because they lack the skills to create games themselves. Of course, this makes the manipulation of a particular design feature impossible. Game programmers often balk at working on this type of research because they want to make a complete game, not several versions of the same game. The second problem is finding funding for experimental work to solve the stimulus design problem. A major funder in the area of games for learning told me that agencies and foundations prefer to fund a complete and 'tested' game as a demonstration of the effectiveness of their funding. They are rarely interested in research that doesn't contain a demonstration game.

Situative Learning

A group of scholars, self-identified as learning scientists, have critiqued the traditional scientific approach, arguing that learning occurs both within the learner's mind and in the mind, body, activity, and culture within which the learner exists.[34] As such, the focus of research and design is shifted from isolated components that predict learning to interaction structures in social and game systems. Under such assumptions, it is not only the learner's playing of the game that is important, but also how that play occurs in the classroom, at home, or in other environments. Additionally, emphasis is placed on how the idea that play and learning are socially constructed in the learner's social system. Is learning valued in the social system? Is it necessary? Are games for learning seen as an intrusion on play space or are they embraced as an alternative way to learn in a formal or informal setting?

For situative researchers, learning takes place in a community of practice and meaning evolves as learners are enculturated to that community. Derry and

Steinkuhler[34(p803)] state that learning "is the gradual transformation of an individual from peripheral participant to central member of a community, through apprenticeship and increased acceptance of community values and increased participation in community practices." Further, Barab & Squire[35(p1)] argue that "learning, cognition, knowing, and context are irreducibly co-constituted and cannot be treated as isolated entities or processes." If learning is conceived as a community practice, the use of massively multi-player games provides the platform within which the community norms can emerge.

In order to study learning within the complex environment in which it happens, situative scholars have developed a methodology known as design-based research. Design-based research examines learning in the types of real-life environments where it occurs and attempts to account for multiple dependent variables such as collaboration among learners, content learning and transfer, use of available resources, and intervention efficacy. To do so, both qualitative (e.g., observational, interviews, focus groups) and quantitative (e.g., content knowledge gain, participation rate, attitude change) methods are employed in a mixed method design. Ultimately, situative researchers hope to develop theory and to make research-based claims about the trustworthiness, credibility, and consequentiality of game-based educational interventions.

Design-based research generally doesn't suffer the funding problems that traditional science does because it typically delivers a complete game and data on an in-class experience. The game may be one fully designed by the research team (e.g., *Quest Atlantis*) or it may be off-the-shelf (e.g., *Sim City*). However, design-based research does suffer from its own inherent set of problems. Collins, Joseph and Bielaczyc[36] note that design-based research suffers from difficulties of capturing the complexity of real-world situations, the difficulty of exacting experimental control, the complexity of analyzing massive and incompatible data from ethnographic and quantitative sources, and the ability to compare across designs.

Designer Driven

A number of game designers have taken up efforts to design games for learning. This is not surprising, as they probably understand better than anyone the amount of learning and puzzle solving that engages gamers. The connection to education is obvious for game designers. In particular, game designers recognize the inherent power of motivation in games. As Prensky[37] writes, games are where "*motivation itself* is the expertise, and is, in fact the *sine qua non*." Many individuals from the game industry have become educational game evangelists, including Marc Prensky, Ian Bogost, Katie Salen, Eric Zimmerman, and Jane McGonigal.

In general, professional game designers are trained in computer science and engineering. As such, they are steeped in the "design thinking" paradigm. Design thinking is an intellectual tradition rooted in architectural and industrial design and that later migrated to the then newly emerging field of computer science. It has been adopted in a number of engineering and business innovation areas. Design thinking teaches that design is an iterative process that involves a defined process of definition, research/empathy, ideation, prototyping, testing, implementation, and testing/learning. By following the design logic, a game solution may be found for just about any situation.[38]

The definition stage consists of defining the learning problem to be solved. This would necessitate understanding all the educational goals of the game intervention, perhaps organized by Bloom's hierarchy of learning. During the research/empathy stage the designer gathers information on the learner: what does the learner know, what obstacles to learning exist, what context will the learning take place in, etc. This may be framed in cognitive task analysis.[39] CTA answers (1) what tasks are associated with the learning goal; (2) what skills are required to perform those tasks; (3) what is the mental model of an expert performing those tasks; (4) what difficulties the learner runs into; and (5) which teaching components are likely to be most helpful.

After definition and research are completed, the team can move on to ideation, prototyping, and testing. In the ideation stage, the team brainstorms possible solutions for the defined learning task. Here they are encouraged to let their imaginations run free, now that they know the problem to be solved. The brainstormed solutions can be prototyped and tested to determine the degree to which the solutions do what they are expected to do. This process iterates until the best solutions emerge and the game can be designed. At that point, the total game design is instantiated into code and implemented in the real world. The educational game can now be tested in a real environment (e.g., classroom) and the designers can learn what works and what doesn't work. If resources allow, the game can be further revised based on these data. Frequently, game designers write a document called a 'post-mortem' detailing the process, the results, and what they learned from the project. Post-mortems of educational games are often shared with others in the larger educational game design community.

Naturally, the biggest problem that game designers face when creating educational games is that they lack a strong background in pedagogy, communication/psychology, and/or the content domain. This can lead to the familiar "fun game, but I didn't learn anything" problem. This problem was so pervasive in the early years of educational games that the entire industry folded.[1] Theoretically, the problem can be solved by recruiting education, communication, and content experts to advise the project. However, new problems can arise. Outside experts often don't understand the constraints and affordances of video game design. They can request modifications that are expensive or even impossible to do. Talking across areas of expertise requires a good deal of humility and effort to understand and translate jargon. Often, either academics or designers lack the kind of humility necessary. Finally, without the type of fine-grained research done by traditional science, experts may not have a recommendation that is anything more that opinion. For example, if a designer wants to know how a five-year-old understands time or transformation in games, there is simply no data to answer that question.

Resolving the Debate?

It has been over four decades since *Oregon Trail* was first played in a classroom. In the time since, there has been tremendous amount of effort and money put forward to figure out how to use games for learning. What do we now know? Do children learn from games? As I wrote earlier, this seems self-evident. Can we point to examples of successful educational games? Yes, but only successful in specific contexts. Do we know why children learn from games? Or what features of the games draw and hold attention? There is very little evidence. Despite the flurry of activity over the past few decades, there is still no clear empirically tested foundation for designing educational games. This situation may largely reflect the lack of interdisciplinary effort dedicated to the development of these games, as reflected by the proliferation of individual labs that rarely communicate outside of their own fields. A simple search of references shows that only a few named scholars (e.g., Gee, Squire, Jenkins) are cited outside of their own field. Meanwhile, companies such as Mattel, Nickelodeon, Sesame Workshop, and others continue to produce proprietary research for game development.

Efforts to bridge this gap have been notably limited. One successful effort was the 2007 *Annenberg Workshop on Games for Learning, Development & Change*. The conference introduced behavioral scientists working in the field to scholars from the mainstream of games and learning. To illustrate the extent of the divide between camps, leading learning games scholar James Gee remarked that he had no idea there were so many behavioral scientists doing such interesting and important work on games for learning (personal communication). The edited book that resulted from the conference, *Serious Games: Mechanisms and Effects*,[40] was filled with optimism for progress moving forward. In 2010, the National Science Foundation sponsored a similarly interdisciplinary conference at Fordham University to reflect on the current state of knowledge about the use of digital games for education and to develop a focused research agenda for STEM learning among child and adolescent students. Attendees at the three-and-a-half-day meeting included STEM game designers, computer scientists, educational technologists, developmental and cognitive psychologists, and communications research scholars representing academe (e.g. Carnegie Mellon University, Georgetown University, USC) and media practice and education policy (e.g. Quest to Learn, Joan Ganz Cooney Center, Fisher-Price, Games for Change).

Consistent themes noted by nearly all attendees was the glaring lack of empirical research attesting to transfer from digital game play to other segments of children's worlds, as well as the paucity of research on the processes involved in learning from games. While game designers and educational technologists were able to identify projects that showed *that* learning had occurred, no one was able to provide empirical evidence for *why* learning had occurred or for transfer to contexts outside the game. Many questions remain: "Which game mechanisms were children most engaged by?" "Would the game engage interest in a non-experimental (informal) situation?" "How much time on task was required for learning?" "Did the observed gains persist and can the knowledge gain be transferred to other similar contexts?" Among the key research areas suggested in the book that followed from the conference, *Learning by Playing: Video Gaming in Education*[41] were (1) the specification of those game aspects, game mechanics, and formal features that seemed to appeal or promote attention to academic content within digital games and (2) examination of how those features might differ by age.

One might argue that most of the progress made to date has been to identify the differences among visions. However, science often proceeds best when different groups attack a problem from a variety of angles. This allows more options to be considered and for comparison to find the best results. In order to make those comparisons, competing ideas typically need to work from the same set of assumptions. In this case, the assumptions are quite different from each other.

Possible Solutions to Gridlock

The problems confronting the field of educational games are not that much different from those that faced the Children's Television Workshop when creating *Sesame Street* and the core principles of television-based learning. Gerald Lesser[30] wrote that one of the biggest challenges the CTW faced was to facilitate productive conversations among the television producers, academics, and community advocates that made up the original team. The advantage that the CTW had was a secure source of funding for two years and a well-connected and inspiring leader in Joan Ganz Cooney. What can be done other than waiting for the next great leader? There are a few options.

Learn to Work Together

The simplest solution would be for representatives from each of the three camps to learn to work together. Many universities house experts from all three areas and they occasionally collaborate. However, the modern university has little patience for the type of research needed to delineate principles for effective design. Instead, professors are pressured to generate revenue through grants. This places the process under control of foundations and national agencies who only want demonstration projects. Additionally, most universities are set up to reward exceptional individuals rather than groups. If there isn't a clear intellectual leader, the university generally won't provide resources or reward. Which camp gets to lead and which researchers are willing to put their own career advancement on hold?

Increased Funding

Funding is important for two reasons: it pays for the work and is a recognizable accomplishment for university administrators. However, designing games for education is an expensive endeavor and funding is limited in the social and behavior sciences where these researchers typically originate. For example, in fiscal year 2013, the US National Science Foundation allocated only 15 percent of its total budget to education and the social and behavioral sciences. Of that total, very little is in programs that can be accessed for creating educational games. Foundations typically allocate smaller amounts than federal agencies. The lack of recognizable achievement compounds the problem by making it more difficult for researchers to argue they will effectively use funds.

A For-profit Model

Both Shuler[1] and Prensky[37] have argued that educational games can be a viable for-profit business. Despite the downturn of the late 1990s,[1] there remains a potential market for both formal games (e.g., schools) and informal games (e.g., home). In fact, Prensky[37] argues that the market is even better than it was during the first era of educational games because more schools and households now have the necessary hardware. But who will provide the seed money for such a risky venture? In personal conversations with Microsoft and Electronic Arts, I found that they are only looking to invest in educational games *after* someone proves that they are profitable. Perhaps new educational games will have to take the same route to success as small independent game makers. But Prensky[37] points out that educational products represent a long-term investment (up to ten years for a textbook). Can a start-up find venture capital and sustain a business with such long product cycles? He suggests an open-source solution with programmers and learners contributing to ongoing projects. Interestingly, he does not reserve a place in his vision for the behavioral, cognitive, or learning sciences.

The Remaining Questions

Who will step up to invest the time or resources necessary to make the first widely used educational game since *Oregon Trail*? Or will we just let the potential pass us by? Will academics remain comfortable in their institutional cocoons while game designers focus on the next big entertainment application? If scientific research is necessary, which academic strategy should win the day?

Will some government around the world make the investment to find out how to make games? Or might a foundation switch strategy and support basic research on games? Perhaps there is another way?

While the concept of learning from games is not debatable, the way we will get there continues to be an ongoing conundrum. Perhaps there are too many visions and not enough action. In any case, it remains an open question and an ongoing debate in the video game world.

References

1. Shuler C. *What in the World Happened to Carmen Sandiego? The Edutainment Era: Debunking Myths and Sharing Lessons Learned.* New York, NY: Joan Ganz Cooney Center; 2012: 1–22.
2. Greenfield PM. Technology and informal education: What is taught, what is learned. *Science.* 2009; 323(5910): 69–71. doi:10.1126/science.1167190
3. Mayo MJ. Video games: A route to large-scale STEM education? *Science.* 2009; 323(5910): 79–82. doi:10.1126/science.1166900
4. Fenichel M, Schweingruber HA. *Surrounded by Science: Learning Science in Informal Environments.* Washington, DC: National Academies Press; 2009.
5. Boyan A, Sherry JL. The challenge in creating games for education: Aligning mental models with game models. *Child Dev Perspect.* 2011; 5(2): 82–87. doi:10.1111/j.1750-8606.2011.00160.x
6. Sherry JL, Pacheco A. Matching computer game genres to educational outcomes. *Electron J Commun.* 2006; 16.
7. Sherry JL. Flow and media enjoyment. *Commun Theory.* 2004; 14(4): 328–347.
8. Common Sense Media. *Zero to Eight: Children's Media Use in America.* 2011. Retrieved December 1, 2011 from www.commonsensemedia.org/research/zero-eight-childrens-media-use-america
9. Entertainment Software Association. *2013 Essential Facts about the Computer and Video Game Industry.* 2014. Retrieved October 6, 2014 from www.theesa.com/facts/pdfs/ESA_EF_2013.pdf
10. Rideout VJ, Foehr UG, Roberts DF. *Generation M2: Media in the Lives of 8- to 18-Year-Olds.* Menlo Park, CA: Kaiser Family Foundation; 2010.
11. Greenfield PM, Camaioni L, Ercolani P, Weiss L, Lauber BA, Perucchini P. Cognitive socialization by computer games in two cultures: Inductive discovery or mastery of an iconic code? *J Appl Dev Psychol.* 1994; 15(1): 59–85. doi:10.1016/0193-3973(94)90006-x
12. Pillay H. An investigation of cognitive processes engaged in by recreational computer game players. *J Res Technol Educ.* 2002; 34(3): 336–350. doi:10.1080/15391523.2002.10782354
13. Blumberg FC, Torenberg M, Randall J. The relationship between preschoolers' selective attention and memory for location strategies. *Cogn Dev.* 2005; 20(2): 242–255. doi:10.1016/j.cogdev.2005.04.006
14. VanDeventer SS, White JA. Expert behavior in children's video game play. *Simul Gaming.* 2002; 33: 28–48. doi:10.1177/1046878102033001002
15. Okagaki L, Frensch PA. Effects of video game playing on measures of spatial performance: Gender effects in late adolescence. *J Appl Dev Psychol.* 1994; 15: 33–58. doi:10.1016/0193-3973(94)90005-1
16. Greenfield PM, Brannon C, Lohr D. Two-dimensional representation of movement through three-dimensional space: The role of video game expertise. *J Appl Dev Psychol.* 1994; 15(1): 87–103. doi:10.1016/0193-3973(94)90007-8

17. Sims VK, Mayer RE. Domain specificity of spatial expertise: The case of video game players. *Appl Cogn Psychol.* 2002; 16(1): 97–115. doi:10.1002/acp.759

18. Spence I, Feng J. Video games and spatial cognition. *Rev Gen Psychol.* 2010; 14(2): 92–104.

19. Green CS, Bavelier D. Enumeration versus multiple object tracking: The case of action video game players. *Cognition.* 2006; 101(1): 217–245.

20. Green CS, Bavelier D. Action video game modifies visual selective attention. *Nature.* 2003; 423(6939): 534–537. doi:10.1038/nature01647

21. Hays RT. *The Effectiveness of Instructional Games: A Literature Review and Discussion.* Washington, DC: Naval Air Warfare Center; 2005.

22. Mayra F. Getting into the game: Doing interdisciplinary game studies. In: Perron B, Wolf MJP, eds. *The Video Game Reader 2.* New York, NY: Routledge; 2009: 313–388.

23. Blumberg FC, Ismailer SS. What do children learn from playing digital games? In: Ritterfeld U, Cody M, Vorderer P, eds. *Serious Games: Mechanisms and Effects.* New York, NY: Routledge; 2009: 129–140.

24. Sherry JL, Dibble JL. The impact of serious games on childhood development. In: Ritterfeld U, Vorderer P, Cody M, eds. *Serious Games: Mechanisms and Effects.* New York, NY: Routledge; 2009: 169–169. doi:10.1080/14753821003679205

25. Dondlinger MJ. Educational video game design: A review of the literature. *J Appl Educ Technol.* 2007; 4(1): 21–31.

26. Oblinger DG. The next generation of educational engagement. *J Interact Media Educ.* 2004: 1–18.

27. O'Neil HF, Wainess R, Baker EL. Classification of learning outcomes: Evidence from the computer games literature. *Curric J.* 2005; 16: 455–474.

28. *Science.* 2009; 23(5910).

29. Fisch SM, Truglio RT, Cole CF. The impact of Sesame Street on preschool children: A review and synthesis of 30 years' research. *Media Psychol.* 1999; 1: 165–190.

30. Lesser GS. *Children and Television: Lessons from Sesame Street.* New York, NY: Random House; 1974.

31. Sherry JL, Rosaen S, Bowman N. Cognitive skill predicts video game ability. In: *International Communication Association Annual Convention.* Dresden, Germany; 2006.

32. Fisch SM. *Children's Learning From Educational Television.* New York: Routledge; 2004: 324. doi:10.4324/9781410610553.

33. Blumberg FC, Almonte DE, Barkhardori Y, Leno A. Academic lessons from video game learning. In: Blumberg FC, ed. *Learning by Playing: Video Gaming in Education.* Cambridge, MA: MIT Press; 2014: 3–14.

34. Derry SJ, Steinkuehler CA. Cognitive and situative theories of learning and instruction. In: Nadel L, ed. *Encyclopedia of Cognitive Science.* England: Nature Publishing Group; 2003: 800–805.

35. Barab SA, Squire K. Design-based research: Putting a stake in the ground. *J Learn Sci.* 2004; 13(1): 1–14.

36. Collins A, Joseph D, Bielaczyc K. Design research: Theoretical and methodological issues. *J Learn Sci.* 2004; 13(1): 15–42. doi:10.1207/s15327809jls1301_2

37. Prensky M. Digital game-based learning. *Comput Entertain.* 2003; 1(1): 21. doi:10.1145/950566.950596

38. McGonigal J. *Reality Is Broken: Why Games Make Us Better and How They Can Change the World.* Penguin Press, New York; 2011: 400. doi:10.1075/ni.10.1.03bro

39. Crandall B, Klein GA, Hoffman RR. *Working Minds: A Practitioner's Guide to Cognitive Task Analysis.* Cambridge, MA: Mit Press; 2006: 320.

40. Ritterfeld U, Cody M, Vorderer P. *Serious Games: Mechanisms and Effects.* Routledge, New York; 2009: 530. doi:10.4324/9780203891650

41. Blumberg FC. *Learning by Playing.* Cambridge: MIT Press; 2013.

8

VIDEO GAMES AND COGNITIVE PERFORMANCE

Gillian Dale and C. Shawn Green

The human brain is an exceptional learning machine. Given appropriate training – including sufficient training time, proper spacing of training sessions, and useful feedback – humans will tend to show improvements on essentially any perceptual or motor task. However, the gains in performance seen as a result of training are very often highly specific to the exact training task and do not extend to untrained tasks or functions.[1] For example, in one classic demonstration of the specificity of perceptual learning, participants were presented with two vertically oriented lines – one above the other.[2] In different trials, the line on top was displaced very slightly either to the left or to the right relative to the line on the bottom. The participants' task was simply to indicate the direction of the displacement. With extensive practice on the task, participants' performance improved substantially (i.e., they were able to discriminate finer and finer displacements). However, when a seemingly minor change was made to the display (it was rotated by 90 degrees such that the two lines were oriented horizontally), participant performance returned to baseline levels, indicating that none of the learning benefits gained during the initial vertical training transferred to the horizontal condition.[2,3] This general finding of task specific perceptual learning has been observed repeatedly over the past three decades, not just for stimulus orientation, but also for myriad other stimulus and task characteristics such as position, spatial frequency, motion direction, motion speed, and even the eye of training.

While the issue of learning specificity has perhaps been most thoroughly documented in the domain of perceptual learning, it is certainly not isolated to this domain. Indeed, task specific learning has also proven to be one of the major obstacles in the domain of cognitive training, where many paradigms designed to more generally "train the brain" instead appear to lead to improvements primarily on the training tasks themselves.[4-7] Even in more complex physical activities, such as clay pigeon shooting,[8] baseball,[9] or tennis,[10] changes have primarily been observed in only those sub-tasks utilized in the activity. For example, following baseball training, changes were observed in Go/NoGo reaction time tasks, which use the same processes that are used when deciding whether or not to swing at a pitch in baseball, but there were no changes found for simpler reaction time tasks.

From a rehabilitative standpoint, the tendency toward learning specificity is a severe hindrance, as it is necessarily the case that in order to be of practical use, the effects of training need to extend *beyond* the strict parameters of the trained task. Interestingly, one intervention that *does* appear to lead to more generalizable improvements in cognitive performance involves an experience that was not originally designed for practical ends – video game training. Video games have consistently been shown to result in global transfer to a variety of perceptual and cognitive measures, from those that tap low-level visual abilities, all the way up to task switching and high-level decision making. Critically, not only are these effects "statistically significant" in the laboratory, but also of a scope and scale sufficient to be utilized in practical, real-world applications.

Early Video Game Research

Specific scientific investigations of the potential effects of video games began to take off in the early 1980s (perhaps not surprisingly, at virtually the same time that the societal popularity of video games began to rise steeply). This early research focused primarily on hand-eye coordination and spatial skills. For instance, Griffith and colleagues[11] examined whether regular video game players, in this case broadly defined as individuals who played 2–59 hours of any video game per week, had better hand-eye coordination than non-video game players. They found that individuals who regularly played video games had enhanced performance on a rotary pursuit task (keeping a wand in contact with a moving dot) as compared to non-players, suggesting that there is an association between video game play and cognitive abilities.

As will become evident throughout the chapter, much of the work on the effects of video games has employed this type of cross-sectional design, which takes advantage of the fact that some individuals freely choose to engage in substantial amounts of video game play, while others play little to no games. One major issue with this type of research, though, is the well-known axiom that correlation cannot be used to imply causation. Thus, in the case of cross-sectional data on video games, one cannot determine whether the act of playing the video games actually caused the observed improvements, or if, instead, individuals who have innately high levels of ability are drawn to video games.

To adjudicate between these possibilities, a well-controlled experiment must be employed. Here, individuals who do not naturally play the video games of interest are specifically trained on those video games over a period of hours, weeks, or months and laboratory measures of perception, cognition, and/or motor skill are compared before and after the training to see the effect of the training. In this vein, Gagnon[12] had a group of participants play two different video games for 5 hours: a 2D game called *Targ*, and a 3D game called *Battlezone*. Spatial abilities (rotation and visualization) were assessed before and after the training. Consistent with the causal hypothesis, playing these games for just 5 hours was associated with improvements in scores on the spatial tasks as well as in hand-eye coordination. Similar results were later observed throughout the 1980s and 1990s using different video games, assessing different populations (e.g., younger children[13,14]), and examining different abilities (e.g., divided attention[15] or mental rotation[16,17]).

Together, this early research provided strong support for the idea that video game play has the capacity to broadly influence perceptual, cognitive, and motor skills. It also provided the framework around which later work was built, from issues related to methodology (e.g., cross-sectional versus experimental methods), to theory (e.g., the relationship between demands of certain games and their cognitive effects).

Effects of Action Video Games

While clearly building on the early research, the research that has taken place over the past fifteen years has also been strongly shaped by changes in the video game industry. As technology has advanced, the graphics, game mechanics, and overall sophistication of video games has rapidly improved. Furthermore, as more and more games were developed, a number of distinct game genres emerged. One such genre, the action video game (AVG) genre, includes games that rapidly present players with an ever-changing, complex array of information across a wide visual field. Players usually need to make quick and accurate decisions and responses in order to stay alive or reach a mission objective, and successful players must possess well-developed skills in a variety of cognitive domains such as selective attention, working memory, task switching, and inhibitory control.[18] Many AVGs use the first-person shooter format (such as in popular series like *Halo*, *Call of Duty*, and *Medal of Honor*), but certain sports and adventure games are considered to be "action" based as well (see Spence and Feng[19] for a systematic description of the characteristics of AVGs). The extreme perceptual, cognitive, and motoric demands of this specific genre have thus made it the focus of the majority of the work in the field. Indeed, there are now numerous documented benefits of playing AVGs to all aspects of cognition, from very low-level visual and attentional processes, to high-level executive functions.

Visual Perception

Action video game experience has been consistently associated with improvements in the ability to utilize low-level visual features of stimuli. For instance, the contrast sensitivity function (CSF) represents the ability to distinguish between slight differences in contrast, or shading, across a uniform background,[20] and is commonly regarded as one of the foundational elements of vision. In Li et al.[20] expert action video game players (AVGPs), individuals who reported having played AVGs for at least 5 hours per week for at least the previous 6 months, were compared to non-action video game players (NVGPs) on a standard contrast sensitivity task. The AVGPs were found to have significantly better contrast sensitivity as compared to NVGPs, meaning that AVGPs were able to distinguish finer changes in gray level than NVGPs.

As discussed earlier, though, the cross-sectional approach leaves open the question of causation. Thus, in a second experiment, action game novices were trained on either an action video game (*Unreal Championship* and *Call of Duty 2*) or a control video game (*The Sims 2*) for 50 hours spaced over the course of many weeks. The control group in such experiments serves a number of distinct purposes. First, the group acts as a control against simple test-retest effects. Experimental training designs involve a pre-test phase, a training phase, and post-test phase. Because the goal is to be able to attribute changes in performance from pre-test to post-test to the intervention, one must first know if there is a simple benefit from taking the test twice. Second, the group acts as a control against various more subtle participant reactivity effects such as the Hawthorne effect, wherein performance can improve simply due to being observed. As such, the control video game in these experiments is chosen to eliminate a number of reactivity-type confounds (e.g., it is chosen to be as engaging and interesting as the experimental game, to lead to an equal amount of identification with the character, to induce a similar degree of flow, etc.). Consistent with the causal hypothesis, a dramatic improvement in contrast sensitivity (43–58 percent) was observed in those individuals trained on the action video game, and this improvement was larger than what was found in the control group. Other low-level visual benefits of AVGP experience have been observed for tasks involving simple peripheral perimetry[21] and dot motion perception,[22] and in terms of basic perceptual processing speed.[23]

Furthermore, although video games are commonly associated primarily with the visual system, the perceptual benefits of AVG experience are not limited to the visual domain. Donohue et al.[24] examined the ability of AVGPs and NVGPs to perform simultaneity and temporal-order tasks in both the visual and auditory modalities, and found that AVGPs outperformed NVGPs in both. Similarly, Green et al.[25] examined perceptual decision making in both the visual and auditory domains, and again found that AVGPs outperformed NVGPs in both (with a causal relationship observed in a 50-hour training study).

Recent research has suggested that the mechanistic change underlying the improved performance across perceptual tasks is in the ability to learn perceptual templates for the task at hand.[26] In other words, AVG experience leads to an enhanced ability to detect what low-level stimulus characteristics are most discriminative for the task at hand, and to utilize this information to make effective decisions.

Attention

A number of attentional processes are also influenced by action gaming. For instance, many studies have now shown clear enhancements in spatial selective attention. Although there are many tasks in the psychological literature that tap spatial selective attention, one common measure in the action video game literature is the Useful Field of View (UFOV) task. In the UFOV task, participants view a briefly presented (e.g., 20 milliseconds) display that contains both a central target and a peripheral target (see Figure 8.1). The peripheral target can appear at three different eccentricities (10, 20, 30 degrees) from the center of the screen. Following stimulus presentation, a strong pattern mask is

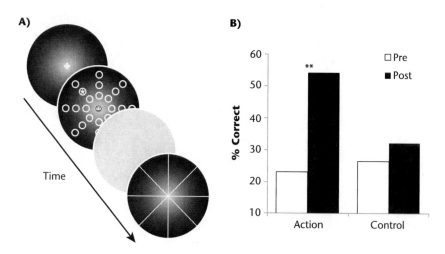

FIGURE 8.1 A) Typical Useful Field of View trial. Participants fixate centrally, and are then presented with a display that contains a central target (i.e., the smiley face), a peripheral target (i.e., the star), and distractors (the white circles). After a variable duration (~20 ms), the display is covered by a noise or pattern mask. Then, participants are presented with a display that contains eight spokes, and are asked to both indicate the identity of the central target, and on which of the eight spokes the peripheral target had appeared. B) UFOV data adapted from Green and Bavelier.[18] Accuracy on the UFOV task (% correct) is compared before (Pre) and after (Post) training for individuals trained on an action game (Action) or on a puzzle game (Control). Only the Action group showed a statistically significant improvement in their accuracy on this task following training.

presented to eliminate afterimages. Participants respond by first indicating the identity of the central target and then the location of the peripheral target. AVGPs have consistently been shown to perform this task more accurately than NVGPs at all eccentricities,[18,27–30] with similar results found in NVGPs specifically trained on action games.[18,27,29]

Similar results have been seen in many other tasks where task-relevant information needs to be selected from amongst distracting information across space. For instance, performance on crowding tasks is thought to offer a measure of the spatial resolution of visual selective attention. In these tasks, individuals are asked to identify a briefly displayed peripheral target (e.g., determine whether a T shape is presented right side up or upside down) that is presented in the presence of distracting shapes. When the distracting shapes are presented far from the target, performance is usually quite good, but when the distracting shapes are presented close to the target, performance decreases significantly. Thus, the distance between the target and the distractors at which an individual can perform the task at a criterion level of performance offers a measure of the "crowding region." Green and Bavelier[31] found that this crowding region is significantly smaller both in AVGPs, and in individuals specifically trained on AVGs, as compared to NVGPs, meaning that AVG experience allows for more effective spatial filtering of distractors.

Finally, several studies have reported enhanced performance in AVGPs on more standard visual search tasks.[32–34] In these tasks, individuals are asked to find a specific target (e.g., either the letter 'b' or the letter 'd') from amongst a field of distracting letters. When the target is presented alongside only a few distractors, participants find the target rapidly. As more and more distracting elements are added, search times increase reasonably linearly. The slope of this increase can thus be taken as a measure of the speed of visual attentional processes. In Hubert-Wallander et al.,[32] the slope of the search function was shallower in AVGPs (i.e., reaction time increased less steeply with each additional distractor added) than in NVGPs, suggesting either more efficient distractor suppression, or overall faster speed of processing.

Beyond spatial selection, the benefits of AVG experience have also been reliably seen in attention across time. Green and Bavelier,[18] for example, examined the effects of AVG experience on the attentional blink (AB) task. In the AB, stimuli are rapidly presented one at a time in the center of a computer screen. Participants are asked to detect/identify two targets from within this stream of stimuli. In the typical AB task, when the two targets are presented temporally close (within ~500ms of each other), accuracy for detecting/ identifying the second of the two targets is markedly decreased as compared to longer target separations. This task is thought to reflect a fundamental temporal limitation of selective attention.[35] In the Green and Bavelier[18] study, while NVGPs showed a typical attentional blink effect, the AVGPs had a much smaller attentional blink effect (with several of the AVGPs having no attentional blink at all). This suggests that the AVGPs either had more processing resources available, or were able to process items more quickly, thus avoiding the typical attentional bottleneck that occurs in this task. A similar effect was found when NVGPs were trained on AVGs, such that individuals who trained on an action game showed a reduction in their AB, whereas those who trained with a puzzle game showed no such benefit. As was true of spatial selective attention, the general finding of enhanced temporal attention has been reproduced in young children,[23] and using a number of other tasks including other rapid serial visual presentation tasks,[36] and in measures of backward masking.[20,37]

A final aspect of visual attention that appears to be enhanced by AVG experience is attentional capacity. For example, individuals who play AVGs have also been shown to perform better on tasks in which they are required to monitor and track multiple objects within a display (e.g., the multiple object tracking task – MOT). Trick et al.[38] presented children from five different age groups (6, 8, 10, 12, and 19 years) with a MOT task called "Catch the Spies" in which they were required to track between 1 and 4 "spies" who were trying to blend in with a crowd. Interestingly, after controlling for age, they found a significant increase in the number of objects tracked by children who played AVGs as compared to sports video game players and non-gamers. Similar results have been observed in a different cohort of children[28] as well in adult populations,[27,39] although only Green and Bavelier[27] showed a significant effect in a dedicated training experiment.

Memory

A number of memory processes have also been shown to be associated with playing action video games. For example, visual short-term memory (VSTM) has been shown to differ between AVGPs and NVGPs. Boot et al.[39] examined differences in AVGPs and NVGPs on a VSTM task originally developed by Luck and Vogel.[40] In this task, participants are presented with a display of colored bars for 100ms, followed by a 900ms blank, and then another display of bars. The second display of bars can either be identical to the first display, or else one of the individual bars can be changed (either its color or its orientation). Participants are asked to determine whether or not the first and second displays were identical. Boot et al.[39] found that AVGPs were significantly better on this task as compared to NVGPs, indicating that they had superior memory performance. This same effect in AVGPs and NVGPs was also seen in McDermott et al.[41] However, it is worth noting that in Boot et al.,[39] individuals specifically trained on action video games did not show similar benefits. It is also the case that no effects of action gaming have been seen in either extremely short (i.e., iconic) or long-term memory.[42,43]

While the above tasks mainly involved simple retention, working memory tasks require both retention and manipulation. One could argue that this is a better match to the demands of AVGs, which commonly require players to not only remember multiple items at a time, but also to be able to continuously and fluidly update what information is being remembered. Using this logic, Colzato et al.[44] recruited 26 AVGPs and 26 NVGPs, and examined their performance on an N-back working memory task. In the N-back task, participants are presented with a series of digits or letters one after another. They are asked to press one key if the current letter is the same as that which was presented N-items earlier. For instance, in a 2-back task, if participants had seen the following letters: A, D, F, G, H, G, K, L, M, L, they would have been expected to answer "yes" on the 6th letter (G – which is the same as the 4th letter) and on the 10th letter (L – which is the same as the 8th letter). This task thus clearly requires that participants monitor and continually update their working memory stores. As expected, the AVGPs were more accurate on the task than NVGPs, suggesting that video game play is associated with the development of a flexible working memory that actively updates and clears irrelevant information from the memory store. However, a similar study found that while AVGPs were faster on the N-back task as compared to NVGPs, they were no more accurate;[41] a finding similar to that obtained by Boot et al.[39] who used an operation span task. As such, it is currently unclear how video games influence working memory capacity, but there is at least the suggestion that action gamers perform differently from non–gamers. This is an area that requires further investigation, particularly given the current interest in video games as a rehabilitative tool for elderly individuals, many of whom suffer working memory decline in old age.

Executive Functions

Lastly, a number of higher order executive functions have been shown to be influenced by action video game training. "Executive functions," also known as "cognitive control," is an umbrella term that describes a collection of high-level cognitive abilities, all of which are goal-oriented, and under top-down, effortful control. For example, planning, inhibitory control, and task switching are all classified as executive functions.

The ability to flexibly change from one task to the next in a rapid manner is vital when playing fast-paced, complex action games, and is one of the most important aspects of cognitive control. Colzato et al.[45] first investigated whether regular AVGPs would differ from NVGPs on a task-switching paradigm (see Figure 8.2). Participants completed a global/local task in which large, global shapes that were composed of smaller, local shapes were presented on the screen, and participants were asked to respond to the identity of either the overall global shape (e.g., a square made of small circles) or the local elements

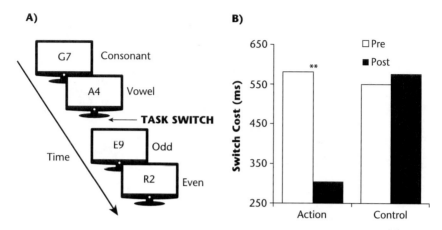

FIGURE 8.2   A) A typical task-switching paradigm. In each trial, participants are presented with a letter/digit pair, and are asked to either classify the letter as a vowel or consonant, or classify the digit as odd or even, by pressing a key with their left or right hand. Critically, participants receive two letter classification trials followed by two digit classification trials, and their response time is recorded. Performance is measured by comparing response time on task-repeating trials to response time on task-switching trials in order to obtain an index of switch costs. B) Data adapted from Strobach et al.[49] Switch costs are compared before (Pre) and after (Post) training for individuals trained on an action game (Action) or on a puzzle game (Control). Only the Action group showed a statistically significant decrease in their switch costs on this task following training.

that comprised the global shape (e.g., the small circles that make up the large square). Participants alternated between four global and four local blocks, and received cues when they were required to switch the level at which they were responding. While AVGPs did not have faster reaction times overall as compared to NVGPs, they showed reduced reaction time costs following the task switch, demonstrating that they were more efficient at switching sets during the task. This finding has since been replicated and extended by using more complex tasks that require goal switches or vocal responses,[46] although it should be noted that this effect disappears when proactive interference on the task is increased by including three possible tasks and rapidly alternating between them.[47] As has been true in other domains, the causal role of action video games in enhanced task-switching performance has been shown in a number of training studies;[46,48,49] an effect that appears to be modulated by genetic polymorphisms related to dopamine degradation.[50] In addition to task-switching performance, AVGPs have also been shown to perform better on measures of general multitasking ability[51,52] (although see Donohue et al.[53]).

There is also suggestion that video games may have an influence on inhibitory control. Oei and Patterson[48] trained NVGPs on one of four video games, and assessed performance on a variety of measures before and after training. One of the measures was a Go/NoGo task in which participants are required to make rapid button presses in response to stimuli presented on the screen on the vast majority of trials, but on a subset of trials participants are required to withhold responding. Withholding a prepotent response requires immense cognitive effort and control, thus this task is a classic measure of inhibitory mechanisms. In this particular task, a false alarm rate (number of times they incorrectly responded on "withhold" trials) is calculated, and higher false alarms are indicative of poorer inhibitory control. Interestingly, they found that only the participants who played the complex action puzzle game showed improvements in their Go/NoGo performance following training, such that they had a reduction in their false alarm rate. Similar benefits in inhibitory control have been seen when comparing AVGP and NVGP participants on the Test of Variables of Attention, which is a test commonly used in the clinical diagnosis of ADHD.[23]

Higher-level visual imagery seems to be affected by AVG experience as well. For instance, in a standard mental rotation task, participants are presented with one test item and four probes. One of the probes is an identical copy of the test item that has been rotated. The other three are mirror images of the test item that have been rotated. The participants' task is to determine which of the four probes is the same as the test item. Typically, males perform better than females on this spatial imagery task, and performance on this task is associated with general spatial abilities.[29] However, training on an action video game can not only result in significant improvements in rotation speed/ability, but game training has also been shown to partially reduce the gender disparity on this task (in that females showed greater benefits of the action video game training than did males).[29]

Lastly, there is evidence that video games may help improve problem-solving abilities. Shute et al.[54] trained participants on an interactive puzzle/action game called *Portal 2*, and examined performance on a number of cognitive measures before and after training. They found that participants who received video game training had higher scores on a number of problem-solving measures.

Practical Applications

Although most publications in the academic domain of training and transfer center on the question of whether effects are "statistically significant," practical applications demand that the effects are of a size that allows real-world benefits to be realized. Because the effects of action video games are reasonably large, several groups have attempted to utilize these off-the-shelf games to produce real-world impact. These attempts can be loosely organized into two areas – rehabilitation and job-related training.

Rehabilitation

Interventions for Elderly Adults

As we age, we begin to show decrements in key cognitive abilities such as visuo-spatial attention, speed of processing, multitasking, and memory.[55] These decreases in cognitive functioning can lead to a number of difficulties in everyday functioning leading to a loss of independence, impairments in mood and subjective well-being, and can generally decrease the quality of life in the elderly.[56] Interestingly, recent studies have demonstrated that video game play may aid in preserving, and even enhancing, cognitive function in the elderly.

In a landmark study, Anguera et al.[51] trained older adults (age 60–85) for 12 hours (3 hours a week for 4 weeks) on an action video game that was developed to enhance multitasking abilities (*NeuroRacer*). They found that, as compared to controls (who showed no improvement over the course of the experiment), individuals who trained on the action version of the game performed better on measures of multitasking following training. Interestingly, they also showed improvements in sustained attention and working memory despite not being specifically trained in these abilities. Critically, these training effects persisted for at least 6 months post-training, demonstrating that video game training can result in cognitive enhancements in a variety of domains that endures long after the training has concluded.[51] Related studies have shown that playing a visual speed of processing game resulted in a slowing of age-related decline, and enhancements in both cognitive functioning and subjective well-being[57] (see also Torres[58]). Outside of the specific action genre, more general video game play has also been shown to lead to improvements in self-reported health and quality of life,[59,60] and elderly participants who regularly play video games have been shown to have higher levels of subjective well-being and positive affect, and lower levels of depression, as compared to non-gamers.[61] As such, video game play can have numerous benefits and can help stave off many of the negative effects of normal aging (see Toril et al.[56] for a review).

Amblyopia

Video games have also been shown to have applications toward the treatment of amblyopia. Amblyopia, which is colloquially referred to as "lazy eye," is a vision disorder that affects approximately 1–5 percent of the population.[62] This disorder typically first emerges in childhood, and results in reduced or blurry vision in the affected eye.[63] Amblyopia is associated with a number of developmental visual issues such as congenital cataracts (deprivation amblyopia), misaligned eyes (strabismic amblyopia), or unequal refractive errors in the eyes due to, for example, astigmatism in one eye (anisometropic amblyopia).[63]

In each case, the brain receives inconsistent input from the two eyes and thus, to some extent, comes to "ignore" the eye sending the poor quality information. Conventional treatment involves the use of eye patch therapy, the success of which is dependent on catching the disorder in early childhood.[63] However, recent studies have demonstrated that amblyopia can be at least partially alleviated through the use of video game interventions, even in adults.

Early video game interventions for amblyopia utilized somewhat simple games such as *Pac-Man* in order to both strengthen the weak eye, as well as to engage and entertain children during treatment.[64] The premise of the treatment program was to stimulate and strengthen the amblyopic eye by presenting different images to the two eyes. For instance, in *Pac-Man,* this may involve presenting the image of the Pac-Man and the ghost enemies to one eye, and the image of the maze to the other eye. While traditional eye patch therapy often takes upwards of 400 hours to show improvements,[63] the interactive binocular treatment method resulted in improvements after only 2 hours of treatment for 87 percent of the children tested. Similar results have since been found using the same technique with adults. For example, Li et al.[65] had adults with amblyopia play the puzzle game *Tetris* with either a monocular or binocular display. While both displays resulted in improvements to vision after two weeks of training, the binocular condition resulted in greater improvements. Interestingly, this same group also found that simply playing AVGs with the bad eye (patching the good eye) resulted in significant improvements in vision as compared to the groups who either played no game (controls), or who played a non-action video game. In some cases, the improvements resulted in vision returning to normal levels (including stereoscopic depth perception). As such, playing video games, particularly AVGs, is potentially an efficient and powerful therapy for amblyopia.

Dyslexia

While the idea that AVGs could be used as a rehabilitative platform for a purely visual disorder such as amblyopia may not be overly surprising, recent research suggests that the benefits may extend to other disorders as well. For instance, Franceschini and colleagues[66] showed that having a group of dyslexic children play a commercially available video game, *Rayman Raving Rabbids,* resulted not only in improved visual and visual attentional skills, but actually improved reading abilities as well. While the mechanism underlying this effect is not currently known, the authors suggest that although dyslexia is classically considered to arise as a result of issues in the language system (e.g., issues with phonology or morphology), part of the deficit may also be visual in nature (in that the visual system is the "front end" of the reading system). They thus argue that the types of visual improvements seen as a result of action video game playing should percolate down to improvements in reading.

Job Skills

Laparoscopic Surgeons

There are a number of occupations that involve substantial visuo-spatial demands for which action video games could be a potentially useful training tool. For instance, laparoscopic surgery is a minimally invasive type of surgery wherein both surgical instruments and a small camera are inserted into the patient and the surgeon manipulates the instruments by viewing them on a television screen.[67] This type of surgery presents a number of unique visuo-spatial and visuo-motor challenges, particularly with respect to the ability to extrapolate the 2D television images to the 3D person on which the surgeon is operating.[67] Several studies have now shown a correlation between laparoscopic surgical skills and video game experience[68,69] (see Ou et al.[70] for a review). In fact, in one correlational study, video game experience was found to be a better predictor of positive surgical outcomes than measures one would have a priori predicted would be more pertinent (such as years of training).[69] Furthermore, specific AVG training studies have demonstrated that training on AVGs results in better performance on laparoscopic simulators, indicating that the relationship is indeed causal.[67] Finally, video game skill seems to be predictive of future surgical ability, suggesting that video game scores could be a useful tool for identifying future surgeons.[68]

Pilots

In addition to surgery, video games have also been shown to improve flying skills in novice pilots. In some of the earliest work on this topic, Gopher et al.[71] took a group of flight cadets and trained them on a video game called *Space Fortress*. This group received feedback and helpful tips during their training sessions. A second group played *Space Fortress* with no feedback, and a third group played no video games (control). Participants in the two training groups played for 10 1-hour sessions, and their flight skill performance was assessed before and after training. Both groups who played the video game had better flight performance following training, with the feedback group showing the largest improvements. Additionally, both groups performed better than the controls, demonstrating that performance on an action video game can transfer to actual flying skill. Another recent study showed that experienced AVGPs performed similarly to pilots on a task that required them to land an unmanned aircraft (drone), despite the AVGPs having no prior experience with aircraft or aircraft software.[72] Finally, AVGs have been shown to have enhanced performance on the multi-attribute task battery (MATB), which is a task that measures operator workload and performance in airline pilots.[52] Together, these findings demonstrate the utility of video games in educational environments, and show that the skills that are developed when training in the complex, fast-paced environment of AVGs may transfer to many other professions, and have numerous real-world applications from training to personnel selection.

Which Processes Do Action Video Games Not Influence?

It is apparent that playing video games, particularly AVGs, influences and enhances a number of cognitive processes from a variety of domains, and that existing action gamers differ in their cognitive abilities as compared to non-gamers. However, not all abilities appear to be equally changed via AVG experience. One domain in particular that one might have expected to be strongly influenced by AVG experience is exogenous attentional orienting. Important information in AVGs often appears briefly in the periphery, requiring an extremely fast orienting response. Thus, it would seem to follow that exogenous orienting should be associated with AVG experience. However, the literature on the effect of AVG experience on exogenous attentional orienting is decidedly mixed. Castel et al.[34] demonstrated that existing AVGPs were faster to respond to targets on a classic Posner spatial cueing paradigm as compared to NVGPs, but both groups showed a similar inhibition of return (IOR) effect. The same basic result was also observed by Hubert-Wallander and colleagues,[73] as well as Dye and colleagues who observed no strong changes in either the orienting or alerting networks using the Attentional Network Task.[23]

However, other studies have suggested that AVGPs *do* perform differently than NVGPs on tasks that involve exogenous orienting. For example, West et al.[74] had AVGPs and NVGPs complete an exogenous orienting task in which irrelevant exogenous cues were presented, and the sensitivity of attentional orienting to these cues was assessed. Interestingly, they found that AVGPs were more sensitive to the irrelevant exogenous cue, indicating that their attention was more easily captured by exogenous stimuli as compared to NVGPs. Conversely, a recent study used an anti-cueing task in which AVGPs and NVGPs were presented with a cue that appeared at the opposite location to a target.[75] The critical measure was the eventual reaction time to the target. Interestingly, the AVGPs were faster on the task, indicating that they were *less* captured by the cue, suggesting that they had better control over exogenous attention.[75] Two other studies showed similar results, such that AVGPs were better at overcoming distraction and capture by an irrelevant exogenous cue,[76] and showed fewer saccades to irrelevant stimuli with a sudden onset,[77] as compared to NVGPs. Together, these results indicate that playing AVGs may be associated with differences in exogenous orienting, although it is unclear whether gamers are more or less sensitive to exogenous cues (or whether the mixed results are due to some studies actually tapping substantial top-down processing demands, which are known to be enhanced via video game training, rather than bottom-up exogenous orienting alone).

What Makes Action Video Games a Potent Training Tool?

Video games, particularly AVGs, have a clear influence on a variety of cognitive processes, and have been shown to have numerous implications for practical, real-world training and rehabilitation practices. Unlike many cognitive interventions, video games appear to have unique properties that allow them to induce general transfer across a wide variety of cognitive abilities. What is it about video games, and AVGs in particular, that makes them such an effective training tool? Many video games, of course, are complex and simultaneously tax a number of cognitive abilities, which likely leads to many of the training effects that we see. However, there are a number of other unique factors that may contribute to their utility as a training program. This section will briefly touch upon some of these factors (see Bavelier et al.[78] for a more in-depth review).

First, unlike many cognitive training programs or laboratory tasks which tend to be dull and tedious, video games are fun, engaging, and rewarding.[79] Indeed, there is numerous evidence to demonstrate that reward circuits in the brain are stimulated, and striatal dopamine released, during video game play,[80] and that this stimulation is the direct result of task engagement.[81] Interestingly, these neural responses are stronger when playing another human being, rather than playing against the computer,[82,83] suggesting that games containing a strong social component (i.e., most action games) are more rewarding than solitary games (i.e., most puzzle games). Activities that are more engaging and rewarding have long been shown to lead to better learning,[84,85] thus it follows that AVGs should result in more learning and transfer than more sterile and less engaging laboratory tasks.

Second, video games are dynamic, with constantly changing landscapes, puzzles, challenges, and goals. Difficulty on these games gradually increases in most cases, but also tends to fluctuate such that some missions/matches/competitions are easier than others. Interestingly, this variety in practice has been shown to increase the probability that a skill will transfer to a new task.[86–88] In addition, because of the complexity and rich storyline of action games, people have a tendency to play the game steadily over the course of several weeks or months (i.e., utilize distributed practice). Several studies have demonstrated that distributed practice, in which trials are divided over several days or hours, leads to better learning and transfer.[89–91] As such, the very nature of action games may lead to practice behaviors that are particularly conducive to learning and transfer.

Third, it has recently been suggested that video game play may lead to many of the benefits we see because individuals engage in "learning to learn" (see Bavelier et al.[78] for a review). The basic idea of learning to learn is that individuals develop a set of dynamic tools and rules that they can then apply to a variety of scenarios or tasks in order to learn faster.[92,93] Bavelier et al.[78]

suggest that when individuals play AVGs, they learn a number of general strategies, probabilistic rules, and models that can then be applied to a variety of different tasks, so long as those tasks share some overlap with AVGs. Generally, because video games are more complex, engaging, and demanding than many training paradigms, they seem to lead to more generalized benefits.

Toward The Future

The finding that video games, particularly AVGs, influence cognition is fairly well substantiated, but more research is needed to understand the precise mechanisms by which video game play affects cognitive change, and to better understand why some cognitive abilities are influenced while others are not. One area in particular that has been largely underrepresented is the study of game genres other than the action genre, such as real-time strategy games (RTS; e.g., *StarCraft II* or *League of Legends*), role-playing games (RPG; e.g., *World of Warcraft* or *Final Fantasy*), and turn-based strategy games (TBS; e.g., *Hearthstone* or *Pokémon*). Indeed, many studies only classify action/first-person shooters as VGPs, and will (perhaps erroneously) classify both non-gamers and gamers of these other genres as NVGPs. However, there is emerging evidence that genres other than action games can influence cognitive performance.

For example, Glass et al.[94] showed that NVGPs who were trained on the RTS game *StarCraft II* performed better on a global measure of cognitive flexibility after training as compared to controls who trained on the simulation game *The Sims*. Similarly, older adults who trained for 23.5 hours on the RTS game *Rise of Nations* showed significantly greater improvements as compared to controls on measures of working memory, task switching, VSTM, and mental rotation.[95] This demonstrates that RTS games may have a similar impact on cognitive performance as action video games.

A study by Wu and Spence[33] provided participants with 10 hours of training on either a first-person shooter game (*Medal of Honor: Pacific Assault*), a driving game (*Need for Speed: Most Wanted*), or a 3-D puzzle game (*Ballance*), and examined performance before and after training on a visual search task. Both the first-person shooter and driving groups showed significantly improved scores on the visual search task following training, but did not differ from each other. The puzzle group did not show any improvements, however, thus demonstrating that a game must be fast-paced in order to lead to improvements.

Finally, Oei and Patterson[96] trained participants for 20 hours on one of five different mini-games (action, spatial memory, matching, hidden object, and a life simulation game). Performance on a battery of cognitive tasks was measured before and after training, and while they found that the group who played the action game improved their scores on measures of cognitive control and verbal span, the other four groups also showed improvements in visual search and working memory. Taken together, these findings suggest that it is essential that the field move away from a purely genre-based classification scheme (e.g., where first-person shooter games and RTS games are placed in different categories) and toward a classification scheme that takes into account the perceptual and cognitive demands of the games.

Conclusion

To summarize, playing video games, particularly AVGs, has been shown to benefit performance on a variety of cognitive tasks and paradigms. After only a few hours of playing commercially available video games, individuals have shown global improvements in perception, attention, memory, and executive functioning, and existing gamers have been shown to possess superior cognitive abilities as compared to non-gamers. These findings have numerous real-world applications, from rehabilitation to job-related training. While not all cognitive abilities are similarly affected, there is enough evidence of cognitive enhancement to encourage the development and use of video games both for fun, and for increased cognitive well-being.

References

1. Fiorentini A, Berardi N. Perceptual learning specific for orientation and spatial frequency. *Nature.* 1980; 287: 43–44. doi: 10.1038/287043a0
2. Fahle M. Perceptual learning: A case for early selection. *J Vis.* 2004; 4(10): 879–890. doi:10:1167/4.10.4
3. Fahle M. Perceptual learning: Specificity versus generalization. *Curr Opin Neurobiol.* 2005; 15(2): 154–160. doi:10.1016/j.conb.2005.03.010
4. Melby-Lervåg M, Hulme C. Is working memory training effective? A meta-analytic review. *Dev Psychol.* 2013; 49(2): 270–291. doi:10.1037/a0028228
5. Owen AM, Hampshire A, Grahn J, et al. Putting brain training to the test. *Nature.* 2010; 465(7299): 775–778. doi:10.1038/nature09042
6. Redick TS, Shipstead Z, Harrison TL, et al. No evidence of intelligence improvement after working memory training: A randomized, placebo-controlled study. *J Exp Psychol Gen.* 2013; 142(2): 359–379. doi:10.1037/a0029082
7. Shipstead Z, Redick TS, Engle RW. Is working memory training effective? *Psychol Bull.* 2012; 138(4): 628–654. doi:10.1037/a0027473
8. Abernethy B, Neal RJ. Visual characteristics of clay target shooters. *J Sci Med Sport.* 1999; 2: 1–19.
9. Kida N, Oda S, Matsumura M. Intensive baseball practice improves the Go/Nogo reaction time, but not the simple reaction time. *Brain Res Cogn Brain Res.* 2005; 22(2): 257–264. doi:10.1016/j.cogbrainres.2004.09.003
10. Overney LS, Blanke O, Herzog MH. Enhanced temporal but not attentional processing in expert tennis players. *PLoS One.* 2008; 3(6): e2380. doi:10.1371/journal.pone.0002380
11. Griffith JL, Voloschin P, Gibb GD, Bailey JR. Differences in eye-hand motor coordination of video-game users and non-users. *Percept Motor Skills.* 1983; 57(1): 155–158. doi: 10.2466/pms.1983.57.1.155
12. Gagnon D. Videogames and spatial skills: An exploratory study. *ECTJ.* 1985; 33(4): 263–275. doi: 10.1007/BF02769363

13. Dorval M, Pepin M. Effect of playing a video game on a measure of spatial visualization. *Percept Motor Skills.* 1986; 62(1): 159–16 2466/pms.1986.62.1.159

14. Subrahmanyam K, Greenfield PM. Effect of video game practice on spatial skills in girls and boys. *J Appl Dev Psychol.* 1994; 13–32. doi: 10.1016/0193-3973(94)90004-3

15. Greenfield PM, deWinstanley P, Kilpatrick H, Kaye D. Action video games and informal education: Effects on strategies for dividing visual attention. *J Appl Dev Psychol.* 1994; 15: 105–123. doi: 10.1016/0193-3973(94)90008-6

16. Okagaki L, Frensch P. Effects of video game playing on measures of spatial performance: Gender effects in late adolescence. *J Appl Dev Psychol.* 1994; 15(1): 33–58. doi:10.1016/0193-3973(94)90005-1

17. Greenfield PM, Brannon C, Lohr D. Two-dimensional representation of movement through three-dimensional space: The role of video game expertise. *J Appl Dev Psychol.* 1994; 15: 87–103. doi: 10.1016/0193-3973(94)90007-8

18. Green CS, Bavelier D. Action video game modifies visual selective attention. *Nature.* 2003; 423(6939): 534–537. doi:10.1038/nature01647

19. Spence I, Feng J. Video games and spatial cognition. *Rev Gen Psychol.* 2010; 14(2): 92–104. doi:10.1037/a0019491

20. Li RJ, Polat U, Scalzo F, Bavelier D. Reducing backward masking through action game training. *J Vision.* 2010; 10(14): 1–13. doi: 10.1167/10.14.33

21. Buckley D, Codina C, Bhardwaj P, Pascalis O. Action video game players and deaf observers have larger Goldmann visual fields. *Vision Res.* 2010; 50(5): 548–556. doi:10.1016/j.visres.2009.11.018

22. Hutchinson CV, Stocks R. Selectively enhanced motion perception in core video gamers. *Perception.* 2013; 42(6): 675–677. doi:10.1068/p7411

23. Dye MWG, Green CS, Bavelier D. The development of attention skills in action video game players. *Neuropsychologia.* 2009; 47(8–9): 1780–1789. doi:10.1016/j.neuropsychologia.2009.02.002

24. Donohue SE, Woldorff MG, Mitroff SR. Video game players show more precise multisensory temporal processing abilities. *Atten Percept Psychophys.* 2010; 72(4): 1120–1129. doi: 10.3758/APP.72.4.1120

25. Green CS, Pouget A, Bavelier D. Improved probabilistic inference as a general learning mechanism with action video games. *Curr Biol.* 2010; 20(17): 1573–1579. doi:10.1016/j.cub.2010.07.040

26. Bejjanki VR, Zhang R, Li R, et al. Action video game play facilitates the development of better perceptual templates. *Proc Natl Acad Sci.* 2014. doi:10.1073/pnas.1417056111

27. Green CS, Bavelier D. Enumeration versus multiple object tracking: The case of action video game players. *Cognition.* 2006; 101(1): 217–245. doi:10.1016/j.cognition.2005.10.004

28. Dye MWG, Bavelier D. Differential development of visual attention skills in school-age children. *Vision Res.* 2010; 50(4): 452–459. doi:10.1016/j.visres.2009.10.010

29. Feng J, Spence I, Pratt J. Playing an action video game reduces gender differences in spatial cognition. *Psychol Sci.* 2007; 18(10): 850–855. doi:10.1111/j.1467-9280.2007.01990.x

30. Wu S, Cheng CK, Feng J, D'Angelo L, Alain C, Spence I. Playing a first-person shooter video game induces neuroplastic change. *J Cogn Neurosci.* 2012; 24(6): 1286–1293. doi:10.1162/jocn_a_00192

31. Green CS, Bavelier D. Action-video-game experience alters the spatial resolution of vision. *Psychol Sci.* 2007; 18(1): 88–94. doi:10.1111/j.1467-9280.2007.01853.x

32. Hubert-Wallander B, Green CS, Bavelier D. Stretching the limits of visual attention: The case of action video games. *Wiley Interdiscip Rev Cogn Sci.* 2011; 2(2): 222–230. doi:10.1002/wcs.116

33. Wu S, Spence I. Playing shooter and driving videogames improves top-down guidance in visual search. *Atten Percept Psychophys.* 2013; 75(4): 673–686. doi:10.3758/s13414-013-0440-2

34. Castel AD, Pratt J, Drummond E. The effects of action video game experience on the time course of inhibition of return and the efficiency of visual search. *Acta Psychol.* 2005; 119(2): 217–230. doi:10.1016/j.actpsy.2005.02.004

35. Raymond JE, Shapiro KL, Arnell KM. Temporary suppression of visual processing in an RSVP task: An attentional blink?. *J Exp Psychol Hum Percept Perform.* 1992; 18(3): 849–860. doi: 10.1037/0096-1523.18.3.849d

36. Mishra J, Zinni M, Bavelier D, Hillyard SA. Neural basis of superior performance of action videogame players in an attention-demanding task. *J Neurosci.* 2011; 31(3): 992–998. doi:10.1523/JNEUROSCI.4834-10.2011

37. Pohl C, Kunde W, Ganz T, Conzelmann A, Pauli P, Kiesel A. Gaming to see: Action video gaming is associated with enhanced processing of masked stimuli. *Front Psychol.* 2014; 5: 70. doi:10.3389/fpsyg.2014.00070

38. Trick LM, Jaspers-Fayer F, Sethi N. Multiple-object tracking in children: The "Catch the Spies" task. *Cogn Dev.* 2005; 20(3): 373–387. doi:10.1016/j.cogdev.2005.05.009

39. Boot WR, Kramer AF, Simons DJ, Fabiani M, Gratton G. The effects of video game playing on attention, memory, and executive control. *Acta Psychol.* 2008; 129(3): 387–398. doi:10.1016/j.actpsy.2008.09.005

40. Luck SJ, Vogel EK. The capacity of visual working memory for features and conjunctions. *Nature.* 1997; 390(6657): 279–281. doi: 10.1038/36846

41. McDermott AF, Bavelier D, Green CS. Memory abilities in action video game players. *Comput Human Behav.* 2014; 34: 69–78. doi:10.1016/j.chb.2014.01.018

42. Appelbaum LG, Cain MS, Darling EF, Mitroff SR. Action video game playing is associated with improved visual sensitivity, but not alterations in visual sensory memory. *Atten Percept Psychophys.* 2013; 75(6): 1161–1167. doi:10.3758/s13414-013-0472-7

43. Cain MS, Landau AN, Shimamura AP. Action video game experience reduces the cost of switching tasks. *Atten Percept Psychophys.* 2012; 74(4): 641–647. doi:10.3758/s13414-012-0284-1

44. Colzato LS, van den Wildenberg WPM, Zmigrod S, Hommel B. Action video gaming and cognitive control: Playing first person shooter games is associated with improvement in working memory but not action inhibition. *Psychol Res.* 2013; 77(2): 234–239. doi:10.1007/s00426-012-0415-2

45. Colzato LS, van Leeuwen PJ, van den Wildenberg WPM, Hommel B. DOOM'd to switch: Superior cognitive flexibility in players of first person shooter games. *Front Psychol.* 2010; 1: 8. doi:10.3389/fpsyg.2010.00008

46. Green CS, Sugarman M, Medford K, Klobusicky E, Bavelier D. The effect of action video game experience on task-switching. *Comput Human Behav.* 2012; 28(3): 984–994. doi:10.1016/j.chb.2011.12.020

47. Karle JW, Watter S, Shedden JM. Task switching in video game players: Benefits of selective attention but not resistance to proactive interference. *Acta Psychol.* 2010; 134(1): 70–78. doi:10.1016/j.actpsy.2009.12.007

48. Oei AC, Patterson MD. Playing a puzzle video game with changing requirements improves executive functions. *Comput Human Behav.* 2014; 37: 216–228. doi:10.1016/j.chb.2014.04.046

49. Strobach T, Frensch P, Schubert T. Video game practice optimizes executive control skills in dual-task and task switching situations. *Acta Psychol.* 2012; 140(1): 13–24. doi:10.1016/j.actpsy.2012.02.001

50. Colzato LS, van den Wildenberg WPM, Hommel B. Cognitive control and the COMT Val(158)Met polymorphism: Genetic modulation of videogame training and transfer to task-switching efficiency. *Psychol Res.* 2013. doi:10.1007/s00426-013-0514-8

51. Anguera J, Boccanfuso J, Rintoul JL, et al. Video game training enhances cognitive control in older adults. *Nature*. 2013; 501(7465): 97–101. doi:10.1038/nature12486

52. Chiappe D, Conger M, Liao J, Caldwell JL, Vu K-PL. Improving multi-tasking ability through action videogames. *Appl Ergon*. 2013; 44(2): 278–284. doi:10.1016/j.apergo.2012.08.002

53. Donohue SE, James B, Eslick AN, Mitroff SR. Cognitive pitfall! Videogame players are not immune to dual-task costs. *Atten Percept Psychophys*. 2012; 74(5): 803–809. doi:10.3758/s13414-012-0323-y

54. Shute V, Ventura M, Ke F. The power of play: The effects of Portal 2 and Lumosity on cognitive and noncognitive skills. *Comput Educ*. 2014; 80: 58–67. doi:10.1016/j.compedu.2014.08.013

55. Van Hooren SH, Valentijn AM, Bosma H, Ponds RWHM, van Boxtel MPJ, Jolles J. Cognitive functioning in healthy older adults aged 64–81: A cohort study into the effects of age, sex, and education. *Neuropsychol Dev Cogn B Aging Neuropsychol Cogn*. 2007; 14(1): 40–54. doi:10.1080/13825580096948 3

56. Toril P, Reales JM, Ballesteros S. Video game training enhances cognition of older adults: A meta-analytic study. *Psychol Aging*. 2014; 29(3): 706–716. doi: 10.1037/a0037507

57. Wolinsky FD, Vander Weg MW, Howren MB, Jones MP, Dotson MM. A randomized controlled trial of cognitive training using a visual speed of processing intervention in middle aged and older adults. *PLoS One*. 2013; 8(5): e61624. doi:10.1371/journal.pone.0061624

58. Torres A. Cognitive effects of video games on old people. *Int J Dis Hum Dev*. 2011; 10(1): 55–58. doi: 10.1515/ijdhd.2011.003

59. Jobe JB, Smith DM, Ball K, et al. ACTIVE: A cognitive intervention trial to promote independence in older adults. *Control Clin Trials*. 2001; 22(4): 453–479. doi: 10.1016/S0197-2456(01)00139-8

60. Wolinsky FD, Mahncke H, Vander Weg MW, et al. Speed of processing training protects self-rated health in older adults: Enduring effects observed in the multi-site ACTIVE randomized controlled trial. *Int Psychogeriatr*. 2010; 22(3): 470–478. doi: 10.1017/S1041610209991281

61. Allaire JC, McLaughlin AC, Trujillo A, Whitlock L, LaPorte L, Gandy M. Successful aging through digital games: Socioemotional differences between older adult gamers and non-gamers. *Comput Human Behav*. 2013; 29(4): 1302–1306. doi:10.1016/j.chb.2013.01.014

62. Hillis A. Amblyopia: Prevalent, curable, neglected. *Public Health Rev*.1985; 14(3–4): 213–235.

63. Waddingham PE, Cobb SV, Eastgate RM, Gregson RM. Virtual reality for interactive binocular treatment of amblyopia. *Int J Disabil Hum Dev*. 2006; 5(2): 155–162. doi:10.1515/IJDHD.2006.5.2.155

64. Eastgate RM, Griffiths GD, Waddingham PE, et al. Modified virtual reality technology for treatment of amblyopia. *Eye (Lond)*. 2006; 20(3): 370–374. doi:10.1038/sj.eye.6701882

65. Li J, Thompson B, Deng D, Chan LYL, Yu M, Hess RF. Dichoptic training enables the adult amblyopic brain to learn. *Curr Biol*. 2013; 23(8): R308–R309. doi:10.1016/j.cub.2013.01.059

66. Franceschini S, Gori S, Ruffino M, Viola S, Molteni M, Facoetti A. Action video games make dyslexic children read better. *Curr Biol*. 2013; 23(6): 462–466. doi:10.1016/j.cub.2013.01.044

67. Schlickum MK, Hedman L, Enochsson L, Kjellin A, Felländer-Tsai L. Systematic video game training in surgical novices improves performance in virtual reality endoscopic surgical simulators: A prospective randomized study. *World J Surg*. 2009; 33(11): 2360–2367. doi:10.1007/s00268-009-0151-y

68. Kennedy AM, Boyle EM, Traynor O, Walsh T, Hill ADK. Video gaming enhances psychomotor skills but not visuospatial and perceptual abilities in surgical trainees. *J Surg Educ.* 2011; 68(5): 414–420. doi:10.1016/j.jsurg.2011.03.009

69. Rosser J, Lynch P, Cuddihy L, Gentile D, Klonsky J, Merrell R. The impact of video games on training surgeons in the 21st century. *Arch Surgery.* 2007; 142: 181–186. doi: 10.1001/archsurg.142.2.181

70. Ou Y, McGlone ER, Camm CF, Khan O. Does playing video games improve laparoscopic skills? *Int J Surg.* 2013; 11(5): 365–369. doi:10.1016/j.ijsu.2013.02.020

71. Gopher D, Weil M, Bareket T. Transfer of skill from a computer game trainer to flight. *Hum Factors.* 1994; 36(3): 387–405. doi: 10.1177/001872089403600301

72. McKinley RA, McIntire LK, Funke M. Operator selection for unmanned aerial systems: comparing video game players and pilots. *Aviat Space Environ Med.* 2011; 82(6): 635–642. doi:10.3357/ASEM.2958.2011

73. Hubert-Wallander B, Green CS, Sugarman M, Bavelier D. Changes in search rate but not in the dynamics of exogenous attention in action videogame players. *Atten Percept Psychophys.* 2011; 73(8): 2399–2412. doi:10.3758/s13414-011-0194-7

74. West GL, Stevens SA, Pun C, Pratt J. Visuospatial experience modulates attentional capture: Evidence from action video game players. *J Vis.* 2008; 8(16): 1–9. doi: 10.1167/8.16.13

75. Cain MS, Prinzmetal W, Shimamura AP, Landau AN. Improved control of exogenous attention in action video game players. *Front Psychol.* 2014; 5(February): 69. doi: 10.3389/fpsyg.2014.00069

76. Chisholm JD, Hickey C, Theeuwes J, Kingstone A. Reduced attentional capture in action video game players. *Atten Percept Psychophys.* 2010; 72(3): 667–671. doi:10.3758/ APP

77. Chisholm JD, Kingstone A. Improved top-down control reduces oculomotor capture: the case of action video game players. *Atten Percept Psychophys.* 2012; 74(2): 257–262. doi:10.3758/s13414-011-0253-0

78. Bavelier D, Green CS, Pouget A, Schrater P. Brain plasticity through the life span: Learning to learn and action video games. *Annu Rev Neurosci.* 2012; 35: 391–416. doi: 10.1146/annurev-neuro-060909-152832

79. Przybylski AK, Rigby CS, Ryan RM. A motivational model of video game engagement. *Rev Gen Psychol.* 2010; 14(2): 154–166. doi:10.1037/a0019440

80. Koepp MJ, Gunn RN, Lawrence D, et al. Evidence for striatal dopamine release during a video game. *Nature.* 1998; 393(6682): 266–268. doi:10.1038/30498

81. Cole SW, Yoo DJ, Knutson B. Interactivity and reward-related neural activation during a serious videogame. *PLoS One.* 2012; 7(3): e33909. doi:10.1371/journal. pone.0033909

82. Kätsyri J, Hari R, Ravaja N, Nummenmaa L. Just watching the game ain't enough: Striatal fMRI reward responses to successes and failures in a video game during active and vicarious playing. *Front Hum Neurosci.* 2013; 7(June): 278. doi:10.3389/ fnhum.2013.00278

83. Kätsyri J, Hari R, Ravaja N, Nummenmaa L. The opponent matters: Elevated FMRI reward responses to winning against a human versus a computer opponent during interactive video game playing. *Cereb Cortex.* 2013; 23(12): 2829–2839. doi:10.1093/ cercor/bhs259

84. Greenwood C, Horton B, Utley C. Academic engagement: Current perspectives on research and practice. *School Psychol Rev.* 2002; 31: 328–349.

85. Bao S, Chan VT, Merzenich MM. Cortical remodelling induced by activity of ventral tegmental dopamine neurons. *Nature.* 2001; 412(July): 79–83.

86. Catalano JF, Kleiner BM. Distant transfer in coincident timing as a function of variability of practice. *Percept Motor Skills.*1984; 58(3): 851–856. doi:10.2466/ pms.1984.58.3.851

87. Fulvio JM, Green CS, Schrater PR. Task-specific response strategy selection on the basis of recent training experience. *PLoS Comput Biol.* 2014; 10(1): e1003425. doi:10.1371/journal.pcbi.1003425

88. Schmidt R, Bjork R. New conceptualizations of practice: Common principles in three paradigms suggest new concepts for training. *Psychol Sci.* 1992; 3(4): 207–217. doi:10.1111/j.1467-9280.1992.tb00029.x

89. Cepeda NJ, Pashler H, Vul E, Wixted JT, Rohrer D. Distributed practice in verbal recall tasks: A review and quantitative synthesis. *Psychol Bull.* 2006; 132(3): 354–380. doi:10.1037/0033-2909.132.3.354

90. Gentile D, Gentile JR. Violent video games as exemplary teachers: A conceptual analysis. *J Youth Adolesc.* 2007; 37(2): 127–141. doi:10.1007/s10964-007-9206-2

91. Baddeley AD, Longman DJA. The influence of length and frequency of training sessions on the rate of learning to type. *Ergonomics.* 1978; 21(8): 627–635.

92. Kemp C, Goodman ND, Tenenbaum JB. Learning to learn causal models. *Cogn Sci.* 2010; 34(7): 1185–1243. doi:10.1111/j.1551-6709.2010.01128.x

93. Perfors AF, Tenenbaum JB. Learning to learn categories. *Proceedings of the 42nd Annual Conference of the Cognitive Science Society.* 2009; 136–141.

94. Glass BD, Maddox WT, Love BC. Real-time strategy game training: Emergence of a cognitive flexibility trait. *PLoS One.* 2013; 8(8): e70350. doi:10.1371/journal.pone.0070350

95. Basak C, Boot WR, Voss MW, Kramer AF. Can training in a real-time strategy video game attenuate cognitive decline in older adults? *Psychol Aging.* 2008; 23(4): 765–777. doi:10.1037/a0013494

96. Oei AC, Patterson MD. Enhancing cognition with video games: A multiple game training study. *PLoS One.* 2013; 8(3): e58546. doi:10.1371/journal.pone.0058546

9

EXPLORING GAMING COMMUNITIES

Frans Mäyrä

It is obvious that digital games and game playing in general carry various meanings in the lives of many millions of people. For some, games are at the periphery of their lives, perhaps just providing momentary escape from daily routines. For others, games can provide a focus on intense interests, with regular investments of time and energy. As such interests become shared, they enter the social sphere, possibly leading to the formation of human relationships that are motivated or catalyzed by gaming activities or interests.

This chapter has its focus on the social networks and communities of digital game players. The concept of community is discussed, and its specific relations to games elaborated: are games capable of supporting true communities, or should we address the social dimensions of gaming and people with games-related interests in different terms? A second issue this chapter explores are the consequences of such gaming communities or social formations: how does the organization of gaming communities affect game playing (game-internal consequences), or has it possibly some consequences to the lives of game players, outside of the gaming reality?

Particular emphasis in this chapter is placed on the potential for gaming networks (offline and online) to promote communication, social networking and peer support. In order to provide the necessary background, important community, and network studies will be linked to both classic and more recent work in social gaming research. The evolving social phenomena of digital gaming will be highlighted through the dual perspectives opened up by general community studies on the other hand, and by the specific studies of game playing and gaming communities.

Communities, or 'social capital' have been associated with both physical health and subjective well-being.[1] In this chapter the complex character of gaming communities will be introduced and interpreted, on the basis of existing research. It is important to note that in the games industry and new media business, it is common to see communities being discussed as something that is produced, and even sold. This kind of perspective that is focused on the commercial design of "community as a service" mostly falls outside of the scope of this chapter. Here, the perspective is primarily on communities as performance, or as social facts. Gaming communities are seen as something that game players do, and their belonging to a community is dependent on their choices and actions, and also defined by the associated sense of belonging to a community. In the public debate surrounding communities there are often conflicting views between what are considered genuine or true communities, and non-genuine or artificial or insubstantial ones. This is a long-standing argument, which is also affecting how gaming communities are discussed and perceived. On the one side is the classic perception of community as something that is fundamental to all human life, and "true community" as something that is essential and highly beneficial to all human sociability. Against such background, the "interest communities" such as gaming communities emerge as novel, borderline phenomena – or as non-essential, optional forms of sociability, not worthy of the name 'community.'

This chapter will aim to respond to key questions such as: are contemporary online or virtual communities similar to offline social communities? How does sociability relate to play and games? How should the nature and character of gaming communities be described, and what are the possible benefits that game players gain from them?

Defining "Community"

"Community" is one of the key concepts in sociology and in human sciences in general. It is also a contested concept, and one that will invariably lead the researchers also to political debates about the standards of the "good life," or about what constitutes an "ideal society," or into discussions about what is wrong with contemporary societal developments. As video games are a similarly contested phenomenon, the discussion of 'gaming communities' emerges as a topic ridden by tensions into several dimensions.

The debates about the character of community and society and their developments can be traced far into history. In antiquity, poets like Hesiod and Virgil wrote about the Golden Age, the age of abundance, which was the mythic era dominated by primitive community and communism – the fruits of nature were all peacefully shared among the people and private property was unknown.[2(p42)] The ancient conceptions of original community were also tightly linked with the idea of degeneration: in Hesiod's version, the Golden Age was followed first by the Silver Age, then by the Bronze Age, each one worse than the previous one. Approaching contemporary reality of social life also meant that the conflicts and ills of society appeared in closer focus.

The classic conceptions of community are thus built upon a distinctive foundation of romantic nostalgia for the past time of happiness, and pessimism about the direction of social development.

In modern scholarship, the German sociologist and philosopher Ferdinand Tönnies is generally credited as introducing the concept of 'community' (*Gemeinschaft*), by differentiating it from 'society' (*Gesellschaft*). In his classic work, Tönnies writes:

> All intimate, private and exclusive living together, so we discover, is understood as life in Gemeinschaft (community). Gesellschaft (society) is public life – it is the world itself. In Gemeinschaft with one's family, one lives from birth on, bound to it in weal and woe. One goes to Gesellschaft as one goes into a strange country. A young man is warned against bad Gesellschaft, but the expression bad Gemeinschaft violates the meaning of the word.[3]

From a contemporary perspective, the main contribution of Tönnies was the analytical emphasis and perspective he opened into the ongoing societal changes: in the nineteenth century, the traditional, "organic" ways of people connecting with each other were being reframed and reorganized in modernization processes that involved urbanization, industrialization, and increasing mobility in many areas of life. Tönnies wrote about "natural will" (*Wesenwille*) as the force that bounds people together in a community, whereas the society is more "artificially" based on laws and contracts of various kinds. In another classic of sociology, Emile Durkheim turned the tables, and argued that it is actually the modern society where more "organic," voluntary, and flexible solidarity is possible between individuals, whereas traditional villages and other small groups of people partake in "mechanical" solidarity, where everyone is tightly bound to do the same things.[4(pp126–131)] The increases in the heterogeneity and in the degree of individual freedom that characterizes modern societies had, however also its downsides, as pointed out by Durkheim's study on suicide. While individuals may suffer in traditional communities from excessive pressure to conform, in the modern society it "is everlastingly repeated that it is man's nature to be eternally dissatisfied, constantly to advance, without relief or rest, towards an indefinite goal."[5(p257)] Durkheim analyzed available statistical data and suggested that it is particularly those who are economically and intellectually free to express their individual desires who are in danger of suicide out of anomie, feelings of emptiness. The individual freedom available in modern society can thus also translate into the lack of community feeling, and feelings of loneliness.

While community has remained a key concept in research for more than a century, there is little agreement on what the defining characteristics of communities are, or on what communities are at their heart. Already by the mid-1950s, George Hillery[6] had quoted 94 different definitions for 'community.' Steven Brint[7(pp3–4)] has provided a useful summary of the community concept theorization, and suggested that there are six key criteria for tight "Gemeinschaft style" communities that emerge from research in this area; such social formations have: (1) dense and demanding social ties, (2) social attachments to and involvement in institutions, (3) ritual occasions, and (4) small group size. Additionally, they are characterized by (5) perceptions of similarity (e.g. in physical characteristics, expressive style, way of life, on in historical experience with others), and (6) by common beliefs in an idea system, moral order, institution, or a group.

Looking at this list, it is immediately clear that most contemporary gaming communities – social gatherings or groupings of varyingly obligating or non-obligating character – do not fill all such tight criteria for 'community.' It actually appears that many important contemporary social aggregates fail to meet all these criteria, raising the question whether "true communities" are in decline, or whether it should be better to revise our definitions of community to fit with the changing social realities. Brint considers that the community concept needs to be applied in a more flexible manner to meet the core, relevant social phenomena. He decides first to divide the existential basis of relationship ties into two main groups, geographic and choice-based. These are then further divided on the primary reason for interaction (activity-based or belief-based), and these are then further split on the basis of how frequent the interaction between members is, or whether the interaction is primarily face-to-face or mediated by character. Such an approach has the benefit of rejecting the monolithic Gemeinschaft community concept Tönnies introduced, and helping to identify the several distinctive forms that community is capable of taking. Brint's analysis identifies eight such general subtypes of communities, providing a useful starting point for further research and discussion: (1) communities of place, (2) communes and collectives, (3) localized friendship networks, (4) dispersed friendship networks, (5) activity-based elective communities, (6) belief-based elective communities, (7) imagined communities, and (8) virtual communities.[7(pp10–11)] There is no reason why games or game playing could not be relevant elements in any or all of these community subtypes.

From Social Play to Culturally Constructed Gaming Communities

The existing research suggests that various forms of play are ancient, and inseparably related to social interactions and significances. The studies of animal play point out that there is plenty of evidence of both locomotor and object play, as well as of social play behaviors among mammals, reptiles, as well as many other animals.[8] Since social play requires complex interplays of communication, interpretations of intention, role-playing, and cooperation, many researchers have suggested that the evolutionary and adaptive or learning benefits of social play explain its popularity.[9(p98)] Many mammals who engage in social play use specific signals to convey their playful intention, thereby engaging in what Gregory Bateson[10] has called metacommunication. The levels of cooperation in advanced social play go beyond simple evolutionary arguments, however, and require more comprehensive appreciation of how consciousness, intentionality, representation and communication relate to each other.[9(p109)] As humans engage with social game play, such activities are also culturally mediated and contextualized.

The Dutch cultural historian Johan Huizinga was perhaps the most important nineteenth-century scholar to argue for a cultural interpretation of games and play. In his *Homo Ludens* he also explicitly linked play with formation of communities:

> Summing up the formal characteristic of play, we might call it a free activity standing quite consciously outside 'ordinary' life as being 'not serious' but at the same time absorbing the player intensely and utterly. It is an activity connected with no material interest, and no profit can be gained by it. It proceeds within its own proper boundaries of time and space according to fixed rules and in an orderly manner. It promotes the formation of social groupings that tend to surround themselves with secrecy and to stress the difference from the common world by disguise or other means.[11(p13)]

Huizinga aimed to identify the nature and significance of play as a cultural phenomenon, and consequently emphasized the role of examples, which clearly differentiate play and games from everyday life. Like "magic circle," another important boundary concept for Huizinga's project, the secret "social groupings" that he discusses contribute to the establishment of play-world as somehow separate and distinctive from common life. There are particular temporal, spatial, and social conditions that make play phenomena stand out most clearly and it is those Huizinga is most interested in. In case of game play communities, Huizinga first discusses the challenges presented by the "cheat" and the "spoil-sport," who present different threats to play. While the cheater pretends to play the game, Huizinga argues, it is the spoil-sport who "threatens the existence of the play-community." As a spoil-sport does not respect the rules and the illusion of the play-world, he must be cast out, if the magic world of play is intended to continue to exist. The socially constructed character of game play is in Huizinga's view intimately linked with the social contracts and groupings that are required to guarantee its continuity. He continues to argue that a "play-community generally tends to become permanent even after the game is over."[11(p12)] The relationships between the game of football and the football clubs, or chess and chess clubs are good examples of this.

The cultural history of gaming communities is usefully approached through traditional examples such as (physical) sports and board games, as the institutional roles in such fields have substantial and long histories. Many ancient societies elevated sports to a central place in the society, as witnessed by such institutions as ancient Greek Olympic Games, or Roman gladiator games. There have been different forms for the social organization of sports among the aristocracy and the peasants in the Middle Ages, and the Modern Era marked the rise in the popularity of team sports, supported by increases in wealth, leisure time, and mass media that supported developments in spectator sports.[12(pp44–70)] Similarly, a board game like chess is the product of a long history in the methods as well as means of play, including both the material objects used for game play, as well as the social and cultural conditions that had an effect on who were capable of playing, when, and where. Chess clubs and written rulebooks, for example, are a rather recent development, rising in popularity in the eighteenth and nineteenth centuries. There is nevertheless evidence from many parts of the world of long-standing gaming communities forming around chess.[13]

Expanding Games: Gaming in Social Life

The social character of gaming, and gaming as a perspective into social life, have been discussed in relation to each other by several scholars, most notably by sociologist Erving Goffman. In his major work *Frame Analysis*,[14] Goffman utilized his interest in theatre, arts, and games to discuss the various "social games" that people engage in to organize their social lives. As in his earlier work, *The Presentation of Self in Everyday Life*,[15] Goffman argues that as we as humans encounter each other, we also perform as social actors, who are conscious of the various contexts that frame our social interactions. In *Frame Analysis*, he discusses how multiple such organizing frames can overlap or conflict in different ways, and how individuals engage in "keying" or managing such frames in their everyday lives. As these social frames are based on rules, like games are, Goffman suggests that the "meaningfulness of everyday life is similarly dependent on a closed, finite set of rules," and that "explication of [such rules] would give one a powerful means of analyzing social life."[14(p5)] The degree of formality of such rules is nevertheless distinctively different in several everyday "play situations" as contrasted with actual games. As Goffman writes:

> There seems to be a continuum between playfulness, whereby some utilitarian act is caught up and employed in a transformed way for fun, and both [in] sports and games. In any case, whereas in playfulness the playful reconstitution of some individual into a "plaything" is quite temporary, never fully established, in organized games and sports this reconstitution is institutionalized – stabilized, as it were – just as the arena of action is fixed by the formal rules of the activity.[14(p57)]

The social formations that organize participation in game play can be called 'gaming communities,' and they can be discussed as a specific phenomenon, while being situated within the social dimensions of play, or "social games" that take place in the society in more general terms. While not completely separate from the surrounding society, such games-focused forms of social life have nevertheless grown into a notable aspect of late modern, network societies.[16,17] In Brint's terms, such formations are primarily 'elective communities,' as they are based on a choice, rather than on such facts as occupation or on living on a certain village or suburb, for example. Often discussed as 'communities of interest,' such social forms have increased in popularity particularly along the increasing use of Internet and its forums for online communication, where the concept 'virtual community' is often preferred.[18,19] With the increases in ubiquity of personal computers, video gaming consoles, smartphones, and other connected digital devices, there are more and more multiform opportunities for communication and thus also for social contact than in the past. The playfulness that Goffman discusses also finds its avenues and new forms of expression in the contemporary communication environment. In contemporary services such as photo-sharing site Flickr, social network services Twitter and Facebook, as well as in location-based services such as Foursquare, it is easy to find evidence that people are using them both for sharing information in utilitarian sense, as well as simply "for fun" – and that such online humor and play is actually a central element in the popularity and use motivations of such services.[20] In addition, large online services like Facebook have grown into important game publishing platforms on their own right, while also providing group discussion areas for people who share a common interest in a particular game.

There are multiple benefits that research has connected with games, play, and playfulness, social or not. Playfulness as a personality trait and as an attitude towards everyday encounters has been linked with an increased capability to recover from anxiety or depression, for example, and playfulness is also noted to promote friendship formation – play acts as a social catalyst.[21–24] As social play and playful communication increases interpersonal exchanges, and as the online environment for such interplay is also rather often international and multilingual by nature, there are reports of language learning, competence building, and socialization into sophisticated communicative practices in online games and Internet forums alike.[25]

The social nature of play is not necessarily always obvious in contemporary digitally augmented or mediated, online and offline play situations. There are multiple ways how social interaction may or may not take place in relation to game play, and even contemporary "social games" are not necessarily intensely social by character, despite their name. In a research article published in 2011 we set forward a model aimed at clarifying how players' social and games-related relationships can be broadly categorized into certain key classes.

The five such fundamental play situations we discussed all take place within the social sphere, but there are different degrees of contact between individual players, those interactions are framed differently, and also the interaction in terms of actual game play varies greatly (see Figure 9.1).

If we adapt this categorization to the maintenance of more permanent social relations, that are necessary for communities to emerge, it can also help us to identify the various dimensions and forms of gaming communities. In the case of single-player games, there is obviously no real-time, co-located community present that would be focused on playing the game together. However, many single-player computer or video games have active fans who connect with each other particularly in online discussions. For example, the most popular discussion forums dedicated to the *Civilization* series of single-player strategy games are running well over one million messages.[27] The more "off-topic" areas in such forums feature discussions that deal with real-life concerns such as politics or mental health, in addition to the more tightly games-focused debates, highlighting the breadth and depth of human contact such gaming communities can serve for their users. The contact and communication between the players of single-player games nevertheless remain mostly mediated and not co-located. There are elements like sharing the top-score lists and other achievements online or in the game client that sometimes frame the play experience, and make even the solitary game player part of a social or communal framework.

Two-player and other multi-player game players, however, need to have some way to get in more direct contact with each other in order to have an effect on the shared game states. A classic example is chess, when played with the help of mail (correspondence chess): even physically remote individuals can engage in prolonged chess matches by passing the information of their moves via posted letters. The game itself does not presuppose a more binding social relationship to exist between players, or existence of a more extensive community of players – even two casual chess acquaintances can play together. The shared interest, and in some cases even passion, in a game can nevertheless explain why gaming communities have grown around popular games for centuries. In the case of play-by-mail chess, for example, the first chess club dedicated solely to postal chess was established in 1870, and numerous correspondence chess tournaments, rating systems, correspondence chess magazines, and other socially based institutions have been formed around postal chess.[28] Today, correspondence chess commonly involves computer-assisted gaming, there are correspondence chess servers that register and transmit the moves, and there is also an increase in the popularity of mobile correspondence chess, where players use smartphone apps to submit their moves. The emergent communities of correspondence chess players are served by formal organizations, such as the Correspondence Chess League of America, which organizes official postal chess tournaments, as well as by online discussion boards in sites like www.chess.com.

Players	Players' Relationship	Description
Single Player	Reflective, Competitive*	• Knowledge of others playing the same game makes the game more social • Social media have made single player gaming more transparent • Play increases gaming capital, made visible through reward mechanisms such as achievements and trophies • Single player gaming can be strongly performative
Two Players	Reflective, Competitive, Collaborative	• Two-player gaming has many forms in relation to time, place and system • Communication channels include face-to-face, in-game channel(s) or 3rd party channel(s) • Competition is often tiered
Multi-player	Reflective, Competitive, Co-operative, Collaborative	• All players have direct effect on each others • Numerous communication channels (e.g. global, team, zone, one-on-one) • External communication channels such as discussion forums and wikis
Massively Multi-player	Reflective, Competitive, Co-operative, Collaborative, Neutral	• Macro-communities, micro-communities, friends • Complex communication channel hierarchy (e.g. global, groups, sub-groups, one-on-one) • Neutral players, players as tokens or props, playing "alone together"
Massive Single Player	Reflective, Competitive, Co-operative, (Collaborative,) Neutral	• Content sharing between players • Little or no real in-game interaction between players

*Single-player competes only via mechanics that are not part of the core game play experience.

FIGURE 9.1   Player Relations[26]

Changing Forms of Gaming Communication and Gaming Community

Community and communication are closely related phenomena. There are scholars who view communication as a crucial element for society to function as a democratic and somehow cohesive whole; Lewis A. Friedland, for example, has applied Jürgen Habermas' theory of communicative action to propose the concept of "communicatively integrated community" as a way of understanding the central role of communication in producing community.[29] The roles and forms that gaming communities have taken historically have changed, as the technologies and cultures of communication have continued evolving. Consequently, the exclusive gaming clubs of the past with their closely-knit communicative practices are very different phenomena from the massive online forums dedicated to some of the most popular digital games today. While the rise of online communication and the expansion of related mediated social networks have been recognized as major forces transforming the societal sphere, the exact role of the Internet has been the subject of debate as well. In the connection of gaming, communication, and communities, it is important to take into consideration both how changes in communication practices affect the social formations surrounding gaming, and on the other hand, how games promote certain types of communication – or even whether game play in itself can be considered as a particular, ludic form of communication.

From the social historical perspective, technologies and cultures of communication have undergone both "revolutions" while also being engaged in processes that suppress or slow down spread of technological innovations.[30] Any process of rapid technological change that is connected with societal and cultural changes is also likely to provoke negative reactions – in the case of media, "media panic" has been a consistent cultural reaction that involves moral issues and power struggles, before "new media" eventually has been domesticated into a more neutral, everyday phenomenon.[31] In the late 1990s, social critiques related to the rise of video games and Internet were starting to appear, probably most notably captured in the book *Bowling Alone* by Robert D. Putnam.[32] Putnam argued that while the first two-thirds of the twentieth century were characterized by deepening involvement of Americans in the life of their local communities, the recent decades have turned the tide. People are growing apart from each other, losing the "social capital" that has long been empowering American communities, and according to Putnam this development can be witnessed by the lessening popularity of traditional card games, parlor games, and the social formations that support playing them together. While such traditional games, played face-to-face, regularly bring people together and stimulate discussions that also focus on important matters for local community, Putnam argues that video games are very different. "My informal observations of Internet-based bridge games suggest that electronic players are focused entirely on the game itself, with very little social small talk, unlike traditional card games."[32(p104)] Rather than visiting each other's homes or public places, the late modern Americans prefer to stay home – a trend that Putnam primarily addresses to the powerfully grown popularity of televised entertainment, but also to the solitary use of video games and the Internet.[32(p223)]

Putnam's views have received their fair share of critique. In his review, Steven N. Durlauf[33] argues that there is conceptual vagueness in what constitutes social capital to start with, and that the causal connections Putnam presents as explanations for the decline in social capital are unconvincing. Sociability nevertheless appears to be changing in the forms it takes, also in connection to game playing, but the interpretations of these changes diverge. Since the concept of community remains fuzzy and hard to define in a unanimous manner, some scholars have suggested abandoning it altogether. Sociologist Barry Wellman has suggested that "networked individualism" better describes the social formations that characterize the social life in what he calls "networked society." From the unified family and shared, local neighborhood as the idealized centers of society in the twentieth century, life in the twenty-first century is increasingly based on more loosely-knit social frameworks. "Untypical" family structures start becoming typical, and rather than sharing the same, tight community ties, individuals grow and maintain their own, individual personal social networks.[34]

This development towards increasing individualization and fragmentation of communities has been described to continue also in online social forums. For example, Paul Hodkinson[35] describes how transition from earlier, rather tightly integrated Listserv or Usenet discussion groups on the Internet to the era of blog writing in services like Livejournal meant a move into a social context that emphasized individual agendas, personal "friends lists," and consequently higher level of personal control over social networking. The transition into the era of Facebook and other social networking services (SNSs) has been claimed to further promote individualization of online sociability, even though it has also been suggested that there are significant differences in the ways people coming from individualistic or collective cultures[36] adopt and use new media like SNSs. In the study by Cho and Park,[37] Korean users used SNSs to reinforce their tight and close relationships with their family and close, real-world friends, whereas the U.S. study participants invited many more people as their online "friends," and consequently also controlled more carefully what kinds of personal information they shared in this more heterogeneous social arena.

Online MUDs and MMORPGs as Gaming Communities

There has been special attention dedicated to the social dimensions of online gaming, particularly to the "massively multi-player online role-playing games" (MMORPGs). This might partly be due to the commercial success and novelty of MMORPGs as a distinctive phenomenon that brings together the social character of game play with audio-visual and interactive, online environment. The earliest computer role-playing games were developed by groups of computer-savvy role-playing gamers for the PLATO system in the University of Illinois already in the early 1970s.[38] The text-based "multi-user dungeons" (MUDs) were the earliest type of games where the social interaction and team play could be transported within the world of digital simulation – every game player accessed and interacted with the same, textually described places, characters and events using their own computer terminals. The early accounts of the culture that was built around these shared digital domains often focused on their radical, socially supportive, and individually liberating potentials. These two dimensions of online gaming can, however, also be seen as inherently conflicting.

Sherry Turkle's book *Life on the Screen*[39] is famous for highlighting the radical, individually liberating potentials of shared virtual gaming spaces such as MUDs. She describes the life of one active MUD user, and claims that it "seems misleading to call what he does there playing." Rather, the intense engagement in virtual game worlds should be seen as "constructing a life that is more expansive than the one he lives in physical reality." Turkle describes the MUD as a "new kind of virtual parlor game and a new form of community," as well as a "new form of collaboratively written literature," where one can construct new selves through social interaction and become "who you pretend to be."[39(pp11–12,193)] The individual freedom of exploration and expression can of course take many forms, and in the area of sexual identity and experimentation, for example, interpretations of permissible behaviors have differed greatly, sometimes dividing the community in question. Julian Dibbell[40] has provided good illustration of this in his account of a "virtual rape" that divided the early community of LamdaMOO in their interpretations of whether everything that is technically possibly in a game is also legitimate behavior – a topic that has also been extensively addressed by David Myers.

In his *Play Redux*[41(p128)] David Myers puts forward a view that solitary, individual and in a social context "selfish" competitive play is the true and basic form of computer game "aesthetic." Opposing Jean Piaget and other social play theorists' views, Myers suggests that there is no inherent reason why individual and selfish motives of play should be forced to adapt into more socially constructive or acceptable behaviors. In order to experiment with this premise in practice, he created a game character, Twixt, in the *City of Heroes* MMORPG, which he played only with an eye towards the goal of winning "without reference to or concern with any social rules of conduct established by CoH/V players outside the PvP game context."[41(p145)] Myers/Twixt particularly used a controversial tactic, which involved teleporting a nearby game character to areas which were guarded by NPC (non-player character) drones that would immediately attack and vaporize the unfortunate victim.

Myers describes how his application of this aggressive teleporting technique was met with increasing hostility by the other players, to the point where Myers/Twixt became the most hated character in the game. Yet, as Myers emphasized, his techniques were not actually forbidden by the game designers;[41(p146)] they were formally valid game strategies, but strictly against the informal social rules of gaming community. Such rules of "fair play" are set up by the gaming community as an important dimension of play, as a completely selfish play style would ruin the fun of the game for everyone else. Unintentionally, Myers' experiment thus affirms the centrality of informal, gaming community created rules for the operation and appreciation of formal game rules and systems.

Like the mainstream attention on online sociability early on focused on virtual communities as a dramatically altered or different form of community, the interest in game communities has also been drawn towards studying massively multi-player games, through their differences, rather than continuities in the range of social phenomena. Social forms of gaming do not take place in isolation, and much of the interactions that take place online are embedded and intermixed with non-online forms of sociability in many ways. The issue whether MMORPGs should be primarily addressed as games (that is, as formal structures, in isolation from real-world social contexts) or as communities has led into diverse research lines. While few game researchers appear to share David Myers' interest in pushing towards "purely rule-based" play, willingly ignoring the social norms that also frame online games, there has been sustained interest in the ways game systems and game design influence certain human behaviors, and discourage others. The branch of humanities-oriented game studies known as Ludology is particularly associated with the formal and text-analytical studies of games, and is also a style of study that is more likely to interpret player behaviors as being implicated by the game system, rather than by their social contexts and real-world motivations, for example. Espen Aarseth[42] has followed the approach adopted in literary studies, where an 'implied reader' has been identified as an element of text.[43] Aarseth[42] correspondingly introduced the concept 'implied player,' which is a role designed and programmed in the game that the actual players must adopt, in order for the game become realized as it was intended to be played. However, Aarseth also pays attention to and provides examples of the manner in which players can resist the role game designers have prepared for them, and engage in various kinds of transgressive, creative, or surprising behaviors in the game.[42] The creative player and communities of active game modifiers, or modders, have indeed gained their fair share of attention from game research, as a category of game players that blur the boundary between game consumer and game creator.[44,45] Celia Pearce,[46] for example, has examined how the voluntary nature of play can contribute towards motivating online game players to commit themselves strongly in a play context, to form online game communities and contribute to collective creativity and sharing. One of the key motivations for such a supportive game community that Pearce lists in her study include the sense of pleasure and happiness deriving from altruism and love of learning, that underlie the culture of that particular gaming community.[46]

Mixed Motivations: Alone Together?

The question nevertheless remains, whether MMORPG games always grow or cultivate communities around them. The studies of sociability in massively multi-player games tell a mixed story. For example, the study Nicholas Ducheneaut and team published in 2006[47] focused on the most popular MMORPG of all time, *World of Warcraft* (Blizzard Entertainment, 2004; "WoW"). Using an innovative methodology, the research team collected both qualitative in-game observations, as well as automatically logged quantitative data gathered from 129,372 unique WoW player characters. Their conclusions suggest that an MMORPG like WoW is not as socially oriented a game as is often thought: the recorded player characters spent typically only 30–35 percent of their play time in groups, and "solo play" was more typical. While the authors recognize the important role that more persistent guild structures and larger raid groups play particularly in the high level play, they suggest that most WoW subscribers tend to be "alone together," as they play surrounded by others, rather than playing with them. But the ambient presence of other people is nevertheless an important factor in online games of this kind. The ability to show off one's achievements and high-level gear to other players is an important rewarding element in itself. Massively multi-player games would therefore not fulfil the criteria of dense, classical communities, but would rather be more correctly characterized as socially saturated environments, where game sub-scribers, "instead of playing with other people, rely on them as an audience for their in-game performances, as an entertaining spectacle, and as a diffuse and easily accessible source of information and chitchat." Even guilds, the more permanent groupings in WoW, tend to have high "churn rates" as old members are constantly leaving and new ones enter; only about 10 percent of guild members actively engage in joint guild activities.[47]

The instrumental character of MMORPG play has been discussed in several studies. For example, sociologist and game scholar T.L. Taylor has studied the "power gamers" of *EverQuest* (Sony Online Entertainment, 1999)[48] and found their play style to be highly goal oriented, or like an interviewed power gamer said: "I want to be [level] 50. I want to be 50 first. I want to be 50 in three weeks. How am I gonna do that?" At the same time, Taylor also notes that the observed power gamers do not fit in the "lone ranger" stereotype of isolated gamer, either. Successful play in an online game like *EverQuest* relies on what Taylor characterizes as "complicated systems of trust, reliance and repu-tation." Even the most goal-driven power gamer needs to rely on maintaining working social relationships and memberships in larger organizations like guilds in order to be able to meet the increasingly massive in-game challenges.[48]

The character and potential consequences of participating in gaming communities are intimately tied into the gaming motivations. There appear to be several, even conflicting, game play motivations, which emphasizes the diverse nature of gaming communities. The early studies into digital game play motivation such as the one by Malone and Lepper[49(p239),50] have referred to the key character of intrinsic motivations, such as need for competence and challenge, optimal levels of arousal or stimulation, as well as control and self-determination. Malone and Lepper also added to these motivational categories other game-content related ones, such as emotional and cognitive aspects of fantasy – vicariously experiencing satisfactions of power, success, fortune, and of mastering "situations that would baffle or be unavailable to us in real life."[49(p241)] They also emphasized that in addition to individual motivations, there are interpersonal motivations such as competition, cooperation, and need for recognition, which provide both extrinsic as well as intrinsic motivations for game play (and for learning, which was the main focus of Malone and Lepper).

When human activities based on complex, intermingling motivations take place in an environment that is computer-mediated and partially based on fantasy, there are rich potentials for diversity of both action and interpretation. While everyone is co-located in the same game environment, the reasons for playing and the interpretations of these activities may differ greatly. Richard Bartle, the co-creator of the first MUD ("Multi-User Dungeon"), was a pioneer to highlight the ensuing motivational space. In his article "Hearts, Clubs, Diamonds, Spades: Players Who Suit MUDs,"[51] Bartle analyzed online MUD forum discussions to outline two main directions of interest for playing: the game environment, or other players. Of his four main "player types," the game environment oriented ones ("achievers" and "explorers") are driven to acting, or interacting and experimenting with, the game environment, and other people are for them of low interest, potentially adding some element of authenticity or competition to the game experiences they are after. On the contrary, those belonging to the player oriented MUD player types are primarily drawn to such shared gaming spaces in order to interact with other players ("socializers"), or for acting on, or humiliating other players ("killers"). It is interesting to note that while players belonging to the last "killer" category might appear anti-social by definition, Bartle actually emphasizes that killers want to demonstrate their superiority, and that their reputation and impact on other players is important for them.[51]

The non-altruistic behaviors of killer or grief-player gamers easily appear somewhat marginal or non-essential for understanding gaming communities, which are after all mostly created around joint interests and willingness to collaborate with other players in a positive manner. However, Foo and Koivisto in their grief play study[52] point out that the online violence and conflict is also one of the motivations for players to group together and form tight knit groups, and to rely on trusted comrades, and guild structures. In their online games design guidebook, Mulligan and Patrovsky defined a grief player as: "A player who derives his/her enjoyment not from playing the game, but from performing actions that detract from the enjoyment of the game by other players."[53(p299)]

Stenros[54] has adapted the frame analysis developed by Erving Goffman to understand the different orientations of play that affect how player-to-player relationships are also defined in game play. In his model, there are three main frames in a gaming situation: frame of the game world, frame of the (game) system, and frame of the ordinary, or everyday reality. The person who engages in game play activities becomes involved in all of these frames, as a participant, as a player, and as a game character, but their orientation regarding these frames may be different. Making reference to psychologist Michael J. Apter's reversal theory,[55] Stenros differentiates between serious and playful mindsets (corresponding to telic and paratelic states in Apter's theory), and then suggests that a paratelic or playful mindset can be adopted in all three main frames, but it will lead to different kinds of play behaviors. While research has mostly focused on either the level where the playful activity is directed towards game world ("playing the game"), or game system (e.g. hacking or cheating to win), there is also the third level, where the playful activity is directed towards other players – "playing the players." Stenros emphasizes that while the victims of killers, or grief players, suffer, for grief players themselves their behavior is still playfully motivated, and they have also been documented to establish griefer peer groups where they document their exploits, and share efficient grief play tactics.[54] "Trolling communities" such as those convening at the popular 4chan anonymous imageboard website can further be analyzed to emerge loaded with internal, conflicting impulses that both celebrate irony, alienation, and aggression, but that also promote paradoxical identity creation for a trolling community through shared, "collective shame."[56]

Positive Community: Participatory Culture and Gaming Capital

Research does not agree on how social, or anti-social, digital game play generally is, and what kind of consequences to socialization the engagement in game play involves. Pew Internet & American Life Project has carried out studies into the use of games and Internet, and their results from a teen video game study[57] suggest that gaming is a diverse phenomenon, where both single-player and lone play settings, co-located social play, online social play, and solitary play online are all common. For most American teens studied, gaming is a social activity, and an important element in their overall social lives. Only about one-quarter (24 percent) of teens only played games alone, whereas the remaining three-quarters played games with others at least some of the time.[57(piii)]

The series of nationally representative Player Baromcter studies our research group has carried out since 2009 in Finland suggest that over half of the Finnish 10–75-year-old population play digital games regularly – circa 53 percent reported playing some digital game at least once a month in 2013. When all forms of play, including non-digital and casual or occasional playing, were accounted for, almost everyone (99 percent) could be categorized as a "game player."[58] In an earlier study, the prevalence of playing alone and playing together were examined, and also in this study the majority of digital game players appeared to be playing together with other people, whereas 30 percent of digital game players only reported playing alone.[59(p75)]

Studying the social integration of game playing and its relation to positive adolescent development, Durkin and Barber[60] reported results where those young people who played either a lot, or moderately, both reported higher levels of family closeness and less risky friendship networks than those teens who did not play games at all. Also the attachment to school was higher in the game player groups as contrasted to the non-player group. The player groups had reported less depression, and higher self-esteem than the non-player group. The conclusion of Durkin and Barber was that game playing can "contribute to participation in a challenging and stimulating voluntary leisure environment," which has positive consequences for social integration and healthy development in adolescence.[60] Recent longitudinal work by Kowert and colleagues[61] uncovered similar findings, as over a two-year period, they found online video game play to contribute to higher rates of life satisfaction, and have no discernible negative impact on sociability, for adolescent players.

The aforementioned Pew study[57] was particularly focused on finding out whether involvement in game play has negative or positive consequences to civic and political participation in a society. As many games require young people to work together as teams, and jointly resolve complex challenges, they have potential to promote what Henry Jenkins has called "new participatory culture."[62(p24)] According to this view, games and the online contexts where they are commented on, such as online fan communities, offer the game players opportunities for participating in community life, engaging in civic debates, and to become political leaders, even if in the alternative contexts provided by massively multi-player games and their online discussion forums. The results from the Pew survey suggest that general involvement in game play does not automatically translate to significant political or civic activism. However, those teens who commented on websites or participated in games-related discussion boards proved to be more engaged civically and politically than those who did not belong to such gaming communities. There were significant differences in such activities as participating in social protests, political campaigning, raising money for charities, and staying informed about current events, all in favor of those teens who play and also contribute to game-related websites, as contrasted to those teens who just play games.[57(pvii,4–6)]

The idea of participation carries many positive connotations in general. Participation in social and cultural affairs signals empowerment and capacity to act in a societal context. Scholars of media culture such as Henry Jenkins often draw attention to the ways in which active fans of games, comic books or television series, for example, are capable of remarkable achievements that challenge the view of media consumers as "victims" or subjects of marketing machinery or various "media effects." The communities of fans in this line of analysis approach media texts actively, poaching for elements that are personally useful or pleasurable for them, and then use them for constructing new texts – or, as in the case of game play, alternative performances.[63] Digital games play a central role in the development towards increasing cultural prevalence of such participatory, or active media culture, as they are after all highly interactive, and in contrast to television, for example, allow much greater degree of freedom for consumers to act upon the mediated or represented world.[62(p133)]

Cultural capital is another important concept that is useful for unlocking the positive dimensions of gaming communities. French sociologist Pierre Bourdieu has identified three key forms of capital: economic, social, and cultural capital, and while money and other classical forms of economic capital as well as the influential connections and memberships of social capital are immediately useful, the forms of cultural capital also are intimately linked to individual's status and capacities to function in society.[64] Mia Consalvo[65] has applied and further developed Bourdieu's thinking with her concept "gaming capital," which provides a flexible way of recognizing and discussing the complex and dynamic significances that games, game playing, and forms of knowledge about such things can hold for groups and individuals alike. When people meet, face-to-face or online, to discuss their game experiences and for sharing tips, tactics or even cheat codes that allow extra lives in a game, they cultivate and shape their gaming capital. Consalvo also emphasizes that such meetings and activities do not take shape in a cultural or economical vacuum. The games industry, including the diverse network of game developers, publishers, distributors, marketers, and gaming press, all also try to gather people around games, and to direct their attention to certain elements in games. It should nevertheless be remembered that instrumental uses of games, such as seeking notable achievements, social recognition, or trying to establish leadership roles in gaming communities are not all that there is in game play. Consalvo underscores that being playful can be immensely satisfying for its own sake, and it may have nothing to do with advancing in the game, or even with gaining a skill.[65(pp4,104)]

An alternative approach to conceptualize the cultural and interest-based connection fans or players of a game share with each other is to treat it as a 'subculture,' rather than as a fully developed community in the sociological sense. Classic studies of subcultures such as Dick Hebdige's *Subculture: Meaning of Style*[66] focus on subculture's differences or deviances from the norms set up by the "mainstream culture" in a society. The research carried out in the field of subculture studies has often focused on groups such as punks or hip-hoppers, who carry signs of their affective relationship to a particular musical style also in their style of clothing, for example. Alienated from the (white, bourgeois, Christian) values of the dominant societal structures, such subcultures provide alternative symbols and a sense of identity and solidarity for groups of excluded individuals. Hebdige points out that a subculture has links to, but is also different from a 'counter-culture,' which exists in explicitly political and ideological opposition to the dominant culture, and also aims to establish alternative institutions, like communes or media outlets of its own.[66(p148)]

The concept or subculture or counter-culture carries similar undertones as the secret, disguise-wearing societies or social groupings that Huizinga associated with games and play. A typical player of a digital game, however, rarely carries in an everyday context such overt signs of his or her affective relationship with a particular game, or of membership in a gaming community. A particular event, such as a LAN party or gaming convention, may however provide a suitable setting for expressing the games-related fan identity with outward signs – the construction and wearing of elaborate cosplay dresses and props inspired by video game characters are probably the most easily detectable type among this kind of game fan practices. Studying the Japanese *otaku* phenomenon, Mizuko Ito[67] has argued that while the field of electronic gaming remained somewhat separate from other forms of media fandom like those of manga or anime, by the 1990s popular game characters such as Mario or Pikachu had become well integrated in the overall media mix. The expansion of fanlike cultural activities and peer-to-peer forms of social organization into the Internet has also encouraged alternative perspectives into how more activist and productive forms of media engagement are perceived in research and public discussion. While the interpretation of passionate game or media fans as infantile, obsessed, or cut-off from normal reality remains, the threshold for participating in fandom as well as in gaming communities is lowering, and the demographics of interpersonal networks are becoming more diverse, while new forms for contact and communication have become widely available.[67]

Conclusion: the Good, the Bad, or the Irrelevant Gaming Communities?

On the basis of research, playing of all kinds, including digital game play, is predominantly a well socially integrated and integrating activity. Dmitri Williams and his research team studied[68] *World of Warcraft* players who belong to guilds – in-game social groupings or communities – and found out that in this kind of MMORPG, there was a large group of players (about one-third) who used the game primarily to strengthen and maintain existing, offline friendship ties. Even a larger group of players (a third to a half) reported using the online game as a casual "third place" (cf. Oldenburg[69]) to generate bridging social capital, but rarely using it for tight, bonding interactions; the anonymous character of online, in-game encounters appears to create an obstacle for many to use it for developing in-depth relationships, or for exchanging advice or emotional support on personal issues. However, a small portion (5 percent) of the *World of Warcraft* players studied reported forming new friendships within the game, bonding, and extending those relationships outside of the game, into their "real lives." However, there were also a substantial number of game players (about a quarter) who were not interested in creating social relationships with other gamers, and saw their utility for them merely as instrumental, necessary for accomplishing some tough game tasks.[68] The character of gaming communities appears to be highly diverse, and translates into different kinds of behaviors and meanings for different people.

As discussed in this chapter, sociability and participation in communities has been associated with several benefits for individuals and groups alike. The advantages for individuals' health, success and general well-being from social ties are well documented. A team or group which functions well together is also likely to perform well, which is important in gaming contexts, as participation in gaming guilds or forums is closely associated with the needs for in-game achievements, as well as with social motivations. The griefer players and the plentiful evidence of online, games-related harassment, however, also point towards the dark side of gaming communities. During autumn 2014, an online campaign was organized around the hashtag #GamerGate, providing an example of how effectively a group of like-minded gamers can form a community to target female game developers or liberal game journalists in a hate campaign. To conclude, both the social forms of game playing, as well as the other forms of games-related sociability all contribute to a highly divergent and extensive field for gaming community studies. For many players, the personal importance of their gaming community for them is the single most important reason why they keep on playing. Also, players regularly report receiving support from their community that goes beyond its in-game origins. However, it is equally important to recognize the casual and instrumental character that games-related communities have for what is perhaps the majority of digital game players. It is also too narrow to see gaming communities only as online communities, even while expanding opportunities for online communications have greatly contributed to the growth of games' social significance. As online and offline lives are increasingly intermingled, games and information technologies continue their proliferation, and various game-like services muddle such distinctions as play versus work, or game versus real life, it will become increasingly difficult to differentiate gaming communities from our other social relationships in the future.

References

1. Helliwell JF, Putnam RD. The social context of well-being. *Phil Trans R Soc B.* 2004; 359(1449): 1435–1446. doi:10.1098/rstb.2004.1522
2. Williams R. *The Country and the City.* Oxford: Oxford University Press; 1975.
3. Tönnies F. *Community and Society.* London: Courier Dover Publications; 1957.
4. Durkheim E. *The Division of Labor in Society.* New York: Simon and Schuster; 1997.
5. Durkheim E. *Suicide: A Study in Sociology.* (Simpson G, ed.). New York: Simon and Schuster; 2010.
6. Hillery G. Definitions of community: Areas of agreement. *Rural Sociol.* 1955; 20(2): 111–123.
7. Brint S. Gemeinschaft revisited: A critique and reconstruction of the community concept. *Sociol Theor.* 2001; 19(1): 1–23. doi:10.1111/0735-2751.00125
8. Burghardt GM. The evolutionary origins of play revisited: Lessons from turtles. In: Bekoff M, Byers JA, eds. *Animal Play: Evolutionary, Comparative and Ecological Perspectives.* Cambridge: Cambridge University Press; 1998: 1–26.
9. Bekoff M, Allen C. Intentional communication and social play: How and why animals negotiate and agree to play. In: Bekoff M, Byers JA, eds. *Animal Play: Evolutionary, Comparative and Ecological Perspectives.* Cambridge: Cambridge University Press; 1998: 97–114.
10. Bateson G. *A Theory of Play and Fantasy: A Report on Theoretical Aspects of the Project for Study of the Role of Paradoxes of Abstraction in Communication;* Approaches to the study of human personality: American Psychiatric Association psychiatric research reports 2. 1955: 39–51.
11. Huizinga J. *Homo Ludens: A Study of the Play-Element in Culture.* Boston: Beacon; 1955.
12. Jarvie G. *Sport, Culture and Society: An Introduction, Second Edition.* Abingdon, Oxon & New York: Routledge; 2012.
13. Murray HJR. *A History of Chess.* Oxford: Oxford University Press; 1913.
14. Goffman E. *Frame Analysis: An Essay on the Organization of Experience.* New York: Harper & Row; 1974.
15. Goffman E. *The Presentation of Self in Everyday Life.* Edinburgh: University of Edinburgh, Social Sciences Research Centre; 1956.
16. Dijk JAGM van. *The Network Society: Social Aspects of New Media.* London: SAGE; 2006.
17. Castells M. *The Rise of the Network Society.* 2nd edn. Oxford: Blackwell Publishers; 2000.
18. Jones Q. Virtual-communities, virtual settlements & cyber-archaeology: A theoretical outline. *JCMC.* 1997; 3(3). doi:10.1111/j.1083-6101.1997.tb00075.x
19. Jones SG. Information, Internet, and community: Notes toward an understanding of community in the Information Age. In: Jones SG, ed. *Cybersociety 2.0: Revisiting Computer-Mediated Communication and Community.* Thousand Oaks, CA: Sage Publications; 1998: 1–34.
20. Mäyrä F. Playful mobile communication: Services supporting the culture of play. *Interactions: Studies in Communication & Culture.* 2012; 3(1): 55–70. doi:10.1386/iscc.3.1.55_1
21. Barnett LA. The playful child: Measurement of a disposition to play. *Play & Culture.* 1991; 4(1): 51–74.
22. Barnett LA. The adaptive powers of being playful. *Play & Culture Studies.* 1998; 1: 97–119.
23. Sias PM, Drzewiecka JA, Meares M, et al. Intercultural friendship development. *Communication Reports.* 2008; 21: 1–13. doi:10.1080/08934210701643750
24. Brown SL. *Play: How It Shapes the Brain, Opens the Imagination, and Invigorates the Soul.* New York: Avery; 2010.
25. Thorne SL, Black RW, Sykes JM. Second language use, socialization, and learning in internet interest communities and online gaming. *Mod Lang J.* 2009; 93: 802–821.

26. Stenros J, Paavilainen J, Mäyrä F. Social interaction in games. *IJART.* 2011; 4(3): 342–358. doi:10.1504/IJART.2011.041486

27. See e.g. "Civilization Fanatics Center" forums at: http://forums.civfanatics.com.

28. See "Correspondence Chess – A History," at: www.chess.com/article/view/correspondence-chess---a-histo

29. Friedland LA. Communication, community, and democracy: Toward a theory of the communicatively integrated community. *Commun Res.* 2001; 28(4): 358–391. doi:10.1177/009365001028004002

30. Winston B. *Media Technology and Society: A History From the Telegraph to the Internet.* Re-issue edition. London; New York: Routledge; 1998.

31. Drotner K. Dangerous media? Panic discourses and dilemmas of modernity. *Paedagog Hist.* 1999; 35(3): 593–619. doi:10.1080/0030923990350303

32. Putnam RD. *Bowling Alone: The Collapse and Revival of American Community.* 1st edition. New York: Touchstone Books by Simon & Schuster; 2000.

33. Durlauf SN. *Bowling Alone:* A review essay. *Journal of Economic Behavior & Organization.* 2002; 47(3): 259–273. doi:10.1016/S0167-2681(01)00212-4

34. Wellman B. Physical place and cyberplace: The rise of personalized networking. *International Journal of Urban and Regional Research.* 2001; 25(2): 227–252. doi:10.1111/1468-2427.00309

35. Hodkinson P. Interactive online journals and individualization. *New Media Society.* 2007; 9(4): 625–650. doi:10.1177/1461444807076972

36. Hofstede GH. *Culture's Consequences: International Differences in Work-Related Values.* Beverly Hills, CA: Sage Publications; 1980.

37. Cho SE, Park HW. A qualitative analysis of cross-cultural new media research: SNS use in Asia and the West. *Qual Quant.* 2013; 47(4): 2319–2330. doi:10.1007/s11135-011-9658-z

38. See e.g. www.armory.com/~dlp/dnd1.html

39. Turkle S. *Life on the Screen: Identity in the Age of the Internet.* New York: Simon & Schuster; 1997.

40. Dibbell J. *My Tiny Life: Crime and Passion in a Virtual World.* New York: Holt; 1998.

41. Myers D. *Play Redux: The Form of Computer Games.* Ann Arbor: The University of Michigan Press: The University of Michigan Library; 2010.

42. Aarseth E. I fought the law: Transgressive play and the implied player. In: *Proceedings of DiGRA 2007: Situated Play.* Tokyo: DiGRA Japan; 2007. Available at: www.digra.org/wp-content/uploads/digital-library/07313.03489.pdf

43. Booth WC. *The Rhetoric of Fiction.* Chicago & London: University of Chicago Press; 1983.

44. Sotamaa O. *The Player's Game: Towards Understanding Player Production Among Computer Game Cultures.* Tampere: Tampere University Press; 2009. Available at: http://urn.fi/urn:isbn:978-951-44-7651-8

45. Postigo H. Modding to the big leagues: Exploring the space between modders and the game industry. *First Monday.* 2010; 15(5). Available at: http://firstmonday.org/htbin/cgiwrap/bin/ojs/index.php/fm/article/view/2972/2530

46. Pearce C. Collaboration, creativity and learning in a play community: A study of the University of There. In: *Proceedings of DiGRA 2009: Breaking New Ground: Innovation in Games, Play, Practice and Theory.* Brunel: DiGRA; 2009. Available at: www.digra.org/wp-content/uploads/digital-library/09287.43135.pdf

47. Ducheneaut N, Yee N, Nickell E, Moore RJ. "Alone together?" Exploring the social dynamics of massively multi-player online games. In: *ACM Conference,* Montréal, Québec, Canada. 2006: 407–416. doi:10.1145/1124772.1124834

48. Taylor TL. Power games just want to have fun? Instrumental play in a MMOG. In: *Proceedings of DiGRA 2007: Level Up.* Utrecht: DiGRA; 2003. Available at: www.digra.org/wp-content/uploads/digital-library/05163.32071.pdf

49. Malone TW, Lepper MR. Making learning fun: A taxonomy of intrinsic motivations for learning. In: Snow RE, Farr MJ, eds. *Aptitude, Learning, and Instruction:* Volume 3: *Conative and Affective Process Analyses.* Hillsdale, NJ: Lawrence Erlbaum Associates Publishers; 1987: 223–253.
50. Malone TW. Toward a theory of intrinsically motivating instruction. *Cognitive Sci.* 1981; 5(4): 333–369. doi:10.1207/s15516709cog0504_2
51. Bartle RA. Hearts, clubs, diamonds, spades: Players who suit MUDs. *The Journal of Virtual Environments.* 1996; 1(1). Available at: www.mud.co.uk/richard/hcds.htm
52. Foo CY, Koivisto EMI. Defining grief play in MMORPGs: Player and developer perceptions. In: *Proceedings of the 2004 ACM SIGCHI International Conference on Advances in Computer Entertainment Technology.* ACE '04. New York, NY, USA: ACM; 2004:245–250. doi:10.1145/1067343.1067375
53. Mulligan J, Patrovsky B. *Developing Online Games: An Insider's Guide.* Indianapolis: New Riders; 2003.
54. Stenros J. Playing the system: Using frame analysis to understand online play. In: *Futureplay '10: Proceedings of the International Academic Conference on the Future of Game Design and Technology.* Futureplay '10. New York, NY, USA: ACM; 2010:9–16. doi:10.1145/1920778.1920781
55. Apter MJ. *Reversal Theory: The Dynamics of Motivation, Emotion, and Personality.* Second Edition, Orig. 1989. Oxford: Oneworld; 2007.
56. Manivannan V. Tits or GTFO: The logics of misogyny on 4chan's Random – /b/. *The Fibreculture Journal.* 2013; (22): 109–132.
57. Lenhart A, Kahne J, Middaugh E, Macgill AR, Evans C, Vitak J. *Teens, Video Games, and Civics: Teens' Gaming Experiences are Diverse and Include Significant Social Interaction and Civic Engagement.* Washington. D.C.: Pew Internet & American Life Project; 2008. Available at: http://eric.ed.gov/?id=ED525058
58. Mäyrä F, Ermi L. *Pelaajabarometri 2013: Mobiilipelaamisen nousu.* Tampere: University of Tampere; 2014. Available at: http://urn.fi/URN:ISBN:978-951-44-9425-3
59. Kallio KP, Kaipainen K, Mäyrä F. *Gaming Nation? Piloting the International Study of Games Cultures in Finland.* Tampere: Tampereen yliopisto, hypermedialaboratorio; 2007. Available at: http://urn.fi/urn:isbn:978-951-44-7141-4
60. Durkin K, Barber B. Not so doomed: computer game play and positive adolescent development. *J Appl Dev Psychol.* 2002; 23(4): 373–392. doi:10.1016/S0193-3973(02)00124-7
61. Kowert R, Vogelgesang J, Festl R, Quandt T. Psychosocial causes and consequences of online video game play. *Comput Human Behav.* 2015; 45: 51–58. doi:10.1016/j.chb.2014.11.074
62. Jenkins H. *Convergence Culture: Where Old and New Media Collide.* New York: New York University Press; 2006.
63. Jenkins H. *Textual Poachers: Television Fans and Participatory Culture.* New York: Routledge; 1992.
64. Bourdieu P. The forms of capital. In: Richardson J, ed. *Handbook of Theory and Research for the Sociology of Education.* New York: Greenwood; 1986: 46–58.
65. Consalvo M. *Cheating: Gaining Advantage in Videogames.* Cambridge, MA: The MIT Press; 2007.
66. Hebdige D. *Subculture: The Meaning of Style.* London: Methuen; 1979.
67. Ito, Mizuko. Japanese media mixes and amateur cultural exchange. In: Buckingham D, Willett R, eds. *Digital Generations: Children, Young People, and the New Media.* Oxon: Routledge; 2013: 49–66.
68. Williams D, Ducheneaut N, Xiong L, Zhang Y, Yee N, Nickell E. From tree house to barracks: The social life of guilds in *World of Warcraft. Games and Culture.* 2006; 1(4): 338–361. doi:10.1177/1555412006292616
69. Oldenburg R. *The Great Good Place: Cafés, Coffee Shops, Bookstores, Bars, Hair Salons, and Other Hangouts at the Heart of a Community.* New York: Marlowe; 1998.

10

NO BLACK AND WHITE IN VIDEO GAME LAND! WHY WE NEED TO MOVE BEYOND SIMPLE EXPLANATIONS IN THE VIDEO GAME DEBATE

Thorsten Quandt and Rachel Kowert

Video Games in the Debate: Between Public Threat and Cultural Asset?

The perception of video games has evolved considerably in the last decades, in sync with changing audiences, content, use, and market structures. What was once considered to be a weird hobby of computer nerds or a part of youth culture in the golden age of arcade games has become a leading entertainment sector of the mainstream culture. However, controversies regarding games are not new, and even in the romanticized 'early' days of gaming, there were heated discussions and bans of games (or attempts to do so). The history of video gaming is full of examples of moral panics revolving around violent, militaristic, or sexually explicit content, addictive qualities of games, and other aspects of games that are considered to be inappropriate or damaging to their users, starting in the 1970s and early 1980s with titles like *Death Race* or *Custer's Revenge*, and certainly not ending with more recent discussions about blockbuster series like *Call of Duty* and *Grand Theft Auto* (see Chapter 2).

The potential impact of video games on the lives of their users has been addressed in many different contexts – there's a sheer endless stream of books, videos, music titles, TV series, and movies depicting games in one way or the other, either as a topic (in movies like *Tron* or *Gamer*) or just as pop cultural reference (like in the song *Juicy* by The Notorious B.I.G. or *Video Games* by Lana del Rey). The news media frequently cover various aspects of gaming as well, more often than not focusing on the potential risks: Sensational stories about players of violent video games committing homicide[1] and addicted gamers dying of exhaustion[2] routinely make the headlines. Some of the more bizarre incidents are also of interest: Somebody marrying a video game character[3] or skills from *World of Warcraft* saving the lives of children attacked by an aggressive moose[4] are safe bets for getting the attention of an audience wondering about the strange world of video gamers. Even courts have shown concern about the potential influence of video games, as school shootings have been linked to games multiple times, claiming that the games contributed to or even triggered the crime (see Chapter 2), at least partially due to their ability to induce aggressive behavior in children and adolescents.[5]

In short, the societal debate about video games is multi-faceted, even confusingly rich by covering many aspects from different viewpoints. Today, there remain some reservations that video games might be harmful, either for vulnerable groups (especially children) or for society at large, as people have long feared that the use, misuse, or overuse of video games contributes to long-term physical, social, and psychological consequences: Do video games make players really aggressive – and more so than other media? Does the effect last? Will children become addicted to games and in turn become obese and dull? Do online games replace real friendships with shallow connections to unknown strangers? Likewise, questions regarding more positive effects – often based on the same assumed, underlying processes – are of public interest: Can we effectively learn something (positive) from games? Are they a more efficient learning agent than other media? Can they help us become smarter, fitter, and more satisfied with our life? Can they form a virtual space to meet friends, and contribute to community building?

It would be easy to denounce the concerns as being solely the result of public confusion due to the cacophony of voices and misleading information by the press and other media. However, the scientific community has long been split in their opinion on whether or not these fears are grounded in scientific fact. In turn, academic answers to the pressing concerns have often been contradictory or remained blurry, at least from the perspective of an interested public. However, it is also the case that some researchers have not taken the concerns seriously enough – remaining in the safety of an ivory tower, preoccupied with academically fascinating topics (that did not always connect to the public concerns at all). In contrast, some public 'experts' gave other, seemingly more easy-to-grasp answers – oversimplifying complex processes and selling assumptions for truth (without much basis in actual research).

However, the questions raised by the public about what is perceived as a 'new' medium are not naive or superfluous and they deserve unbiased, well-researched answers: Societies need to know about potential sources of danger, especially for groups that need to be protected (like children) for their well-being and long-term survival, and their concerns and questions are legitimate. While video games are certainly not new in historical terms (see Chapter 1), their more recent mainstream success has made them relevant for many directly or indirectly affected persons in many societies around the globe.

The aim of this volume was to elucidate some of these concerns and overview the scientific literature relating to the physical, social, and psychological impact of video game use. Naturally, it can only address a few selected topics – the ones we expected to be the most relevant for the public debate and current research. As the scientific analysis of video games has grown considerably during recent years, this overview is also not exhaustive. However, some general trends can be identified in the wealth of insights video games research offers. In the following sections, we will summarize some of the findings as outlined in more detail in this book and draw some conclusions – both for science and the public debate on video games.

Negative Influence: Are Gamers Lonely, Unhealthy, and Addicted?

The questions regarding the negative influence of video games often focus on very general or broad effects. For example, in the public discussion, it is sometimes implied that video games per se make all gamers aggressive. The assumption of such a 'fits 'em all' effects model is typically not discussed in research however, as it is inherently based on the idea of humans being similar to machines. That is, if you press a button, a pre-defined action will happen. This concept is certainly wrong on many levels – there are many different genres, a diversity of game playing groups, and even one and the same person reacts differently to a specific game under varying circumstances. It may even be argued that – in contrast to other media that are not dynamically reacting to user input – there is no *one* content to react to. The concept of 'impact' or 'effect' may even be misleading, as it implies a stimulus-response logic rather than active use. Still, it can be discussed with regards to (very) young children, persons with low self-control or a clinical impulse control disorder, whether the direct effects model has some validity, and it is still worth debating whether long-time exposure might 'cultivate' certain viewpoints and behavior according to the 'role model' of the games content. However, it is important to contextualize these questions and make clear what groups are affected under which circumstances and by which game.

The authors in this book discussed the effects of video games in a differentiated way, taking these considerations into account. Unsurprisingly, they found the influence of video game play on its users is minimal at best when it comes to an 'overall' population of people playing games. If there are effects, then they are primarily limited to specific populations, such as the most avid users, maybe even addicted ones, or people in problematic life situations (unemployment, illnesses, etc.). The everyday impact of games is higher within these groups, as the games also occupy a more central place in their lives. However, in many cases it is likely that this is not a direct 'effect' of the game, but rather the outcome of the overall life situation including a lack of other goals and meaningful occupations. Given the argument above – that effects are group-specific, depending on the game and the context – these findings are probably to be expected.

The health concerns over games – for example, regarding obesity among heavy players – can be discussed in a much more nuanced way when taking a more complex model of the human being seriously: It is not the game that 'makes' the player overweight but the lack of movement and sport, as well as unhealthy food and co-morbidities accompanying a mostly sedentary activity that leads to such problems. Gaming may be the object of an unhealthy fascination but the reasons for engaging with this medium to the extent that one's health begins to suffer likely lie deeper. Similarly, depression, sleep deprivation and resulting other, negative psychological effects have been related to overuse of games, but this, in turn can also be related back to a lack of competing goals and motivations. In the end, it is more important to ask why the player turns towards the game instead of other occupations and why nothing else can motivate her/him more than gaming, rather than blaming the game – as taking this agent out of the life of the users might not change the underlying behavioral problems (i.e., the person might simply acquire a different excessive habit). So in that sense, the discussion on excess gaming might be turned into a discussion of a lack of other orientations. That said, the connection between video gaming and health problems is not even consistently supported by the research literature, so one has to be careful to not over interpret such a discussion (as noted in Chapter 3).

This is not meant to downplay the concerns over excessive forms of use and video game addiction (and more specifically, online/Internet gaming disorder, which is regarded as being a central problem, especially in relation to MMORPGs and competitive multi-player genres). Indeed, the reports on the existence of such problems are consistent. As discussed elsewhere in this volume (see Chapter 5), there has been ample research on this topic and the sophistication of this research field has been growing considerably in recent years. However, there is no consensus on the criteria to identify such a condition, despite some movement into the direction of using similar criteria that are considered to be central for the definition and identification of video game addiction. What we do know from this line of research is the existence of a small group of game players that show signs of addiction and, in some cases, with considerable negative effects on their daily lives. It needs to be pointed out that these highly problematic cases display symptoms of a clinical condition and indeed there are patients treated for video game or Internet gaming disorder in some countries. It is also important to note that an overwhelming percentage of video game players show no signs of this at all (most studies identify very low rate (less than 10 percent) of affected persons, or even less, depending on the group under analysis) – so these findings are probably not the material to start a moral panic; nevertheless, it is important for prevention purposes to find out what differentiates the people with excessive behavior and problems from the large majority of unsuspicious users and what contributes to starting and reinforcing a problematic behavior.

However, it is not only excessive or addicted users that can experience negative repercussions due to video game play. Some authors have discussed negative social outcomes of gaming, claiming that 'virtual life' contacts (for example in online games) might replace 'real life' contacts (or to put it in another way, 'online' contacts replace 'offline' contacts). Research so far has shown it is unlikely that the use of games substantially negatively impacts the social lives of users or one's general ability to socialize in non-mediated contexts (see Chapter 6). In reality, other social factors are typically – and under normal circumstances (i.e., non-excessive use) – much stronger. For example, when controlling for age, gender, socio-economic status, education, and other social and personal factors, the impact of games becomes relatively small. Nevertheless, there is some evidence that loneliness, depression, social anxiety, poor social skills, and other problematic conditions can contribute to (online) video game play and, in turn, become worse due to the displacement of offline with online contacts or an overall shrinking number of social contacts. Such disruptive effects on the social lives of users seem to be rare though and (based on the assumption of pre-conditions) most likely limited to cases that already have shown problems before starting to play.

Finally, and as already noted above, much of the debate on video games has been dominated by the question whether violent content – and there is undeniably a lot of it out there – has a negative impact on the users, and if this content makes them aggressive and more likely to commit acts of violence themselves. There are a lot of studies out there that have found short-time effects of games that point into that direction, especially in laboratory settings. Longitudinal studies are much less consistent and the effects measured there are typically small (if existent at all). As discussed elsewhere in this book (see Chapter 4), there are some serious doubts as to whether this is sufficient to claim direct effects of violent games on societal violence and 'real life' conditions. Again, it can be argued that human beings are not machines. As such, the violence in a game does not translate into an imitation of the behavior among all users – the processes involved here are much more complicated. This does not necessarily mean that there are no effects at all – but the concepts and research need to be refined to cope with the complexity of the phenomenon under analysis.

Positive Influence: Can Anything Good Come Out of Games?

Arguably the major part of (empirical) research on video games up to date has been guided by a protectionist perspective on potentially dangerous effects that might affect vulnerable groups in society. Such a focus in the public debate – and in parallel, in the social sciences – is understandable when taking into account that societies need to protect themselves from negative influences that might endanger their proper functioning, and especially groups that are easy targets to disruptive (media) effects. This focus is particularly strong when the 'source' of such effects is perceived as relatively new, as is the case with video games – at least when portraying them as a central part of mainstream entertainment media, which is a fairly recent development. Naturally, having no previous experience leads to uncertainty and a cautious approach to the new medium.

In contrast to these studies, some researchers have focused on positive effects of video games, especially with regards to health, learning, and community building. In many ways, the respective studies look at the same basic processes and sometimes even follow similar theoretical models as the negative effects studies outlined above – but with a completely opposing 'mind-set' about what to expect from games, with different outcomes of the studies and with different interpretations. It needs to be noted, though, that this does not mean that all these studies contradict each other – both negative and positive influences may happen at the same time.

This is obvious for positive, health-related effects: As discussed previously in this volume (see Chapter 3), video games can be successfully used as a motivation to do sports and to become more mobile, for example when used among elderly people. While, grosso modo, 'exergames' have not been found to perform better than actual sports when comparing them directly, such a comparison misses the point: Typically, they can be used in contexts where normal sports is out of question or where the access through games can motivate persons to train who would normally not participate in demanding physical activities. Naturally, it needs to be evaluated in each individual case whether exergames really perform better than alternative treatments. The positive effect of exergames also exposes the shortcomings of looking at video games from just one angle: While some games, played by specific groups under certain conditions (i.e., heavy gamers playing competitive online games in an excessive fashion over long periods of time) may contribute to health problems (e.g. obesity), other games, played by other groups under other conditions (i.e. elderly persons playing exergames with motion controllers on a regular basis) may have opposite effects.

Research also supports positive health effects for clinical cases: For example, games can contribute to fighting serious illnesses through (indirect) psycho-physiological effects. A prominent example, the game *Re-Mission* – where the patients fight cancer in a shooter game – shows that games can have beneficial effects on self-efficacy and the patient's emotions, and they can actively support healing processes. While the effects here are partially indirect, by improving the patient's feelings about chemotherapy as well as backing resistance and fighting against the illness, there are also learning effects at play here.

Indeed, video games can be powerful learning tools. From specific training programs to tools for rehabilitation, video games are seeing a growth in terms of their application as learning devices for a range of skills. The reasons for the effectiveness of games as learning devices are manifold, but immersion and dynamic learning environments that react to user input and skills certainly play an important role here. These effects can be, and have been, measured on low-level neural processes, where game training can directly improve reaction to input and other cognitive abilities (see Chapter 8). Games can also be used to train complex tasks in flexible learning environments, which makes them more interesting, demanding, and effective as compared to unresponsive learning media.

However, it needs to be noted that while there is no doubt that games can be used as learning tools, it is much less clear on how the learning processes function, in what context, how they can be amplified, when they do not work at all, and how to effectively use this knowledge to design games with defined learning outcomes (see Chapter 7). As discussed in this volume, the reasons for this lack of specific knowledge may lie in silo thinking and the lack of cross-disciplinary cooperation, but also missing benefits and motivation to do so on a professional basis: Games with an explicit 'learning' component are still regarded as being unattractive for the industry (i.e., being not profitable enough) and as being less fun for the users (i.e., by explicitly marking something as 'learning,' it might be equaled with 'work' and not a leisure activity, and become less interesting; see the so called "broccoli-coated chocolate" effect[6]). As it stands today, we do know that games can have beneficial learning effects – but the details of the underlying processes still need to be researched in much more detail.

There is also a flipside to the work on learning from games: While research proves that games can be used as educational media, this also feeds some suspicion that the very same underlying effects can be used in a negative way. If one claims that games can strengthen the processing of specific input on a neural basis, have an impact on emotions, train specific behavioral reactions, and even complex patterns, mustn't this also mean that the very same basic processes might be responsible for inducing hostile or aggressive behavior and cultivating prejudice? Again, the question here is not so much whether games can be used for learning and training per se (and indeed this includes also negative influence), but who is the subject of the influence, what type of learning medium is used under which circumstances, and what is the basis of the learn-ing process? Furthermore, under everyday life conditions, we cannot suspect every member in a given population to be affected by direct negative influences, simply because not everybody will use the respective game (in contrast to a 'prescribed' use of learning games, for example in school contexts or in therapy). This also means that the analysis of media selection (and more specifically, genre and video game use) might become more relevant when realizing that learning effects are indeed powerful (which is not fully supported by the current status quo of research, as noted in Chapter 7).

This may be one of the central 'take home' messages of this volume: The contextualization of game use in everyday life matters, even when looking at games from the angle of a 'media effects' approach. This is even more so the case when focusing on gaming communities.

As discussed in the previous section, a lot of public discussion around video games in an online world has focused on the displacement of real life connections by virtual life connections, which are deemed as being less valuable and shallow. However, many studies have demonstrated the opposite: Players regularly report receiving support from their community that goes beyond its in-game origins and extends into 'real life' (see Chapter 9). Indeed, online video gaming communities can become personal contacts in everyday life contexts (through modality switching) and extend and enhance players' social circles. It has also been noted that for many players, the personal importance of their gaming community is the single most important reason to keep playing. So online video games are inherently social games and also regarded as being part of 'normal' life by their users. As such, the portrayal of an oppositional, mutually excluding online vs. offline world, as often discussed in the public debate, seems to be a misleading approach. This is also obvious when looking at the beneficial effects of social online game play: As studies have shown, participation in gaming communities has been associated with several individual and group benefits relating to health, life success, and general well-being – so there is a transfer from the game to other aspects of the everyday life of the users.

However, it is possible for the beneficial effects that stem from playing with communities to be turned into negative effects (as is the case with other effects, as discussed above): If personal commitment and social obligations within gaming environments are, indeed, not virtual in nature, then their binding effects may be no less important for the user than that of social connections in other (i.e. 'real life,' out of the game) contexts. For example, an appointment for a 'raid' or playing a specific 'instance' of a dungeon in a MMORPG may be perceived as an important engagement and failing to join the player group at a given point of time may be perceived as a breach of confidence. So conflict between in-game and out-of-the game obligations may occur, especially if the online/offline friendship circles of the user do not overlap, and indeed such conflict is highly likely as long as gaming appointments are deemed to be virtual, and thus, unimportant by other social contacts.

This example also points to the complexity of analyzing games in context – what might be considered positive in one case (community contacts) might be problematic in another case (conflicting obligations, tension). The complexity will most likely grow in sync with the differentiation of games, devices, and the growing potential to play anytime, anywhere, with anybody (for example through mobile, networked devices). Research needs to acknowledge this complexity, and raise the ante: While there is considerable and very insightful research on videogames, as outlined in this volume, there are also some limitations of scientific work in this field so far.

Limitations of Research: The Difficulty of Giving Easy Answers to Easy Questions

After overviewing the literature evaluating the impact of video game use, it is clear that a number of theoretical and methodological concerns need to be addressed in future research. As noted in several chapters of this book, methodological inconsistencies between studies make it difficult to compare findings and draw clear conclusions. As a result, research often cannot give any easy answers to seemingly easy questions posed in the public debate.

Even if the goal of research is the same, the concepts and the respective instruments to measure them differ more often than not. A prominent example of this is the research on the effects of violent video game content (see Chapter 4): There are many different experimental setups and scales to measure aggression as an effect of such content, and even the experimental stimulus varies on many levels. As a result, one could argue that by using different instruments or versions of instruments, it would be possible to show there is an effect, no effect, or a positive effect at play[7] – obviously, this leads to contradictory findings and essentially, a confusing situation for third parties who rely on dependable research (like policy makers, educators and parents, the industry, and many other societal groups affected by gaming). More thorough development processes and testing of instruments is needed. In turn, validated instruments should be used more consistently in order for measurements between studies to become comparable. Researchers need to also be more mindful of the fact that the assessments and conclusions drawn from studies are restricted to the measures that were utilized and the situations under which they were tested – given the contextualization of video game play, as discussed in the previous sections, a transfer to other situations and generalization need to be carefully carried out. This does not mean that no inference is possible – but in the past, it was often done without enough caution, resulting in wide-reaching assertions being discussed in the public (with typical general statements in the style of "video games make their users XYZ" or "gamers (in contrast to non-gamers) are XYZ").

It goes without saying that the same care needs to be applied to the sample selection. The samples from which the participants are drawn from vary greatly across studies and areas of research focus, which can contribute to a substantial amount of variance across results. For instance, samples that are drawn from game-related forums and websites are likely composed of more avid players than school-based samples or general population samples. While representative samples are ideal, it is not always possible to recruit them due to financial or time constraints. We are not suggesting that other samples are sub-par, but rather that researchers need to remain mindful of the effects that the source of their participant pool may have on their results and conclusions. For instance, if one's hypotheses were centered within the populations of more avid players, then drawing from a game-centric online sample may be ideal. However, if one aims to evaluate game players more generally, and draw conclusions about the *average* player, samples should be drawn from avenues that will produce a sample across the gaming spectrum (e.g., from highly involved players to less involved casual players).

Financial restrictions are also relevant for another limitation of current research: Most of the studies are cross-sectional in nature (i.e., they do not track changes over time). Naturally, longitudinal surveys and experimental studies that observe behavioral changes over time are much more expensive, and in many cases, not feasible at all. Even in cases where longitudinal designs are possible, the choice of observation time or time in between measurement repetitions may affect the outcome – for some effects, the exact choice of research interval may be crucial (for example, effects might not develop in a too short observation time, or they may have already disappeared with too much time in between observation intervals). Currently, there is virtually no information available on the time-dependency of effects in video games research – although this may be a central aspect when researching dynamic entertainment media such as games.

The biggest limitation so far, however, is the lack of contextualization in the approaches, and as a result, in the overall video game debate: As discussed earlier in this chapter, one major problem lies in overgeneralizations from oversimplified models of video game use. It is crucial to understand that the specifics of the analyzed cases and concepts do matter and that this consideration has both theoretical and methodological repercussions.

The Future of Video Game Research

Video games research has developed considerably in recent years. While in the beginning, the analysis of what was perceived a 'nerd' hobby was an equally nerdy scientific topic, the success of games in the mainstream was paralleled by a growth of research. The focus has also shifted away from a preoccupation with negative effects and potential threats to the users, especially in psychology and communication studies, in favour of a more balanced, neutral approach, that acknowledges the potential benefits and challenges. It can be argued that approaches rooted in cultural studies, ludology, and the humanities in general had a broader perspective from the start, but the focus of that type of research was also different (i.e., not primarily focused on media effects).[8,9]

The concerns connected to video games were not even unique, as games were just the latest target in a long row of new media that were deemed to be dangerous – we saw similar discussions in relation to comic books, TV, and movies (as discussed in Chapter 2). The advent of such entertainment media did not mark the downfall of humanity, as it was sometimes implied by public doomsayers (although some still say this will be the case, even though with some delay), and it is unlikely that games will fulfil the dark prophecies of a deep cultural demise. This does not mean that video games cannot have a negative impact per se – but sensationalist warnings overestimate the potential influence of specific media and underestimate the complexity of social life, often on purpose for the sake of clear messages that will make the headlines of news media. Media use is just one influence among others, and typically, users do not restrict themselves to one type of medium but consume many sources of information and entertainment. And even if a user would turn to only one medium for a certain period of time, then its content would be processed on the basis of individual experiences, knowledge, and cognitive patterns (i.e., it would be related to an already existing wealth of previous influences). In short, media influences are never experienced in a vacuum. They are situated in complex personal and social contexts and processed by humans who are not simple stimulus-response machines.

Accepting this complexity and contextualization as a theoretical premise in video games research also means that we have to live with seemingly contradictory observations: Games can be beneficial and harmful at the same time, they can improve and damage health, they can fascinate up to worrying addiction-like effects, but also bore users, have notable aggression effects, or remain completely ineffective according to scientific measurement. The outcomes are dependent on the given focus and situation. This is one central insight of this volume: *The game and genre, the player, and the context matter.*

Game and Genre Matters!

In the public debate, scientific findings are often presented in a generalizing way: "Study A has proven that video games have effect X." When looking more closely at the respective studies, these are often limited to effects measured on the basis of a very specific game or genre. For example, aggression research is often based on violent and gory first-person shooter games (and in most cases played in single player mode against AI controlled bots), as this material is thought to be extreme enough to induce measurable effects and it is also somewhat easier to control and modify than more complex games and genres. While this is totally acceptable for some research questions, the overall scientific preoccupation with this type of games leads to the false impression that it represents games per se (although research has shown that FPS are among the least preferred genres among the overall video game player population[10]). If TV research would work in an analogous way, content analyses and effects research in that field would solely focus on violent crime series and the public discussion about TV would revolve around the claim that "Television is violent and makes its user aggressive." However, it is obvious that there are other aspects of television programs that are violence free and can have beneficial effects (such as learning effects).

Similarly, game and genre matters – depending on what type of game an individual selects to play, there will be totally different user experiences and potential influences. A basketball game will not have the same effect as a comic jump and run, a gory dungeon crawler, or an abstract puzzle game. While this seems to be a trivial point, it is crucial and cannot be stressed enough when findings from research are still subject to glaring overgeneralizations.

Players Matter!

The overgeneralization regarding video game effects does not only stem from ignoring genre and game differences, but also different player types and individual player characteristics. We know from many studies discussed throughout this book that differences between individual players and groups of players produce stark contrasts in the effects that are measured. For example, while some people will develop addiction-like behavior excessively playing one specific game, others will show no signs of problematic or deviant behavior at all. This may seem to be following a common sense insight: While some people like some games, others hate them – and probably do not play (such) games at all. However, this also means that under real life conditions, as selection predates use, individual preferences will make a fundamental difference. This seems to be an obvious finding, but it needs to be remembered when evaluating studies that claim effects on whole gamer populations, or at least complete subgroups. While some games might elicit similar reactions in experimental subjects, it is not a given that the very same effects will be observable in everyday contexts (as the experimental subjects would never choose to play the stimulus game or they would play it in a completely different context).

It has also been discussed in several chapters throughout the book that there are notable patterns in genre preferences, everyday embedding of playing, perception of and reactions to games, social context of gaming, etc. that correlate with specific personal characteristics of the players – age, gender, educational level, occupational status, and various personality traits all seem to matter. However, this does not mean, for example, that *all* men play shooter games and *all* women play puzzle games – again, one should abstain from over-generalization. The complex combination of factors leads to comparable player groups that transcend the boundaries of simple socio-demographic differentiation. Still, widespread similarities may exist within larger socio-demographic groups – again, this is not a contradiction. So, in short, it seems to be necessary to raise the awareness regarding these potential player differences in light of a discussion that often lumps all players together, measuring them by the same yardstick.

Context Matters!

From the above argument, it should have become obvious already that the context of game use in everyday life matters. We learned that different players prefer different games (or not), and they use and react in a different way according to their personal characteristics. And even one and the same person may show different behavior under different conditions: Research on excessive gamers, for example, shows that there are some life situations and events (like illness, unemployment, divorce, change of city/occupation, etc.) that may contribute to the opt in and opt out of excessive gaming.[11] So one could differentiate that even further – context can refer to several aspects of the gaming situation, but also the embedding of gaming into the life of the user, i.e.: *Situation matters! Interaction (between players) matters! Stage of life matters! Playing environment matters! Social context matters!*

And it is not only the gaming itself that is important here, but also other, competing orientations and meaningful processes: For example, as noted above, it is not only because of the fascination of a game that a player might develop excessive behavior, but there might be a lack of other meaningful occupations (i.e., a personal 'void' that is filled by the gaming). The 'outcome' of such a situation can only be fully understood when looking at the whole setting under which the behavior evolved into its current state.

Concluding Thoughts

The insights and criticisms discussed here regarding the status quo of the public debate are not meant to imply that previous research has not been useful, and that some types of research are not fruitful and valid approaches as such. On the contrary, it is important to approach the phenomenon 'video game play' from different angles. Our argument is rather directed against a reductionist, overgeneralizing perception and interpretation of research findings in public. In short: There is not *one* type of games, not *one* type of gamers, not *one* type of gaming!

It would be easy to pass the buck to the media and blame them for not reporting on research in an appropriate way. Actually, it would be too easy – the truth is that some video game researchers have also contributed to a black-and-white discussion, pushing sensationalist findings as they 'sell' better. However, the various articles in this book do not paint video gaming solely in black and white and also not in a uniform gray. It's rather a vibrant, multi-colored picture. We hope that future games research will embrace this richness, steering the video game debate into new and exciting directions.

References

1. News BBC. Chinese gamer sentenced to life. *news.bbc.co.uk*. 2005. Available at: http://news.bbc.co.uk/1/hi/technology/4072704.stm
2. Associated Press. Chinese man drops dead after 3-day gaming binge. *foxnews.com*. 2007. Available at: www.foxnews.com/story/0,2933,297059,00.html?sPage=fnc/scitech/videogaming
3. Lah K. Tokyo man marries video game character. *CNN.com*. 2009. Available at: www.cnn.com/2009/WORLD/asiapcf/12/16/japan.virtual.wedding/
4. Cavalli E. Boy survives moose attack thanks to World of Warcraft. *wired.com*. 2007. Available at: www.wired.com/2007/12/boy-survives-mo/
5. Bushman BJ, Gollwitzer M, Cruz C. There is broad consensus: Media researchers agree that violent media increase aggression in children, and pediatricians and parents concur [online ahead of print]. *Psychol Pop Media Cult*. 2014. doi: 10.1037/ppm0000046
6. Breuer, J. Broccoli-coated chocolate? The educational potential of entertainment games. In: Kaminski W, Lorber, M eds. *Gamebased Learning*. Köln, Germany, Kopaed, 2012: 87–96.
7. Elson M, Mohseni MR, Breuer J, Scharkow M, Quandt T. Press CRTT to measure aggressive behavior: The unstandardized use of the Competitive Reaction Time Task in aggression research. *Psychol Assess*. 2014; 26(2): 419–432. doi: 10.1037/a0035569
8. Aarseth E. Computer game studies, year one. *Game Studies*, 2001; 1(1). Available at: www.gamestudies.org/0101/editorial.html
9. Williams D. Bridging the methodological divide in game research. *Simulat. Gaming*. 2005; 36(4): 447–463. doi:10.1177/1046878105282275
10. Scharkow M, Festl R, Vogelgesang J, Quandt T. Beyond the "core-gamer": Genre preferences and gratifications in computer games. *Comput Human Behav*. 2015; 44: 293–298. doi: 10.1016/j.chb.2014.11.020
11. Domahidi E, Quandt,T. "And all of a sudden my life was gone . . .": A biographical analysis of highly engaged adult gamers [online ahead of print]. *New Media & Soc*. 2014. doi: 10.1177/1461444814521791

CONTRIBUTORS

Nicholas D. Bowman, PhD is an Associate Professor of Communication Studies and Research Associate in the Interaction Lab (#ixlab) at West Virginia University, Morgantown, USA. His research examines human interaction and communication technology, including social media and video games. He has published over four dozen original research reports, written two dozen book chapters, and presented nearly 80 conference papers on the topic. He is on the editorial board of several academic journals, including *Media Psychology*, *Journal of Media Psychology*, and *Psychology of Popular Media Culture*.

Mark Coulson, PhD is an Associate Professor and Reader in Psychology at Middlesex University. He gained his first degree in Psychology from Nottingham University and his PhD in Biological Sciences from Cambridge. He has a wide range of research interests, spanning emotional expression and communication, stalking and domestic violence, video gaming and online behavior, systematic review and meta analysis, and positive psychology and mindfulness.

Gillian Dale, PhD is a postdoctoral fellow at the University of Wisconsin-Madison. She received her PhD from Brock University in Canada, and has published several research articles on individual differences in selective attention. She is currently examining how individual difference factors predict outcomes following simple and complex visual training

Christopher J. Ferguson, PhD is Department Chair of Psychology at Stetson University. He has written dozens of articles on the topic of video game violence and was recently given an Early Career Scientists award by the Media

Psychology Division of the American Psychological Association. He has also written a novel, *Suicide Kings*. He lives in Casselberry, Florida with his wife and son.

C. Shawn Green, PhD received his BA, MA, and PhD in Brain and Cognitive Sciences from the University of Rochester. His PhD work, advised by Daphne Bavelier, examined the effect of playing certain fast-paced and cognitively demanding commercial video games on human perception, attention, and decision making. He then completed a postdoctoral fellowship focused on machine learning, reinforcement learning, and computational modeling of cognitive processes at the University of Minnesota under the guidance of Daniel Kersten and Paul Schrater. He is now an Assistant Professor in the Department of Psychology at the University of Wisconsin-Madison where his lab focuses on factors that determine the rate, depth, and transferability of perceptual and cognitive learning.

Mark D. Griffiths, PhD is a chartered psychologist and Director of the International Gaming Research Unit at Nottingham Trent University. He has published over 400 refereed papers, 3 books, 70 book chapters, and over 1,000 other articles (mainly in the area of behavioral addiction). He has won 13 national and international awards for his work on gambling and gaming.

James D. Ivory, PhD is an associate professor and Director of Research and Outreach in the Department of Communication at Virginia Tech. He earned a PhD in Mass Communication from the University of North Carolina at Chapel Hill in 2005. Dr. Ivory has served as head of the Communication Technology Division of the Association for Education in Journalism and Mass Communication and as chair of the Game Studies Division of the International Communication Association.

Rachel Kowert, PhD received her PhD in Psychology from the University of York (UK), where her research focused on the relationships between social competence and online video game involvement. She recently completed a two-year research post working on the EU-funded project SOFOGA (the social fabric of virtual life: a longitudinal multi-method study on the social foundations of online gaming). She also serves on the board of DiGRA (Digital Games Research Association) and the International Communication Association (ICA) Game Studies Division. For more information about Rachel, and her research, visit www.rkowert.com.

Frans Mäyrä, PhD is the Professor of Information Studies and Interactive Media, with specialization in digital culture and game studies in the University of Tampere, Finland. He heads the University of Tampere Game Research Lab, and has taught and studied digital culture and games from the early 1990s. His research interests include game cultures, meaning making through playful interaction, online social play, borderlines, identity, as well as transmedial fantasy and science fiction.

Cheryl K. Olson, PhD was the principal investigator for a two-year, $1.5 million Harvard research project to study the effects of video games on young teens, funded by the US Office of Juvenile Justice and Delinquency Prevention. Based on that research, she coauthored a popular book, *Grand Theft Childhood: The Surprising Truth about Violent Video Games and What Parents Can Do* (Simon & Schuster, 2008 and 2011), which has been translated into Japanese, Korean, and Lithuanian. Dr. Olson cofounded and was co-director of the Center for Mental Health and Media at Massachusetts General Hospital. She received her Doctor of Science degree in health and social behavior from the Harvard School of Public Health.

Thorsten Quandt, PhD holds the chair of Online Communication at the University of Münster (Germany) and is a distinguished scientist with extensive experience in digital games research. Quandt is a proficient teacher in the field of digital games studies and the principal investigator of the EU-funded project SOFOGA. He is an ECREA (European Communication Research and Education Association) board member and the founding chair of ECREA's temporary working group on Digital Games Research. Formerly he served as an officer in the ICA (International Communication Association).

John L. Sherry, PhD is an Associate Professor in the Department of Communication and a faculty member in the Cognitive Science program at Michigan State University. He is the founder and former chair of the Game Studies Special Interest Group of the International Communication Association. His expertise is in the use of media for education, using cognitive information processing approaches to understand the way that players interact with video games and other media.

INDEX